THE
FUTILITARIANS

THE
FUTILITARIANS

Our Year of
Thinking, Drinking,
Grieving, and Reading

ANNE GISLESON

Little, Brown and Company
New York • Boston • London

Little, Brown and Company
Hachette Book Group
1290 Avenue of the Americas, New York, NY 10104
littlebrown.com

First Edition: August 2017

Little, Brown and Company is a division of Hachette Book Group, Inc. The Little, Brown name and logo are trademarks of Hachette Book Group, Inc.

The publisher is not responsible for websites (or their content) that are not owned by the publisher.

The Hachette Speakers Bureau provides a wide range of authors for speaking events. To find out more, go to hachettespeakersbureau.com or call (866) 376-6591.

Excerpts from this book, often in different form, originally appeared in the *Oxford American; Okey-Panky; Where We Know: New Orleans as Home,* edited by David Rutledge (Seattle and Tokyo: Chin Music/Broken Levee, 2010); *The Cairo Review of Global Affairs;* and *NOLAFugees.*

Excerpts from "Dies Iraes," "Searching," "Sharing Bread," and "The Gift" by Clarice Lispector, translated by Giovanni Pontiero, from *Selected Crônicas,* copyright © 1984 by Editora Nova Fronteiro, translation copyright © 1992 by Giovanni Pontiero. Reprinted by permission of New Directions Publishing Corp.

"Conversations with Myself at a Street Corner," from *I Hope It's Not Over, and Good-by: Selected Poems of Everette Maddox* (2009), reprinted with permission of the University of New Orleans Press.

ISBN 978-0-316-39390-4
LCCN 2017932689

10 9 8 7 6 5 4 3 2 1

LSC-C

Printed in the United States of America

for
John, Kristin, Susan, Soren, Amy, Rachel and Rebecca

and most especially
for Mom and Dad

The search is what anyone would undertake if he were not sunk in the everydayness of his own life.... To become aware of the possibility of the search is to be onto something. Not to be onto something is to be in despair.

— Walker Percy, *The Moviegoer*

CONTENTS

PREFACE   3

JANUARY *All Is Vanity*   11

FEBRUARY *World of Stone*   31

MARCH *The Belly of the Whale*   53

APRIL *The Last Suffer; or, The Way of the Crisis (Via Dolorosa)*   73

MAY *The Dark Wood*   99

JUNE *Voices over Water*   119

JULY *The Least Dead Among All of Us*   131

AUGUST *The Metaphysical Hangover*   145

SEPTEMBER *The Walled City*   165

OCTOBER *The Unwalled City*   181

NOVEMBER *Nineveh*   203

DECEMBER *Sharing Bread*   227

NEW YEAR'S EVE *Tanks Versus Chickens*   245

ACKNOWLEDGMENTS   255

APPENDIX: WORKS CITED   257

THE
FUTILITARIANS

PREFACE

From the deck of a pleasure boat in the Yokohama harbor, I watched the world's largest clock recede through an early-June drizzle. The Cosmo Clock 21 is a digital display mounted in the center of an enormous Ferris wheel swirling with carnival lights. Time as amusement-park ride. It disappeared as we motored into the glittering nocturnal realm of the Shiohama Canal, whose intricate skyline of smoke and steel reflected shakily on the black water around us, intensified by low storm clouds. My husband, Brad, and I were on a nighttime industrial jungle cruise with a group that included two expat friends from New Orleans I hadn't seen in years. We passed by refineries, oil terminals, and steel mills along this dredged shipping channel of the Sumida River, cut through with a network of canals and man-made islands. The yellow logo that adorned the tour company's brochure had transformed its Japanese characters into stylized pipes, valves, and smokestacks. Language as refinery.

The crew served up a toxic-green complimentary drink, the name of which translated as "Night of Deepening Memory." Brad joked that this sounded like something we'd serve at the ECRG. Adjusting our hats and jackets in the tumult of the wet salt air, he and I explained to the others that six months earlier, at the start of the year, we'd struck up what we called an Existential Crisis Reading Group with some friends back home in New Orleans. The usual response: a blend of bemusement, appreciation, skepticism. Invoking the ECRG within that ethereal nightscape, amid massive civilization-powering machinery obscured by the eerie romance of steam and sodium lights, seemed appropriate. The ECRG had become part of how we engaged with the world, had begun to inform our lives and experiences in so many ways.

Brad went to the lounge belowdecks to see if he could get a refill of Deepening Memory, and my friends huddled with a crew member by the bridge, trying to get more information, since the tour was given in effusive, staticky Japanese and we didn't really know what was going on. I didn't mind, though, was even comfortable in the disorientation, watching girls in neat cardigans clutch the rail, holding their short skirts down against the harassing wind, and pose unsteadily in front of the brilliant menace of the gargantuan TOWA refinery. The pleasure boat lingered there, listing as couples and grinning young women rushed starboard to have their pictures taken with the backdrop of the miles of trusses and angled pipes made eloquent by light and steam.

Halfway across the planet from my home, halfway through this first year of the ECRG project, I was filled with both wonder and dread by this heightened moment, feeling its searching pull, attentive to my own reactions. This curious tour on the Sumida River seemed a fitting end to a trip to Japan defined by disaster and novelty. I'd been here to participate in an academic post-disaster symposium at a Tokyo university where one of my New Orleans friends taught. At the conference and in the bars, scholars from all over the world theorized, analyzed, and relived various individual and regional disasters, both natural and man-made, focusing on how people negotiate the aftermath, move forward. This urgent sharing of ideas and findings, the collective preoccupation with destruction and survival, the drinking, were all ground we covered during any given ECRG, only this was on a different scale, on a different continent.

As we sailed deeper into the shipping channels, it was easy to succumb to the unreality of it all, to let our minds swerve and detour. My friends joined me at the stern. At a Japanese railroad company's energy hub, enormous gantry cranes stood motionless at the water's edge, surrounded by piles of coal that looked almost scatological. One of my friends said the cranes reminded him of Cerberus guarding the gates of hell, another said a giraffe. To me, they just looked prehistoric and expectant, heads raised against the glossy night. Then we became silent and entranced again, lost in our own interpretations.

Our friend Chris had set the ECRG in motion back in December. Manic and intensely thoughtful, he would often show up at our house unannounced, his existential angst trailing and puffing restlessly around him like the dirt clouds attached to the Peanuts character Pigpen, or at other times swirling Tasmanian Devil–style, with dizzying urgency. But he's hardly cartoonish or two-dimensional, just vivid and physical, with an extra dose of animation that's deeply, internally driven. Mortally tormented and Boston Irish, Chris had spent most of his adult life in New Orleans, as an actor, burlesque MC, nonprofit administrator, and construction worker. Our house usually welcomes his particular injection of agitated anima, especially if I'm making dinner and feeling sorry for myself. Chris is a commiserator in the condition, though the trappings of our respective conditions are very different. I write, teach, have kids and a husband and days tightly bound by *responsibility*. Chris is like an emissary from a land I left years ago, and sometimes remember fondly, who brings exotic, weary tales of its customs — frequent, ill-advised hookups and all-night benders, and more current rituals like sexting and Facebook feuds. He had recently asked if I'd want to do some reading with him, sit down and talk through some philosophical issues one-on-one. I immediately said no, my life was already a thicket of personal obligation, but I'd be happy to do it as a group, open it up as a social venture.

So, a few weeks before Christmas, at the Hot Wok Buffet in a suburban strip mall, Brad and I made a list of names on a paper napkin. Beneath the branches of a fake tree reaching toward a chandelier galleon with Lucite sails, we discussed people we thought might be interested in an existential crisis reading group. Our two sons, twelve and five at the time, made frequent trips to the all-you-can-eat serving islands steaming and glistening with immediate gratification. Some people on the list were shoo-ins, others debated, a few eventually scratched off. The boys returned to the table with plates full of anarchy: pizza slices, sushi rolls, Jell-O cubes, and, since we live in south Louisiana, a couple of whole shrimp to dismember.

As we made the list, we realized that there did seem to be a need for something like this among our friends. Flux was the norm — divorces, jobs lost, jobs gained, children birthed, children considered, sustained economic insecurity, and unexpected windfalls. People were on edge as 2011 was winding down, and 2012 seemed to carry some portent. Chris had sent us a handmade postcard featuring the etched disc of the Mayan calendar: *Let's do this! Hang on in 2012. It's going to be a wild ride.* Another friend, Case, showed up at our house one day with his forearm tattooed with the admonishment *Yes in 2012.*

And the time felt right for me personally. My father was two years into worsening leukemia. His illness called for frequent hospital visits. Parking meters, frigid corridors, small talk with a chronically pissed-off dad, clenching fear in an elevator descending from the oncology ward, people in scrubs just doing their jobs. Weekly breakfasts with my mother, who needed someone to listen to her. Our kids were getting older and the demands of parenting becoming more complex. I found myself in the unanticipated fulcrum of midlife: balancing youth and age in my body, in my head, in my family. But, of course, there was no balance, only low-grade near-daily skirmishing.

Besides, much of my adult life had been gouged with crises. I'd crawl out of one trench only to be kicked down into another. In my late twenties, soon after I'd finished graduate school and thought I was embarking on a more accomplished, or at least certified, life, my youngest sister, Rebecca, committed suicide. A year and a half later, just as I was beginning to feel normal again, her identical twin sister, Rachel, did the same. There were eight of us growing up. Now there were six, four sisters and two brothers, a fourth of our brood gone. Losing a sibling, especially in youth, is a particular blow, a lateral loss of shared history and DNA that lacerates your identity. Your old narrative is shattered. Your new narrative becomes shapeless, full of confusion and pain. Double that.

When the worst of the grief was over and life opened up again, I met a kind, funny, creative, handsome man named Brad. Brad had suffered his own traumas. His partner had died from a brain tumor the year before, at the age of thirty-three, and left him with a three-year-old son to raise on his own. Both of us knew grief well, but were committed to living. We married within the year. Barely unpacked from our Mexican honeymoon, we were forced out of our home when Hurricane Katrina made landfall and destroyed much of the city. Stunned exiles, we forged our new family on the road, with a kind of refugee freedom and clutching love. When we were finally able to return home, our new life was overtaken by not only destruction, but also creation, as we discovered that on that Mexican honeymoon, somewhere in Oaxaca between bottles of excellent mescal, I'd gotten pregnant. In the first few years after the storm, we were in survival mode, raising young sons, engaged in civic triage and the exhausting work of reconstruction.

By 2011, life had settled. The kids were fine, our jobs were good, the city was recovering in its imperfect way. There was ample love and sometimes even happiness. Finally, some space in the aftermath for contemplation, for reckoning. It was in this space that I felt a persistent, daily, unsettling dread. I would become hollow at the checkout counter, watching items being scanned, or dazed in traffic with the kids in the backseat, convinced, vaguely, that everything was wrong, this route, my parenting, humanity. Later, through the ECRG, I would learn a name for it: the Metaphysical Hangover. When Chris approached me about the readings, it seemed like a possible remedy.

With our Hot Wok list finished that day, Brad and I paid our check beneath the glittering galleon, bellies full, anticipating an afternoon of gastric regret. Some shared qualities among the people on the list turned out to be: an oft-glimpsed sad or jittery introspective bent, niceness, a sense of humor. Some had a tendency to haunt the periphery, but a few were moths to the spotlight. All seemed to be searching, just in different places. Many of them were strangers to each other. We were wary of our own project, which we knew could by turns seem pretentious, goofy, or totally necessary. Over the next week, we approached some of the roughly twelve listees in person and sent emails to others.

Having been a little sheepish in our invitations, we were surprised at the enthusiasm of the responses. Some said yes seconds into our rambling pitch, others asked cautious questions. What do you mean by "existential crisis"? *You know, an urgent moment of questioning, a desire to search for meaning or purpose.* How depressing is this going to be? *It doesn't have to be depressing at all. Existentialism is really about optimism and engagement, not despair... I think?* How would it work? Each month someone would choose a reading, then hopefully the next month's reading would naturally arise from the discussion, keep the dialogue ratcheting forward month after month. A few names for the gathering were thrown out there — the Futility All-Stars, Existentialists Anonymous, and my favorite, the Futilitarians — but we would remain generically identified and subsequently just refer to ourselves as the Existential Crisis Reading Group. One recruit asked if we'd have a secret handshake. *Sure, why not?* We decided on an earnest grip, a too-long gaze, and a deep sigh.

We would head home to New Orleans the day after the pleasure cruise, which gave the night a valedictory feel. Toward the end of the tour, the boat captain asked the passengers for a show of hands as to which color of lights they had preferred, the red or the white. White won. He was pleased and talked about the spiritual healing powers of the white light and white smoke. One friend translated this as some of us furrowed our brows, skeptically. Throughout the tour, my friends, who'd also grown up in south Louisiana, kept remarking how much it reminded them of home, of the clusters of light and fire rising out of the swamps along I-10 and lining the Mississippi River like intense little cities. The same distant, intermittent drama of the flare stacks, the same petro-sharp smells that changed properties with the wind. Deepening Memory indeed.

But spiritual healing?

"People can find spiritual healing anywhere," Brad said. "Besides, this is like a night journey. A transformation that can only occur at night, outside the context of your regular life." He was referring to an ECRG reading from a few months back.

As usual, I was burrowing toward the darkness while Brad was digging toward the light. As usual, he was right. The tour did feel transformative — images that we see in our everyday lives we were now re-seeing in a different way, from a different angle, informed by new thoughts and influences, a dreamlike metaphor for the year of the ECRG. This trip to Japan, which I thought would be a break from the grief and stress of the past six months, was instead punctuating it, certifying that this truly was a time of deepening, of interrogating life.

Tomorrow, we'd cross over the international dateline, feeling scrambled and anxious to reach home, to shower gifts on our sons, to scroll through pictures and try to pass on to the boys the amazingness of everything we'd seen. Brad gathered us high school friends together for a picture on the slick deck in front of a structure that looked like a rocket launchpad about to blow. It occurred to me that we hadn't all been together like this for over twenty years, since goofing around for our senior-prom photo at a downtown hotel, masquerading as fancy adults. And here we were in a dazzling and seething shipping channel in eastern Japan. I felt a flickering amazement at how life in its arborescence keeps reconnecting us to our pasts in unexpected branching ways.

With the tour over, we headed back, weather-battered, to the pier, back to the illuminated office buildings and high-rise hotels of Yokohama, back to the Cosmo Clock 21's dizzying, spectacular countdown.

JANUARY

All Is Vanity

Nearly everyone showed up on time, odd for a New Orleans social gathering. Friends parked and turned off headlights, or shackled their bikes to our old iron fence. The wooden porch collected and amplified their footsteps. The seven-thirty convergence was rung in by the off-key bells of the church tower near the corner on Dauphine Street. A few years earlier, the church had changed its name to Blessed Francis Xavier Seelos, in honor of a local priest who died tending to yellow-fever victims after the Civil War. Although he was a near saint, in canonical limbo, the legitimacy of his alleged miracles had yet to be ratified by Vatican bureaucracy. The records agreed he was deeply beneficent, holy even, but was he magic?

Wine bottles congregated on our living room's low table, and bodies settled onto the couches and oversized pillows on the floor. Our project seemed to call for some good scotch, an elevated example of human production — the species proving its worth — and Brad and I had bought a bottle of single-malt Aberlour. This first meeting did not have any clear expectations, though, much less a definite agenda, so no one knew quite how to start.

Drinks were poured and names were traded among the dozen of us. With the exception of my younger sister Susan, and Chris, whom

I'd met during the dark years around my sisters' deaths, the others were all people Brad and I had befriended since we'd met each other about eight years before. We knew them from different spheres in our lives — work, art, kids. In addition to Chris's eclectic résumé, we had a few writer/teachers, poet/musicians, a couple of visual artists, a construction manager and former journeyman plumber, and one psychology professor with a private practice on the side who'd long referred to himself as an "existential plumber."

Chris preambled with a little background information. He'd chosen the initial readings because he wanted to go way back, to hear from the ancients, get to the root of existential thought — at least the Western root — with a letter from third-century-BCE Greek philosopher Epicurus to King Menoeceus on "how to live well" and with Ecclesiastes from the Old Testament, believed written not long afterward. Brad and I had scanned the texts and emailed them out, so everyone either had printouts they'd made notes on or, in a couple of cases, a phone they'd scroll through to find passages. Then there were the conflicting legacies of both Epicurus and Ecclesiastes, Chris continued. Some scholars have claimed there were possibly a few different authors of Ecclesiastes, which would explain the inconsistencies, contradictions, and wafflings of the book's speaker, the Preacher, commonly thought to be old King Solomon, son of David, looking back on his life and sharing what he'd learned. Epicurus had a reputation for being a cultlike leader, holed up in his garden commune with his followers, and his name has become wrongly attached to lavish hedonism. In fact, he advocated moderation and making do with little in order to better appreciate more prosperous times. His pursuit of pleasure was more connected to the absence of pain, not excessive sensuality.

Chris read aloud from a section of Epicurus called "The Importance of Studying Philosophy," leaning assertively on his Bostonian vowels. Comfortable behind a mike and in front of crowds, he reined in his performance persona, sized it to the room:

"'So, both for young and old, it is imperative to take up the study of philosophy. For the old, so that they may stay youthful even as they are growing older by contemplating the good things of life and the richness of bygone events. And, for the young, so that they may be like those who are advanced in age in being fearless in the face of what is yet to come.'"

The promise of remaining youthful through philosophy was appealing to me, as nearly every day I was helplessly discovering signs of the disappearance of my younger self. If that self's spirit could be captured and nurtured, then maybe it would be easier to let her body go, accept the inevitable. The oldest among us, Kevin, the bearded, laconic existential plumber, already seemed to have attained a dispassionate agelessness through his dedication to the workings of the metaphysical. Our sons were best friends, and if we ever found ourselves together at a five-year-old's birthday party, I never had to worry about getting trapped in grating parent talk of car pools and charter schools; I could rely on Kevin to lead me down some hushed conversational tunnel about Nietzsche or the construct of authority, far away from the fracas.

The two youngest in the room, Nate and Sara, strangers to each other, both writers in their twenties, newish to the city and to adulthood, already seemed way more advanced in age than I recall ever being back then, even comparatively fearless with their life choices and trajectories. Nate, the only person I've ever met from Wyoming, had been a student in my community writing class at a local university and was so smart and passionate I once ceded most of a class on a George Orwell essay to him. He's a writer and editor who'd lived in too many places and had too many lives for someone his age, enjoying a picaresque early twenties, DJing in Buenos Aires, slam-poeting in Salt Lake City. Quiet and receptive, keeping to the background like the steady blues bass player she is, Sara already had a master's degree at twenty-four and a profound expectation of poetry and the importance of it in her life.

Post-Katrina New Orleans had become a trampoline for some millennials to get momentum and "experience" before vaulting off to better opportunities in more reasonable cities. We'd seen earnest waves of them come and go, with their temporarily funded post-disaster projects and nonprofit jobs. Surprisingly, Nate and Sara had stuck around. I didn't know how they'd gotten so advanced so young, but Sara was having a quarter-life crisis and told me she was glad to have been invited to the group. I didn't quite understand the concept of a quarter-life crisis, as I'd chalked up that whole decade to a sort of inchoate *crisis of becoming,* mostly spent in bars and bad relationships. I was a little envious they were getting the benefits of an ECRG at so young an age. Would it give them some kind of advantage going forward in life? I was hoping it would give me an advantage in just getting through the week.

We began with the abyss. While both the Ecclesiastes and Epicurus were didactic, prescriptive texts about how to live one's life, both were also contingent on acknowledging the void beyond our sensory perception, aka death. Chris said that some speculate that the spirit of Ecclesiastes may have been influenced by Epicurus and other Greek thinkers who sought to grapple with the nature of temporal reality, the here and now, and who discounted an eternal existence of the soul and seemed to struggle with the role of deities in the human condition. Influential to later philosophers, both these texts were considered radical and even dangerous. Epicurus was demonized well after his death. Dante placed his followers in flaming tombs in the sixth circle of hell, reserved for heretics. And "the whole duty of man" section at the end of Ecclesiastes is thought to have been tacked on much later — an attempt to make the near nihilism of the book's message conform to the rest of the Bible's teachings of adherence to God's law.

One of the first things that struck the group was our unwitting familiarity with Ecclesiastes, one of the more quoted and literarily raided books of the Old Testament. Melville draws from it repeatedly in *Moby-Dick*. It's where Hemingway lifted *The Sun Also Rises* from; Henry James, *The Golden Bowl;* the Byrds, the entirety of "Turn! Turn! Turn!" ("To every thing there is a season . . . a time to be born, a time to die"). Everyone owns "fly in the ointment" and "Eat, drink, and be merry." On Ash Wednesday, the ostensible rationale for Mardi Gras, when the priest thumbs the coarse ash onto our aching heads, he reinforces our mortality with "All go unto one place; all are of dust, and all turn to dust again." My favorite aphorism from Ecclesiastes doesn't seem to have gotten much traction, literary or otherwise: "For to him that is joined to all living there is hope: a living dog is better than a dead lion."

The phrase "All is vanity" jackhammers throughout Ecclesiastes, by turns hectoring and exasperated and resigned, and is the book's ultimate punctuation. Some of us gathered in the living room found this nihilism jarring alongside all of the lesson-teaching, others found it liberating. Either way, "All is vanity" became the running joke of the evening. Acknowledging the void, we could make fun of the void. Only an hour into the evening and already despair was seeming more manageable. Most people appeared both relaxed and eager to engage in the big talk. A few didn't say much, but seemed to be attentively reading along on their printouts, or maybe they were inwardly dismissing the whole enterprise?

I brought up the ending of James Joyce's "Araby," where the word "vanity" first stained my consciousness as a teenager. The young narrator is in love with Mangan's sister, who lives down the street, and

Joyce expresses the infatuation as a turn-of-the-twentieth-century adolescent Dubliner might have felt it, conflating Catholic ornamentation with romantic desire: "I bore my chalice safely through a throng of foes. Her name sprang to my lips at moments in strange prayers and praises which I myself did not understand." Raised in a Catholic family in a Catholic city, I could relate, having been jammed into the pew every Sunday morning with my seven brothers and sisters, all of us born within eight years of each other—John, Kristin, me, fraternal twins Susan and Soren, Amy, identical twins Rebecca and Rachel. I'd be on my knees before the Lord with the rest of the family, but most of our bowed heads were confused with hormonal surgings and Saturday-night reverberations.

In "Araby," the smitten narrator is on a mission to buy an exotic gift for Mangan's sister at the Araby bazaar. After his uncle promises to give him money to go, but then forgets and comes home late, the narrator arrives at the bazaar just as everything is closing, stall workers counting their money, the lights in the great hall shutting down all around him. The story ends with the epiphany: "Gazing up into the darkness I saw myself as a creature driven and derided by vanity; and my eyes burned with anguish and anger." As a teenager, I knew instinctively to be moved by the one-two punch of music and meaning, the poetic import. As an adult whose adolescent vein of melancholy and self-loathing is still alarmingly rich, I read those lines and I think: *Oh God, here I am, still empty-handed, still gazing into the darkness!*

At least now, that darkness has become familiar, circumscribed by adult responsibility and experience, but retaining those shadowy contours of longing and frustration and questioning. As I rediscovered that night of the first ECRG, it seems any lengthy discussion of the search for meaning leads inevitably to "desire," that opulent hologram, thus creating a flurry of conversational flourishes on the subject, like:

"We live in fear that our desires won't be fulfilled."

or

"We live in fear of losing desire."

or

"Pleasure is the end of desire, and pleasure is the end of pleasure."

or

"You're just a hungry ghost, nothing but your spirit and your desire; you are insatiable."

or

"And what about manufactured desire, the world of advertising constantly telling us what we desire?"

We were starting to sound French, but no matter how heady our discussion became, references to materialism seemed inescapable, as if our souls were sticky with the problem of *things*. As twenty-first-century first-worlders, caught up in a vortex of vanities, how could we really expect to free our selves?

Case, a construction manager, writer, and former journeyman plumber, kept bringing up an ex-girlfriend's emotional attachment to a pair of shoes and how she had once become disconsolate when they were ruined in a rainstorm. Kevin said that this was completely valid, as the subjectivity of pain always is. But Case said that he couldn't get past it, even though she was really hot, because this was after Katrina, when the whole city was suffering so much actual loss.

One of the few ECRG members Brad and I met as a couple, right before we got married, Case seemed on an itinerant sweep through New Orleans, via a spread-out life that ranged through a graduate program in Mississippi, a young adulthood in the Southwest, and a childhood in Alaska. But Case stuck around after Katrina and threw himself into the city's rebuilding—intellectually, artistically, and physically—with the same intensity he put into most things. He practiced what he called plumber's yoga and occasionally wrote poems and stories on joists underneath the houses he was working on.

While Case was in the gritty trenches of rebuilding, he, Brad, my sister Susan, and I had started a nonprofit that put on community events—readings, art shows—in the largely empty city. During that same wild, hopeful period, we also met Case's new girlfriend, Nina, who worked on her own projects, elaborate floats and oversized sculptural puppets, in a massive abandoned school building commandeered by a few dozen artists. Tattooed and blue-eyed, tough with long blond ringlets, Nina was sitting next to Case on the couch, focusing a fierce gaze onto her printouts of the readings. Everyone else tried to steer the talk away from the hot ex and the shoes, but it was like a boomerang Case kept throwing into the conversation.

Both Ecclesiastes and Epicurus had warned of the scourge of materialism, which has now brought the planet and its humans, including our friend Case, to a point of crisis. Seems that since people stopped roaming, settled down, and starting shaping jars from cliffside clay to hold their stuff, it's been a problem for our souls. The Preacher-King was especially "vexed" by it and claimed that even though he had had it all during his lifetime—houses, gold and silver, "the peculiar treasures of kings," orchards, vineyards, men servants and women servants, men singers and women singers—none of it mattered, *all is vanity,* because he's going to die anyway, and after he dies, all of his labor will be left to the guy who comes after him. *I'm here to tell you,* he basically says, *don't even bother with it all.*

Nina, already on edge, was especially rankled by the patronizing tone of Ecclesiastes. She was independent, following her interests and ambitions all over the world, and I'd often wondered how she and

Case were faring. "For thousands of years, old men have been telling us what's best for us — it gets wearying and boring. And of course, wouldn't we rather bother with it and find out for ourselves? If even one of those things softened the blow of mortality, one jar of silver, one manservant or singer, a couple of fruit trees, wouldn't it be worth it?"

Susan nodded her head in agreement as Nina spoke. She had enthusiastically accepted the invitation to participate in the ECRG, as she had just endured a difficult divorce and was suffering other protracted life trauma. She rarely let the wear show, and if anything, I thought her suspiciously cheerful. Since we'd grown up together, close in birth order, it was a comfort to have someone else in the room to wordlessly connect to, someone who shared blood, the vagaries of a crowded childhood, the ever-present loss of two sisters, and Dad's illness, which kept us anxious from month to month, vacillating between cautious hope and fear.

"Maybe the Preacher-King just had too much," Susan said. "That's what Epicurus seemed to be saying to King Menoeceus, too. Quality over quantity is what brings true pleasure."

It was Epicurus's definition of pleasure, for him meaning merely "the soul is free of distress," that Ellen wanted to question. Ellen is an artist who sometimes worked with Brad as a scenic painter for the movies, with sharp, elegant features and a south Alabama accent that tears opens her words so wide they seem to accommodate a different meaning. "But is it good to be free of distress? And do we even want to be free of *all* distress?" Some of us in the room, especially the passionate and acerbic Ellen, were very attached to our distress, thought that it was often an appropriate response to being human and to being connected to other humans. I pointed out that existentialists like Sartre claimed, "Anguish is natural to man. It means this: the man who involves himself and who realizes that he is not only the person he chooses to be, but also a lawgiver who is, at the same time, making a

19

choice for all of mankind as well as for himself, cannot therefore escape the feeling of his deep and total responsibility."

I read that quote aloud from *A Concise Dictionary of Existentialism,* a thin, gray hardback with brittle foxing pages, published in 1960. During our discussion, when I couldn't articulate my thoughts or was stymied by my intellectual failings, or when the wine was slackening the connection between mind and mouth, the dictionary was my crutch. I found it years before in graduate school when I helped run an estate sale out of a crumbling old storefront in the French Quarter. I sorted through used, smoke-damaged books that the lawyer I was working for believed were cursed, because their deceased owner, a shady book collector, had not been a very good person and because bad things, most recently a mysterious fire in an adjacent storage unit, happened near wherever the books ended up. The collector supposedly had young male lovers pose as college students and steal valuable old books from the local university libraries. The lawyer told me the collector shot and killed one of these young men, claiming he mistook him for a burglar. Whenever I came across a three-hundred- or four-hundred-year-old tome with a ragged rectangle cut low on the thick vellum spine where the call number might've been, I wondered if it was somehow connected to the murdered book thief–lover.

Alphabetical entries in *A Concise Dictionary of Existentialism* begin with "Americanism" — "A monstrous complex of myths, of values, of formulae, of slogans, of symbols, of rites … the great myths of happiness, that of progress, that of liberty, that of triumphant maternity; there is realism, optimism; and then there are Americans who at first are nothing, who grow among these colossal statues and disentangle themselves as best they can" (Sartre) — and end with "Youth" — "Youth as the period of highest vital efficiency and of erotic exaltation, becomes the desired type of life in general. Where the human being is regarded only as a function he must be young; and if youth is over, he will still strive to show its semblance" (Karl Jaspers). (*See also:* Old Age; Past and Present.)

Chris connected Sartre's anguish about contingency, how our individual actions reflect on all of humanity, to Epicurus's "immortal goods." Epicurus defines that phrase as being truly alive, paying attention to the people and world around us, and acting accordingly, and he claims it's the best we can hope for. That all seemed reasonable and doable to us, even though today, thousands of years after Epicurus lounged in his garden with his acolytes, we have an infinite number of distractions between us and our "immortal goods."

For most of the evening, Brad had been rather quiet. Listening, hosting, running interference with the boys, who kept raiding the snacks people brought, and handling bedtime. But he was the one who pointed out that both of the evening's readings embraced another basic value: enjoyment of life through simple fellowship, one of the highest uses of our brief time here in the world.

Which, many people agreed, we were already doing that evening, under the tall ceiling of our living room and the kind, indirect lighting, around a low metal table magnetized by the bottles, glasses, snacks, and our talk, which was building up time around it like good conversation does. It would be nice to describe the blue of that table as a mythic Aegean, but it's actually an iridescent Malibu blue, chosen from an auto paint catalog and airbrushed on by Brad, more West Coast hot rod, a chunk of twentieth-century America weighing down the middle of the room, anchoring us with context even as our minds and talk got all timeless and universal.

The evening wound down with a tentative though satisfying sense of something beginning, a night class we were all auditing, and an agreement to create a monthly curriculum guided by the vagaries of the group. Since there was some dissatisfaction with the abstract nature of the talk that evening, even though ostensibly that's what we were there for, and some of us craved a little narrative, for the next meeting Case suggested "This Way for the Gas, Ladies and Gentlemen," by Tadeusz Borowski, evidently agitating to push us to the extreme of modern societal evil. It's the title story from a beautiful and brutal postwar collection by a Polish writer and journalist who was imprisoned and put to work in Nazi concentration camps, was liberated, wrote about it all, and committed suicide at the age of twenty-eight. But *sure,* we collectively shrugged in assent, and, this being the Age of Impulse, when forethought and waiting are less and less acceptable, Case tapped at his iPhone, accessed the vast shared cyber brain of human knowledge, found the link, and instantly sent the horror of Auschwitz straight to all of our inboxes while we talked and drank.

A tiptoe procession bore crumb-laden platters and glasses down the hallway, past our sleeping boys' bedroom, to the kitchen. Empty wine bottles clanked discreetly into the trash can under the sink. Bikes were liberated from the fence, and parking spots opened back up in front of the house. It was late. Brad and I left the dishes in a precarious pile on the counter until the morning and went to bed, minds buzzing and happy, surprised about how well it had gone, grateful for our friends.

The search had begun, and it was already so affirming and fun. As mother, daughter, wife, teacher, I directed much of my day toward the needs of others. Yes, I could carve out time alone to read and write and replenish the mind and soul, but the ECRG provided the bonus of so many other viewpoints to embrace and invigorated my own experience of the reading, minus the competitiveness and insecurity I'd often felt in school. That night we'd contrasted Epicurus's claim that the attainment of knowledge was necessary for one's "soul-health" with the Preacher-King's warning: "For in much wisdom is much grief: and he that increaseth knowledge increaseth sorrow." I was used to sorrow, didn't even mind sorrow, but the possibility of a hybrid "soul-healthy sorrow" felt useful. This communal investigation of living felt useful, and necessary. I set my alarm for too early, turned off the bedside lamp, and burrowed under the covers, feeling something like relief.

A few hours later, in the early morning of January 6, Nina would leave Case. "Damn the Existential Crisis Reading Group," Nina said repeatedly as she packed up her things. We had sensed the tension between them before, and apparently all the talk of intentionality and the ex-girlfriend had set her off. But still, Brad and I agreed later that day, it wasn't such a great sign for the beginning of the ECRG. Then again, it was a reminder that the search could lead to all kinds of outcomes. January 6 is also the Feast of the Epiphany, celebrating the Three Kings' discovery of baby Jesus, son of God, in the manger, an important day not only on the Catholic calendar but also the New Orleans calendar, because it marks the beginning of the carnival season, pops off the cork of the year. I always loved our celebration of the Feast of the Epiphany as a kid because it meant more presents, and then later as an adult for the import, the celebration of discovery and hope. Joyce secularized the Catholic use of "epiphany" for literary purposes, and humanity co-opted it for personal uses, to put a name to those rare, gleaming revelations that sometimes travel from afar to change our understanding of ourselves or the world.

On that same morning of the Feast of the Epiphany, my dad, with almost no immunity due to his chemo treatments that week, took the long drive to the Angola prison, tucked into the crook of the state near the Mississippi border, to visit his pro bono client on

Death Row and fell ill upon returning home. Days later, he died a patriarch's death in the Touro Infirmary with all of his remaining children around him, prayer working its binding magic among us, even though most of us held only the barest vestige of faith, and really only when it seemed to serve us. He'd been unconscious for most of the day, and all there was to do was attend to the running down of the animal machine, anticlimactic, exhausting.

———————

A couple of days later, taking a break from the death chores, five of the surviving siblings went to lunch at the Rib Room, table 5, Dad's table, to drink with his fresh ghost. We had collectively grieved before, but with a different quality. This was a father's death, a shifting of the axis. Without the shock and horror and self-recriminations of our sisters' suicides, which bound us so tightly to *the events* of their deaths, we faced a chasm, a great unmooring.

During lunch, a reporter from the *New Orleans Times-Picayune* called the oldest of us, John, also a lawyer, who'd made it from Pittsburgh to the deathbed just in time. The paper was doing one of those article-length obituaries it publishes for people of some civic prominence and wanted to ask a few questions about our father's life. John and my older sister, Kristin, a politician at the time, passed the phone back and forth, answering the reporter's questions with a fuzzy magnification brought on by lunchtime martinis, the power siblings in collusion, the rest of us holding in our laughter. I sat across from them in the padded booth, the mortified middle child, mouthing "Stop it" over my Beefeater, Dad's drink.

Dad had held court at table 5 for over twenty-five years, since we were teenagers. The place had hardly changed. Waiters in maroon jackets eternally placed hot French bread in paper wrappers onto white tablecloths. The balcony-sheltered windows kept the noon sunlight golden, the bare bulbs of sconces and chandeliers merely embellishing the light. Church-high ceilings with faux-Tudor rafters, walls veneered with veiny green and black marble meeting a polished flagstone floor. The usual architectural suggestion — affluence as some sort of ancient privilege, anchored by the prizes of geology. Reproductions of nineteenth-century levee lanterns were mounted high on the walls of the Rib Room, names of the towns along the Mississippi painted in black on their glass: Vacherie, Houma, Verret. Table 5 resided between Belle Chasse, christened "the beautiful hunt" by the French in the early eighteenth century, and Bayou Goula, named for the Indian tribe that had been spearing deer on Delta land since before Christ. I loved the idea of the beautiful hunt, not the initial European awe of the land's wild bounty, which quickly and inevitably turned exploitative, but the possibility of a lifelong beautiful hunt, which I always associated with long lunches with my father at table 5.

I never quite understood Dad's attachment to the place. I could only figure his weekly ritual was his reward as a self-made man, a rust-belt refugee who got his first job, at a grocery, at age ten, worked as a grinder in a foundry at nineteen, and by twenty-nine was the youngest strike-force chief against organized crime for the Department of Justice. Through childhood and adolescence, he'd had a terrible stutter, which he vanquished at Notre Dame with hours of practicing speeches in front of a mirror. As a young federal prosecutor he invited his mother to watch him present an opening argument in court, which he executed flawlessly, and which she beamed about for years.

Not just a reward, though. His hard-won presence at the Rib Room, a working-class liberal midwesterner among the New Orleans moneyed elite, or at least the trappings of it, was also a perverse "fuck you" to the establishment, as he rebelled against any and all establishments, especially ones he was associated with. His white-shoe law firm, the government, the Catholic Church. Amy, the sixth and youngest sibling since the twins' deaths, never liked the Rib Room and never went, saying she related to Dad's blue-collar side, while the Rib Room represented his white-collar ambitions. She would embrace the blue collar literally, by becoming a New Orleans cop, working some of the most dangerous streets in the country.

Also: Dad nurtured a grudge like a bonsai tree, tending and shaping, maintaining its diminutive, eternal perfection. Back in the 1970s, as a young federal prosecutor, he'd wanted to pick up the check at the Rib Room to celebrate a department victory. But he was a struggling government employee with eight children, and his credit card was declined. The humiliation lodged and stuck. Eventually, he gave up the job with the Department of Justice that he loved and turned to the private sector — corporate defense. Maybe it was a consolation prize, becoming a regular at the Rib Room. Pouring his Beefeater from a martini pitcher with *Gisleson* etched in the glass, picking up checks at table 5 for the next couple of decades.

Lunches with Dad at the Rib Room were about interrogation, debate, revelation, judgment, and telling stories. My father asserted himself on us in a rather formalized way. Table 5 was a malleable space, could shrink down to the claustrophobic dimensions of a confessional or expand to theater, or courtroom, with Dad playing to the cheap seats or a jury.

Part of the ceremony of the Rib Room was that we weren't even allowed to look at a menu for the first half hour or so. Dad's regular waiters knew this and wouldn't bring a menu to the table unless he asked for it. We couldn't order until about an hour of talking and drinking had transpired. This was to demonstrate that food and time, usually the defining characteristics of lunch, were incidental, nearly irrelevant to my father at table 5. Another Rib Room lunch tradition was reminiscing about dishes that hadn't been on the menu for years. Like the Oysters Rockefeller and the Roti Assorti and the glassy, fragile crème brûlée. The trap of growing up in New Orleans: you're often preoccupied with what's been lost while clinging to a grand, cobbled present — part wreck, part fantasy, part regular civic striving, but always under construction.

And it was at this table that I had my last real conversation with him, a couple of weeks before he died. I told him Brad and I were starting an existential crisis reading group, which I thought he'd get a kick out of, having studied in the Great Books program at Notre Dame. Near the end of lunch, he gazed down Royal Street, toward the white marble steps of the courthouse where he had tried some of his biggest cases as a young prosecutor. I realized long ago that his looking-out-the-window gesture often augured one of those moments in conversation in which the speaker speaks more to himself than to others, an earnest though slightly stagey aside.

"Have you seen the scrapbook that your mother made of our first year of dating?" he asked.

I did remember seeing it as a child or maybe teenager, wedged on a crowded shelf between the leatherette photo albums that archived all eight of our parallel childhoods, some albums more complete than others. Mom and Dad met in 1962, when they were both sophomores in college. Dad was at Notre Dame, scraping by financially but thriving in his double major of math and philosophy. He hauled his books from South Beloit to South Bend in produce boxes proudly supplied by Mick and Dick Zick from the Black Hawk Grocery, where he worked all through high school, while admiring other students' leather-bound trunks and matching luggage. Mom, from New Orleans, was studying Christian culture at Saint Mary's, where women still had curfews, wore uniforms, and always donned coats over their tennis clothes when crossing campus to the courts.

Mom put the scrapbook together on vacation with her parents at Fort Walton Beach, Florida, while stuck inside the cottage nursing a bad sunburn. Funny that my Walton grandparents vacationed at Fort Walton, as my mother once told me that Walton (also my middle name) means "walled town." This makes perfect sense for my grandparents, who were distant, unaffectionate, and inaccessible, but not for my mother, who is more a thatched hut in a sunny meadow — open and nearly glowing with fully expressed love. Along with the name, I inherited a certain cautious, judgmental Walton reserve. I have no idea how my warm and giving mother escaped the ramparts, became someone who would make that scrapbook, carry it back to college while riding coach on the City of New Orleans train, and present it to her delighted midwestern boyfriend. Ever since I can remember, Mom, even with the brood swirling around her, has always created and commemorated with scissors and Elmer's glue, beautiful handwriting and a cheerful generosity.

"I had forgotten about it for forty years," Dad said, "and she just brought it out of mothballs from somewhere. Did you see that first page? The first page says, 'Rick is from Illinois, but not much more is known of him. He is very mysterious.' I looked at that, and I thought, 'You know what? Forty-odd years later I'm the same way. She still doesn't know me. People still don't know me.'"

I related this to my brothers and sisters after John and Kristin hung up with the reporter. We agreed that it was a good, Dad-like mix of melodrama and truth. Either way, burying an enigma seemed even more crushing than burying a man we imagined we knew well. Answering a reporter's questions with any authority seemed absurd. But then again, so did his death.

It was also here at table 5, about ten years earlier, that my father had forbidden me to ever write about the deaths of Rebecca and Rachel. Intimidating in size, intellect, and absolute paternal power, he told me that if I did, he would never forgive me. He would take the affront to his grave. So, over the years, I never really did write about them, except for a cagey reference here or there. One very short story in a very small journal, invisible to him and, frankly, the world. I complied because enough damage had been done to our family by those two suicides. As unnatural as it felt, it was a casualty I was willing to sustain.

But it was also such a great, unfair contradiction that here, in this place where he encouraged me to question authority and think critically, he also demanded I shut myself off creatively from the most affecting experiences of my life. Or more precisely, I could scribble away in a journal, I just couldn't share it with the world. A phenomenon one writer I know described as chewing and not swallowing.

The golden light of the Rib Room was cooling now with afternoon, the shadows among the tables and pillars gathering depth. The dining room was empty of patrons. Busboys were changing linens and resetting tables for dinner, straightening the silverware, centering the white peaks of napkins. I thought about my obligation to honor the wishes of the dead. In this town, the dead can take up a lot of real estate, both physical and mental. But what about honoring the wishes of the irrational dead?

As I sipped my Beefeater, I realized that Dad had, in fact, taken his mandate to his grave, and I could write about whatever the hell I wanted to write about now. I felt a guilty tremor of lightness. I felt kind of mean. How horrible was it that as I sat here with my siblings, sickened with loss, I was thinking about this particular liberation? It's tricky, that impotent vindictiveness reserved for the dead. With no solid target, you either end up absorbing the poison or expelling it altogether.

As the lunch ended, we living dogs toasted our dead lion. Then this wounded pack of sons and daughters, dressed up in the baroque drama of grief and dark tailored clothes, took off into the French Quarter to drink at the bars where our father always had — Harry's Corner, the Chart Room, the Old Absinthe House — retracing and sniffing out the dank trails of old sins and past adventures, heading into the jungly chaos of our first fatherless year.

That night I returned to a house humming with the special quiet of sleeping boys. Bleary, spent, drinking water out of the kitchen faucet, I saw Chris's postcard of the Mayan calendar tucked into the crisp new Saturn Bar calendar on the wall. *Hang on in 2012.* He was right. The wild ride had already begun.

FEBRUARY

World of Stone

Grieving during carnival season was an odd enterprise. Somewhat like grief, carnival's chief tension is between ritual and chaos. And also like grief, it involves breaking out of daily rhythms and getting in touch with something more communal. The season of *carne vale,* or "farewell to the flesh," lasts for weeks, from the Feast of the Epiphany to Mardi Gras, or Fat Tuesday. The same parades have been parading the same nights of the week in the same sequence for years; people have appointed days for throwing and attending certain parties. The same families escape town for the week of Mardi Gras; after all, not everyone enjoys the massive crowds, the traffic, the excess. Most schools in New Orleans, both Catholic and secular, close for the week of Mardi Gras Day, or at least part of it. Regular business is suspended, unless your regular business is the service industry or law enforcement.

During the controversial first post-Katrina Mardi Gras, held when the city was still mostly broken and depopulated, our family's unofficial slogan was from theater critic John Lahr: "Frivolity is the refusal of the human species to suffer." After Dad died, instead of abstaining from carnival that year, as might've been wise, I threw

31

myself into it. I wasn't refusing to suffer, I deeply needed to suffer, I was just letting the celebration invade my grief, and vice versa. Our dad's death was still unreal and still near enough that it shaded all of our actions with a self-conscious though real poignancy. Death brought its own unbearable clarity to scenes often left gauzy or shrouded with activity. We brothers and sisters brought our kids to the parades, caught beads and trinkets alongside them, and did not cancel our parties. Dressed up in formal attire, we went to the Mayor's Ball at Gallier Hall fronting St. Charles Avenue, a neoclassical edifice of Tuckahoe marble built in the mid-nineteenth century. The double rows of huge columns with scrolled Ionic capitals, in the South, are a style of architecture often associated with oppression as much as authority. That night we watched the krewe of Pegasus parade down the avenue in viewing boxes erected on the steps of Gallier Hall for the mayor and the members of the city council, including my sister Kristin.

A light rain was dissolving the hairdo I'd paid to have done that afternoon, so I picked the bobby pins out one by one and threw them down into the street between gaudy papier-mâché floats, marching bands, and sips of champagne. I gave myself a whole new look for the evening — a collaboration between the best efforts of my hairdresser and the elements. We were begging beads from masked riders and dancing when a local high school band stopped in front of the mayor's box, as bands and marching clubs traditionally do, and the mayor in his tuxedo acknowledged the recent death of someone from their community. As they played a solemn tribute, some of the baton twirlers and band members started crying right there on the avenue. These children, too many of whom bear the brunt of the city's historical ills, stood at attention with their instruments and flags, in their spiffy blue-and-gold sequined leotards, tasseled boots, and transparent rain gear — all post-Katrina donations from a famous

Hollywood actress to replace their flood-destroyed old ones. We adults in our tuxes and gowns with our plastic champagne glasses, necks heavy with cheap shiny beads, were tethered with the children to a moment before they resumed their marching and we our partying beneath the antebellum portico. Feeling wretched and shamed by the world, I hid my champagne glass below the viewing stand's bunting and plywood façade until the band passed. It was one of those moments your soul feels like a fist, clutching disparate strings of experience, time, emotion, whatever, holding them all together and then letting them all go to separate out again.

Convening an Existential Crisis Reading Group meeting during carnival season also felt odd. Chris had wondered if it was even necessary, since carnival itself can be a salve for the existential hurt. Identity is transcended, normalcy is transcended, and then on Ash Wednesday, back to Ecclesiastes, the gray smudge of the mortal reminder on our foreheads. "All are of dust, and all turn to dust again," ushering in the always-welcome Lent.

But we all decided it was even more important to meet, since this month's gathering would be laden with loss. Dad's death had left Susan, Brad, and me raw and sad, our friends in the room deferential and tender. Case and Nina had both quit the group after breaking up the night of the first meeting, but since Case had already chosen and sent the reading to us, the discussion was driverless. Was the ECRG endeavor already off-track? His selection, "This Way for the Gas, Ladies and Gentlemen," was intense, and there was an itchy energy in the room that kept people reaching across the table to refill their wineglasses.

Tadeusz Borowski's 1946 autobiographical short story is pretty much about what the title almost symmetrically implies: man's capacity for evil, the sham of civilization in the face of that evil.

"This Way for the Gas, Ladies and Gentlemen" is about a prisoner who volunteers to unload transports into the camp for the reward of the food and clothing left over from the "passengers" after they are trucked to the crematoria or work camp. The action transpires over a hot summer day, narrated in an unnerving present tense.

The horrors that he and others encounter on the platform, the acts they believe are necessary to survive, I don't feel the need to recount. It's heavily charted nightmare territory. As are the terrible things done to children in the story. In his introduction to the collection in which the story appears, Borowski biographer Jan Kott calls the book "one of the cruelest of testimonies to what men did to men, and a pitiless verdict that anything can be done to a human being."

It was a long night of talking about our complicity in different systems, the experiment of civilization, the reaches of brutality. The complicity part fed into my lifelong Catholic project of how much guilt to assign myself in any given situation, and I sat on the floor listening, indulging in the ideas, calculating.

"But the system doesn't work without your compliance."

"We're talking about the distribution of responsibility."

"Crowds can't be morally trusted."

"That part about history being let off its leash…"

"The debris and tragedy formed an adjusted worldview."

"That's why modern existentialism thrived in the aftermath of World War Two. The fertile ground of questioning. The suffering and the witnessing."

My sister Susan, grounded in the material significance of things, offered, "I think Case chose this story because of the shoe connection. The pile of shoes from the prisoners. The narrator needs new shoes from the new arrivals."

There was another reading that Case had chosen and then abandoned us to discuss without him that night, a short excerpt from *Existential America,* by George Cotkin, grainy trenches of darkness down the gutter of the poorly photocopied pages. In this section, "The Era of French Existentialism," Cotkin defines the canon of existentialism — Kierkegaard, Sartre, and Camus — and identifies some of its major themes, like subjective truth, estrangement, existence and nothingness, existential anguish and nothingness, existence and death.

No wonder bottles kept opening and getting drained and crowding the table. The void was among us — in the Borowski story, in these French existentialists, in Dad's death. I found and read aloud a quote from my *Concise Dictionary of Existentialism,* which had a whole section titled "Nothing."

" 'Nothingness lies coiled in the heart of being, like a worm' " (Sartre). (*See also:* Dread; Future; Past and Present; Suicide; Transcendence.)

A brief debate followed about whether it was the size of that worm coiled in the heart of your being or its voraciousness that mattered more. Mostly folks thought it was your relationship with the worm. Did you ignore it, accept it, nurture it?

"My worm positively *defines* me," Ellen drawled. "In a good way. The world wouldn't be nearly so interesting without it."

As the conversation continued, I followed the admonition to "*See also:* Suicide," since Rebecca and Rachel are never far from my thoughts during discussions like these. There was only one entry under that heading, by Karl Jaspers: "One should at least recognize if not comprehend that suicide is a way of positive approach to nothingness." (*See also:* War; World.)

Bullshit, I thought, though I understood where he was coming from, that suicide could be viewed as man's ultimate assertion of will over the absurdity of existence. Taking nothingness into his own hands. But what about the existential ideal of contingency, about being responsible for others? If our individual actions are connected to all of humanity, then wouldn't suicide be an act of genocide? Wouldn't all the damage done to others in the suicide's wake be enough for existentialists to condemn it? (In fact, it was, and some prominent existentialists did end up denouncing suicide on those grounds.)

But the twins' suicides were not elegant philosophical statements. I doubt many are. They were impulsive and confused and messy. Though their deaths were a year and a half apart, they mirrored each other in method (hanging) and toxicity (cocaine and alcohol in their systems). From the outside, the deaths of these two beautiful and outgoing young women from a large, loving family must've looked baffling. A little closer in, Rebecca's troubles were better known. Rachel was in danger by association and sometimes collusion. From the inside, their deaths were the final missteps to end all missteps. And maybe, in their last moments, that's what they wanted. We could never know. They were so mysterious, so hard to communicate with, since as twins, as the youngest, they primarily communicated with each other. As toddlers, they had developed their own language, dropping sounds that were too hard to pronounce or creating whole other words unintelligible to the rest of us. In a family where education and achievement were default ideals, neither of them had finished high school, though both eventually received GEDs, Rebecca's under court order after she'd forged one of Dad's checks at sixteen. We'd marvel at how they even had different accents from the rest of the family, looser somehow, from another part of town, and at how they seemed to know so many diverse networks of people and were always being given free stuff, from appliances to luxury eyeglasses. Like most twins, they also strained to separate themselves from each other, in appearance and interests, and could become envious and wary of each other. They were enigmas to us, but then again, how hard did I try to reach out to them? I was far away in college when their troubles first began, in middle school. I remember coming home and buying them books for Christmas, but now I'm not sure if that encouragement wasn't tinged with condescension.

"There is a forest of bottles on this table," Chris pointed out. We cleared off the empties, lined them against the wall, and kept talking. We had to keep on with the work of confronting the worm. After all, for the existentialists, nothingness was a call to action, and to attention, not despair. According to them, we were born without meaning and had to create our own "essence." Some felt it was a task that not everyone measured up to equally. Simone de Beauvoir, in response to Voltaire's admonition for each of us to "cultivate our garden," wrote that this was unhelpful advice, that there "are men who try to plow the entire earth, and there are others who would find a flower pot too great." That's how I often thought of the twins, stymied or overwhelmed in some way. Forgetting to water their beautiful potted flowers, not giving them the right amount of sun.

Case assigned us the Cotkin reading to establish a little more of a foundation of existentialism and also show how the movement never really took off in the United States. One American existentialist thinker, Ralph Harper, tried to temper the perceived harshness and nihilism of the movement by formulating a more palatable "dynamic existentialism" that was at heart spiritual and even religious. It was heavily influenced by French theologian Pierre Rousselot, a Jesuit priest who died in battle in England in 1915 when he was only thirty-six. He espoused a "loving intellectualism" that focused on love and caring and awareness. This awareness was composed of "willing (desire, energy), possessing (intellect), and feeling (emotion) — all three."

Most people in the room were dismissive of Harper and Rousselot, thought Harper was too soft and that he bastardized the general existential tenets, but I gushed about how hopeful it made me, this definition of awareness, this approach to the task of living. And I appreciated having things broken down like that for me to consider. *All three: willing, possessing, feeling.* This was a trinity I could get behind, one that I did not have to worship but rather could enact.

Eager to get back to Borowski and leave "loving intellectualism" behind, Nate asked what everyone thought about the blond girl with the gold watch in the story.

"Oh, the blonde!" everyone murmured and riffled through the printouts, looking for her. Nate, who spends long days immersed in mute text, likes to read aloud, drawing out emphasis, modulating meaning:

And suddenly, above the teeming crowd pushing forward like a river driven by an unseen power, a girl appears. She descends lightly from the train, hops up on to the gravel, looks around inquiringly, as if somewhat surprised. Her soft, blonde hair has fallen on her shoulders in a torrent, she throws it back impatiently. With a natural gesture she runs her hands down her blouse, casually straightens her skirt....Here, standing before me, is a girl, a girl with enchanting blonde hair, with beautiful breasts, wearing a cotton blouse, a girl with a wise, mature look in her eyes. Here she stands, gazing straight into my face, waiting. And over there is the gas chamber: communal death, disgusting and ugly. And over in the other direction is the concentration camp: the shaved head, the heavy Soviet trousers in sweltering heat, the sickening, stale odour of dirty, damp female bodies, the animal hunger, the inhuman labour, and later the same gas chamber, only an even more hideous, more terrible death....

Why did she bring it? I think to myself, noticing a lovely gold watch on her delicate wrist.

She asks the narrator directly what the situation is; the narrator is unable to respond.

"I know," she says with a shade of proud contempt in her voice, tossing her head. She walks off resolutely in the direction of the trucks. Someone tries to stop her; she boldly pushes him aside and runs up the steps.

Out of all of the blunt descriptions of violence and squalor and degradation, Kevin, our existential plumber, said that the blonde radiated "symbol." But of what? Michael, an exquisite classical-realist illustrator and Edgar Allan Poe scholar, was primed for this question. Michael lived alone in a large two-story house on an oak-sheltered street in the French Quarter, his daily uniform a painterly white linen shirt and khaki pants. Even his mysterious sadness seemed anachronistic to me, a torment from another century, of a different hue and timbre, but always near the surface, as accessible as his sense of humor and gentility.

"In art," he said, "truth and beauty and light are often connected. She saw the truth of the situation and her blond hair and gold watch reflected the light, separated her out from all the darkness." More possibilities ricocheted around the room: culture, youth, virtue, Western civilization, desire, sensuality, courage...Almost everyone else in the story was acting so wretchedly, but she was singled out as brave and dignified; all the more muddying was her Aryan quality, something exalted by the Nazis.

Christine, a chain-smoking historian and writer, instigator and prodder, had a thick reddish bob and an intense aura of patchouli that would linger exotically in my living room until the next morning. She had always intrigued me, as years before I'd met her when she was working at a crusty, decrepit hardware store on Elysian Fields Avenue, but then one day I saw a really good short story by her in an anthology of local writing. One of those necessary reminders that people everywhere have full and surprising lives, have things to say beyond "Here's your change." She said the blonde reminded her of Cordelia, the beautiful daughter in *King Lear,* who shows unwavering devotion to her aging father even after being disowned for refusing to compete against her sisters in a contest of who could most extravagantly express her love for him. Her truth-speaking voice, "ever soft, gentle, and low," made her murder by hanging even more devastating. In both stories, virtue and truth are something beautiful and desirable, deeply affecting the characters around them, shining an honorable and attractive light on humanity. But both these young women take their good looks and dignity to an early grave, become part of both stories' inexorable carnage.

"Did anyone read Borowski's bio?" Ellen asked. She was especially intrigued by the part about his relationship with a young girl before his suicide. Ellen was often interested in relationships, even though she herself seemed suspicious of romantic attachment and relished her own social freedom. Whenever we'd see her out at parties, there seemed to always be a rejected suitor somewhere nearby. Maybe, she thought, there was some connection with "the young girl" and the blonde?

Borowski's life story is as compelling as anything he ever wrote and has caused some to place him in a category of writers whose biographies not only belong "to the history of literature but are also literature themselves — that is, human destiny epitomized," noted biographer Kott. In Nazi-occupied Poland, Borowski studied literature at an underground university in the Warsaw Ghetto, risked his life to publish pamphlets and his own poetry, and later worked to the limits of body and soul in the camps. Throughout it all he had one of those epic wartime romances: underground intrigue, Nazi traps, arrests, separation, letters. Assignment to the same camp, Auschwitz, where he caught glimpses of his beloved, her bald head and scabies-ravaged body, as he repaired the roofs in the Frauen-Konzentrationslager. More separation and long months of desperate searching after the end of the war, beseeching letters for her to return to Poland from Sweden. Reunion and their first night of marriage spent in a repatriation camp.

He was considered the hope of Polish literature in the postwar generation, but ended up working as a journalist for the Communist party, later becoming disillusioned with it, confiding to friends that he had "stepped on the throat of his own song." In a mysterious bit of biography, actually more like a crevasse, shortly before his death he had "entered into a liaison with a young girl," wrote Kott. One afternoon, he visited his wife and three-day-old daughter, their first and only child, in the hospital. Later that evening, at home, he turned on the stove's gas valves and sealed himself in the kitchen.

Why do some suicides complete the act just as a new phase of their life is opening up? Why did both of my sisters hang themselves shortly after moving into new domestic situations? Why did Cordelia have to die by hanging and not merely be strangled? What point was Shakespeare trying to make? What point were my sisters trying to make? Why was the proximity between "suicide" and "transcendence" in that "Nothingness" entry bothering me so much? What did Borowski want from that "liaison with a young girl"? Why did the deaths of the blonde, Cordelia, even the twins, suddenly feel sacrificial, youth and beauty crushed by the world's brutality? But sacrificed to what end? To intensify everyone else's suffering?

My questions never entered the conversation, just stayed in my head, where they connected like gears and wore me down with their whirring insistence. I'm usually grateful for how good conversation stirs up my head, in ways that solitary thinking or reading alone cannot. I usually appreciate the unpredictable interaction with different consciousnesses and experiences. But though I tried to be buoyed by the discussion, it could not relieve my feeling of unresolvable dread, especially regarding Borowski's death. I thought about his poor wife, and how she must've felt, having just undergone the animal glory and trauma of childbirth only to be greeted by its opposite, her husband's death by his own hand. I wondered if she'd had a reaction similar to my sister Kristin's after Rachel's death. She immediately stopped breast-feeding her six-month-old. Not of her own choice — the milk just wouldn't come. It's always been so sad and fascinating to me, that grief could interfere with your body's natural cycle like that, could prevent it from creating nourishment. When my sisters died, I was single, with time to focus on my own spectacular pain, to indulge in the outlandish tragedy of losing two sisters to suicide. When my dad died, I grieved with children for the first time, had to be more circumspect, careful not to frighten them with spontaneous crying jags at the dinner table, to include them in the grief but not suffocate them.

All evening my younger son, Otto, kept padding down the hall in his LEGO Darth Vader blanket sleeper, stealing cookies from the table and sitting in my lap while we talked our weighty adult talk. I held my son's lean, taut, and oblivious little body, kissed his blond hair as he munched the pilfered cookies, felt that protective ache of wanting to shield him from the worst of the world but also prepare him for the worst, knowing that neither was likely possible.

Maybe coincidence, maybe part of the osmotic nature of families, one afternoon, around the same time I was reading "This Way for the Gas, Ladies and Gentlemen," Otto asked from the backseat of the car:

"Mom, can I get a LEGO Nazi mini-figure?"

"I'm pretty sure they don't make those."

"Yeah, they do. There's a site that makes custom military LEGOs and stuff."

"Still no. They were the really, really, really bad guys."

"But they have the cool uniforms."

"That was part of the problem."

This was the first time I'd heard his little-boy voice say the word "Nazi," courtesy of the vast parallel universe of the online LEGO community. The dissonances were many: his absolute unknowing of the word's meaning and the absolute evil it evoked, the context of toys and play with agents of genocide, and the sometimes-disturbing crux of grown-up and kid in the virtual world. Plus, driving the car, eyeing him in the slot of the rearview mirror as he talked to the back of my head, I wasn't ready to have the conversation about Nazis and the problem of evil, nor make the cognitive and associative leaps necessary to contemporary parenting, especially as the Internet underscores how enmeshed childhood and adulthood are.

During this time, LEGOs trailed like crumbs from the car to the front door and scattered through every room in our old house, which is pretty much the opposite of tight LEGO construction and Danish design. A couple of blocks from the Mississippi River, it was built in the 1850s by carpenters who paced out measurements, pounded hand-hewn nails into planks hauled from disassembled barges, sometimes using corncobs as filler in the holes the barges' rods left in the thick wood. I do not believe there is one right angle in this home. And there are gaps — between heart-pine floorboards, in doorsills, baseboards — where the hard little plastic squares, rectangles, heads, weapons, get wedged. The detritus of the endless cycle of creating and destroying that's encoded in childhood.

This compulsion to create and destroy deluged my boys when they searched "LEGO" online, millions of offerings materializing, some official advertisements but mostly homemade videos, school projects, little dramas, lots of battles, posted in places from the Czech Republic to Thailand. Content and production values ranged. Some were burnished by special effects, others played out on bedsheets with the family dog sniffing around. The boys would find LEGO renderings of everything from the Book of Genesis to the March 3, 2011, tsunami and Fukushima Daiichi nuclear meltdown. Whole detailed worlds, like Coney Island; London; a geographically accurate conference-room-sized archipelago of the Philippines; canted bombed-out ruins of nineteenth-century town houses crumbling into perfect LEGO squares; the Twin Towers, about three feet tall, right after the planes hit but before they fell, billowing blackly but still erect. All technically masterful but begging for texture. Someone once told me he'd seen a LEGO reenactment of the Nuremberg trials, but I couldn't find it online when I looked. And since there are scores of World War II LEGO battle re-creations, I'm hopeful the Nazi mini-figure modification Otto referred to and so wanted is a nod to verisimilitude and not something else.

But the Internet is iridescent in that it can go shiny or dark with a single gesture and we can't always be within reach of the mouse, cover our kids' hands, and guide them away from danger. They have so many more worlds to navigate and synthesize than we did growing up, each one endlessly complex and atomized and volatile. One afternoon, as Otto was gliding across the surface of YouTube like a water bug, click to click, clip to clip, it didn't take long before he was hearing grating techno and someone singing "We like them girls with functioning vaginas." I grabbed for the mouse, but not before we saw a blond LEGO girl in a LEGO strip club with a missing leg pole-dancing, illustrating a line about how girls don't even need both legs, as long as they have, you know… I like to think exactly none of that soaked into his spongy brain. The video was stupid and unerotic, but also painful. I'm sensitive about the subject of stripping, as my sons' aunt Rebecca was a dancer at the time of her death. How did we arrive at this point in our culture where my five-year-old, his favorite toy, misogyny, stripping, and the sad context of my sister's suicide would all merge into the same moment?

A few days after Dad died, Otto presented me with a green LEGO cross, "in honor of Big Daddy." It was a solemn, spontaneous gesture, a kid trying to comfort his sad mom, maybe comfort himself by *making* something. But by the end of the day the cross had been absorbed into some other project or lost in the shag rug in the living room, a reminder of the easily dismantled illusion of order, something we are no strangers to in this city.

It was also a reminder that the kids were grieving, thinking about death as well. Our older son, Silas, tried hard to sound reassuring, talking adultly about how, yes, we would all miss Big Daddy. He gave me awkward hugs and a wide berth. The day after Dad died, Otto said, "Hey, today is Big Daddy's first day in heaven. Do you think he'll see Shadow and that kitten from Dauphine Street?" Shadow was their cousins' dog, found mysteriously dead in the backyard, covered in leaves with no visible sign of trauma. A few months earlier, on an otherwise-lovely walk to school, we'd seen a run-over kitten in the middle of the street before I could avert his eyes. It was a gruesome little scene. I couldn't eat for most of the day. He'd brought up the mutilated kitten out of the blue a couple of times since, so I knew it was still lingering near the surface of his mind, accruing portent, probably becoming one of those foundational memories that will keep bobbing up, *shiny black fur and entrails,* unbidden, over the years.

Similarly, I was thinking about the twins, wondering if in Dad's last moments, he was reunited with them. As galaxies of neural systems disintegrated and collapsed, maybe the most potent memories of people remained, floating as fragments in the burgeoning darkness. Or was there an actual uniting of their spirits? Or were they now just united in nothingness? Easier to conjure what Otto was probably envisioning: Big Daddy in a celestial recliner, peacefully stroking a cute, reconstituted kitten, with Shadow dozing by the raised footrest. Then I remembered that Dad really hated cats, was, in fact, allergic to them.

That night at the ECRG, all of those questions about the blonde, the "liaison," and the deaths by hanging still swirling and darkening in my head, I withdrew further from the discussion and held my little son tight, probably too tight, understanding guiltily that I wanted some of his soft, pure unknowingness to comfort me. And it didn't feel fair. It made me think about what adults need from children and the trappings of childhood, some adults being needier than others. But just for that moment I wanted to lose myself in the absolute of maternal physical connection and reemerge into the conversation softened by that melancholy buzz.

I guess Brad thought Otto was distracting me from the discussion, being too clingy, and he offered to do bedtime with him to give me some space. While I appreciated his intent, I excused myself instead to go read the bedtime story and do the tucking in, first checking on his older brother, who was dutifully finishing his homework at the kitchen table and completely uninterested in what the adults were talking about in the living room. Lying there in the boys' darkened room, with light from the hallway illuminating the transom high up, we could hear the voices down the hall in all their grown-up gradations, low to high, masculine and feminine, accents ranging from eastern Massachusetts to southern Alabama. The talking and laughing were muffled by the house's old barge-board walls and heavy cypress doors. Indistinct conversation circulated out of range. I had wondered what of this monthly living room talk Otto was going to retain (Silas willfully tuned us out), and now I thought I had my answer. From his bed, sound and light and meaning were diffuse, as though that evening's meeting had already become future memory. All these blurred voices, often urgent, often laughing. *What were they going on about all those nights?*

At some bedtimes, dread and affection weigh equally. Kids always look so cute in their PJs, so cozy-warm next to you, that connection so total and bodily fulfilling, and as their consciousness slips toward sleep they say amazing things, philosophical non sequiturs, snatches of playground drama, and then they are out, gone. And you lie there heavily, cloaked in the whole weight of the day, in the dark nagging of futility. Or worse, the promise of another day in about ten more hours. Often you can't find comfort in your sweetly nestled child, in fact sometimes the opposite. After the twins' deaths, my older brother, John, would inspect his sleeping daughters' young features for traces of Rebecca and Rachel, as if an inherited slope of the nose or cheekbone could portend self-destruction.

But sometimes you can find comfort elsewhere around you. Many nights, post-story and pre-sleep, my eyes have been attracted to the light-suffused transom over the door. There have been many times when I've received solace, or rather reassurance, from the heavy hand-hewn trim around the door, the architectural details of an old house that someone felt compelled to build more than a century and a half ago, with bargeboard floated down the Mississippi, made from trees chopped down and milled by someone maybe in Indiana or Ohio. Generations of parents have put their children to bed in this house and even if I haven't quite figured out the why and the how of living, others have found reasons to keep moving things forward. In quiet moments I can feel the collective push of these ghost-hands on my back, nudging me on.

This comfort of humanity's anonymous nudging is something

that Borowski seemed to feel, I guess just not strongly enough. In rereading his collection *This Way for the Gas, Ladies and Gentlemen* to get ready for the night's discussion, I had been especially struck by the final story, "The World of Stone." The story's opening describes one of those familiar moments of cosmic anxiety, the kind that arrive at 3 a.m. when you're untethered from the activity of the day:

> For quite some time now, like the foetus inside a womb, a terrible knowledge had been ripening within me and filling my soul with frightened foreboding: that the Infinite Universe is inflating at incredible speed, like some ridiculous soap bubble. I become obsessed with a miser's piercing anxiety whenever I allow myself to think that the Universe might be slipping out into space, like water through cupped hands, and that ultimately — perhaps even today, perhaps not till tomorrow or for several light years — it will dissolve for ever into emptiness, as though it were made not of solid matter but only of fleeting sound.

He tries to bring himself out of this state of free-floating fear by focusing on the activity of the people around him. After the suffering and atrocity of the war, people are moving on with the work of civilization, building, repairing, cooking, cleaning. He summons Rousselot's trinity: willing, possessing, feeling. *All three* inspire him toward his own work of trying to record, and understand, his moment here on the planet. Knowing Borowski's fate makes the narrator's efforts particularly heartbreaking. "The World of Stone" ends like this:

> And since today the world has not yet blown away, I take out a fresh piece of paper, arrange it neatly on the desk, and closing my eyes try to find within me a tender feeling for the workmen ham-

48

mering the rails, for the peasant women with their ersatz sour cream, the trains full of merchandise, the fading sky above the ruins, for the passers-by on the street below and the newly installed windows, and even for my wife who is washing dishes in the kitchen alcove; and with a tremendous intellectual effort I attempt to grasp the true significance of the events, things and people I have seen. For I intend to write a great, immortal epic, worthy of this unchanging, difficult world chiselled out of stone.

Though I was moved by the narrator's search for affection and connection with these other lives, I was also a little confounded that, in the end, he deemed the world static and rigid, when he'd been describing so much of life's flux and movement. What was so "unchanging" about this "world chiselled out of stone"? Our brutality toward each other? That we'll build everything up just to see it all torn down again? What happened to the expanding soap bubble?

That sense of confusion with the ending reminded me of my dad, but then again, during that time, anything I found particularly affecting, especially ECRG readings, did. He often seemed to have similar conflicting impulses about life. Just a few months before he died, he came home one afternoon with some sacks of blue crabs and shrimp, having happened upon a small seafood joint he'd never noticed before and stopped at on a whim. Dumping the crabs into trays on his kitchen counter, ashen but animated, he described the terrifically nice family who worked behind the counter, the freshly cleaned linoleum floors, even the lighting, with such vivid enthusiasm. Life could still surprise you, he was demonstrating, if you paid attention and took advantage.

This seemed in opposition to how dark and fatalistic he could be, feeling his own world was made of stone. I think after the twins died, something in him began to calcify. He became even more attached to the recliner and his remote control, self-medicating with enormous gin and tonics, televised sports, and a weird *Wheel of Fortune* addiction, which always seemed so beneath him. Though now as a working parent I totally understand the need to put your brain in neutral and lose yourself to glittering low-stakes, small-screen spectacles. Six feet three and supine in a recliner is the dominant image I have of him from childhood until his death. It was a sacred zone, exempt from the demands of decor, though at least, thankfully, the recliners became less ugly over the years: terrible, scratchy polyester-blend plaid to maroon Naugahyde to puffy velour and, finally, his last one, a tasteful Mission-style brown leather.

In the big houses he was always so proud of, there was nothing much else that we associated with his personal tastes or proclivities. The rest was Mom, antiques she inherited from some other big house, furniture she found and restored from a thrift store or garage sale. Besides the recliner, his other sacrosanct spot in the house was the head of the sprawling dining room table, where mandatory Sunday dinners were more debates and cross-examinations than meals. Choice discussion topics during the '80s were women's rights, the death penalty, nuclear energy, and whatever political circus was entertaining the state of Louisiana. Table 5 at the Rib Room was the third panel of the patriarchal triptych, outside the domestic sphere, where he operated on his terms only, no managing a hungry, unruly tribe, no compromising with my mother, who never went to the Rib Room or knew the extent of the time he spent there. The Rib Room was the cornerstone of his double life.

We all colluded in keeping our lunches with him a secret from Mom, believed we were simultaneously protecting his privacy and her innocence. (Another reason my sister Amy boycotted the Rib Room.) At the time it seemed normal, harmless, even. Back then, it was a father's privilege, after all, to have his own space out in the world, while my mom's time and attention seemed wide open and always up for grabs. She was home in the morning and the afternoon, for homework help and parent conferences and doctor's visits. I never thought of her as needing privacy or having a private self. The secret lunches were a way of aligning ourselves with our far more mysterious father, who wasn't around much, gaining his favor and confidence, a glamorous introduction to the adult world of martinis and courtroom drama and politics. It all seems so unnecessary now, as Mom was more tolerant and understanding of Dad's need for freedom than he gave her credit for. We didn't really realize that we were helping maintain the existing wall between our parents' parallel lives. Even into our adulthood, when we *did* realize that's what we were doing, out of habit and deference to Dad we still never told Mom.

But the turning point for me in how I viewed the place's role in my relationship with him was that long table 5 lunch when he'd asked me how my writing was going and I mentioned working on a piece about Rebecca and Rachel but, I don't know, maybe it was too soon, not the right time. Dad had a special way of shutting us down with a sudden, efficient ferocity. He leaned across the white tablecloth and the elegant clutter of our meal, formidable in his suit and tie, attitude taut with litigator focus, and said that there would never be the right time for me to write about it because nothing good could ever come from their deaths. Their deaths could not be transformed by art into something positive or affirming ("Suicide; Transcendence"), and he announced that if I ever did attempt to do so, he would never forgive me, that he would take it to his grave if I ever did, which I did not doubt.

For whatever reason, my dad needed their deaths to stay chiseled and unchangeable tragedies. Maybe it was just easier for him to possess their memories, their deaths, that way. Not to mention contain the shame and the pain. I once visited his office and was puzzled by what seemed to be dried-flower arrangements lining a set of shelves against the wall. It seemed an odd decorating choice for a man who cared nothing about decorating. On my way out I noticed a note of condolences on one of the arrangements. These were flowers people sent after Rachel died, over a year before, that he could not bring himself to throw out. That, oddly, his secretary didn't touch either. Brown lines from water long evaporated ringed the bottoms of the glass vases. A sad tableau that he probably didn't even notice any-more, had just become absorbed into the clutter of his office, his life.

I knew he was being irrational in demanding I not write about it, but having two daughters kill themselves is irrational. I remember having no adequate response except to flush warmly, reach for my wine, and look out the window in mute acceptance, suddenly oppressed by the padded booth and black marbled walls. Feeling stuck and wanting to get the hell out of there. Luckily, it was the end of lunch, when things materialize in accordance with the regular rhythm of the meal. The de rigueur Drambuie in snifters would have arrived, throwing quivering amber shadows on the table, and soon after, the check would come and go without Dad even looking at it, a wordless understanding with his waiter. We would go our separate ways into the afternoon. I knew which bars in the French Quarter Dad frequented and would steer clear, go to my own bars in my own neighborhood.

Soon after Dad died, I ran into an ex-boyfriend, a long mistake whom it took me several confusing years to extricate myself from, who told me how he'd overheard a couple of men in a golf clubhouse reminiscing about the legendary Rib Room days and their post-lunch benders. One of the men said that he was often tasked with keeping track of Gisleson, because he had a tendency to just disappear.

MARCH

The Belly of the Whale

On the morning commute to Otto's school, we'd sometimes pass a bar, a twenty-four-hour joint with its door propped open to the daylight. Often the threshold framed a patron on a stool, usually an older guy, maybe smoking, who had either been there all night or was starting very early. Behind him, redly glowing light fixtures on the low ceiling, the jittery screens of video poker machines, that sweet, dread touch of Christmas lights strung above the bottles. Unused cash registers with neat squares of rags covering the buttons. George Jones on the jukebox back by the pool table.

Sometimes we would get stuck in traffic in front of that bar and watch one of the patrons gazing outside. I'd wave and one of the guys would wave back. Once Otto asked why I did that, wave, and I said, "I'm just saying hi." Then thought to myself, *Saluting the Tragic Plane on the way to kindergarten drop-off.*

Because of our March ECRG reading, an excerpt from Arthur Koestler's 1964 opus, *The Act of Creation,* I had become attuned to life's Tragic and Trivial Planes. In *The Act of Creation,* which explores the nature and purpose of creativity in life, novelist/journalist/anti–death penalty activist/suicide Koestler outlined what he believed are the two essential planes of existence: the Trivial and the Tragic. The

Trivial Plane is where most of us spend a great deal of our lives, doing the work of survival and civilization: repetitive labor, commuting, running errands, and general life maintenance. In the Trivial Plane we are held down by "the grip of convention," and the possibility of self-transcendence diminishes. We experience the Tragic Plane when we fully connect to metaphysical forces like love, despair, and death, but if we spend too much time in "the belly of the whale," which tends to "disrupt all logical operations," we become lost.

The Koestler reading was chosen by Tristan, born on a barge on an Amsterdam canal, a former bookseller and editor and now a carpenter. He'd been one of the first to arrive at the warehouse when our nonprofit held a drawing marathon in the half-deserted, art-starved city after Katrina, along with the National Guard. A stranger to us, he stayed most of the twenty-four hours, even helped clean up the huge mess the following morning. He's been a steady partner in projects and a generous friend ever since. That evening he described how about twenty years before he'd taken a nine-month job in Antarctica, painting the walls of the McMurdo Station, an American research center. The average temperature was always below zero and there were only about a hundred people there, the paint crew cloaked in white suits, against the white walls, atop the white continent. He said that the sensory and emotional isolation was intense but that he learned to recognize fellow workers by their gestures and gait, an industrious band of ghosts whose moods he could sense by the way they held a paintbrush or traversed the camp. When he finally went on leave to Christchurch, New Zealand, he was so overwhelmed by the intensity of daily life — the colors, the sounds, the expressions on people's faces — that he felt like a newborn baby, experiencing everything for the first time, wandering the town near tears.

Koestler posited that both the Tragic and Trivial Planes are necessary to live a fully engaged life, and that each plane can only be truly grasped through contact with the other. The seam, or tightrope, between them is where human creativity, whether personal, artistic, or scientific, exists. While the Tragic Plane feeds our minds and souls, the Trivial Plane provides the necessary "social and intellectual stability" needed to create and function.

There's something to be said for putting a name to a condition, a certain comfort in common recognition. After reading the Koestler piece, I started evaluating my days in terms of the Tragic and Trivial, how much time I spent on either plane. I could've charted it out like an EKG reading. In the morning, on Trivial lockdown getting everyone fed, ready, and where they need to go; late morning, if I'm writing, I check in with the Tragic; early afternoon, at work teaching, the planes are interlocked; afternoon safely back on the Trivial with pickup, homework, dinner. Though often, around five o'clock, it's like someone walks up and hangs an anvil around my neck, which maybe explains the universal cocktail hour. Then everyone shuffles sleepily toward nighttime oblivion. With enough luck and self-medication, no night terrors at three in the morning. But there are always places in life where these dichotomies fall apart. For me, it's caring for my children and husband, when affection breaks through the chores, times when making dinner and folding laundry also feel like love.

At March's ECRG, we talked about how difficult it can be to negotiate the planes, like when you're, say, shopping at Target, but deep in some anxiety or despair, and you run into an acquaintance who asks how you're doing and you can only smile and lie, white-knuckling the edge of the Trivial Plane. We talked about how some people we know seem to firmly inhabit one or the other, about people we'd lost outright to the Tragic Plane, dragging others down with them for a while. I wondered if Rebecca and Rachel knew, on some subconscious level, that their suicides awarded the rest of us siblings lifetime memberships to the Tragic Plane, wondered if spite figured at all in the blackness of those last moments of preparation and descent. Most likely not, but they always seemed so united in their aggrievement. We thought they were spoiled, our tired parents too lax with discipline, with curfews, with money, after already raising six children. The twins thought that as the youngest they were getting the scraps of a big, noisy, energetic family.

Koestler wrote that whole communities can be relocated to the gusty Tragic Plane through catastrophes like war and natural disaster. We agreed and talked about how after Katrina, it was extraordinary to live in a city where people were so blasted open and vulnerable, charged with frustration and purpose. For the first year, it was a town without small talk, everyone eager to connect with each other, share their sad, crazy tales. So much work and worry; people seemed exhausted all of the time. In addition to all the authentic human interaction, hope, and generosity, this Tragic Plane was also distinguished by the exodus of friends, the premature loss of many of our elderly, vultures of all stripes, suicide, and divorce.

But, Koestler continued, these communities "soon succeed in banalizing even tragedy itself and carry on business as usual among the shambles." Also true. Just two months after 80 percent of the city had flooded, and was still mostly empty, my older sister, Kristin, insisted on celebrating her husband's birthday with a big dinner at a nice French Quarter restaurant, one of the few that had reopened by October. Restaurants, five-star to one-star, had limited menus and were serving everything on paper, plastic, or Styrofoam because the water system was still wrecked, and everyone was understaffed. Kristin couldn't abide that, despised drinking wine out of plastic, so she brought her own case of wineglasses to the restaurant for us to drink from, then took them home and washed them herself.

That night Brad and I were sitting next to a man I'd known for years who had lost his father, house, and job during Katrina. He had a look that had become familiar during that time, a loose, tired quality acquired from your life being mangled and imperfectly reassembled, wife and children suddenly shoehorned into a small apartment in a part of town you'd never liked but that hadn't flooded, and working a job you'd never wanted but that paid. In the tawny glow of the grand dining room of the Bourbon House, our plastic cutlery might've squeaked against the Styrofoam plates, just like it did against the containers we lined up for at the Red Cross trucks when we first came back to the destroyed city, but we were toasting my brother-in-law and the strength of our troubled region with my sister's wineglasses, clutching the delicate stems.

Spending so much time on the Tragic Plane alters your relationship to the world. Obsessions and patterns emerge that were not available to you before. My first extended visit there was when Rebecca died, in 1998. We buried her in the half-crumbling Lafayette Cemetery No. 1 in an aboveground tomb that had been given to my great-grandfather to pay off a debt. The tomb at Lafayette No. 1 was merely a piece of real estate like any other, and thus contained a whole other family of strangers. My grandparents and five previous generations on my mother's side are buried in a tomb in a Creole section of St. Louis No. 2 on Esplanade Avenue, on the same street where my grandmother was born. My grandfather had been interred there about six months before Rebecca died, and according to certain Latin burial practices in New Orleans, you're supposed to wait a year and a day before reopening the brick-and-mortar seal on the vault. So my mother asked her mother, alive at the time, if the auxiliary Lafayette No. 1 tomb could be used for Rebecca.

It hadn't been opened for well over a hundred years. Walking the crushed oyster-shell lanes toward the interment, we passed a few tombs engraved DIED OF YELLOW FEVER. When we arrived at what was about to become our family tomb, our grief was momentarily pushed aside by curiosity about the freshest vision of history we'd probably ever see. As my older brother held the urn with Rebecca's ashes, we peered inside and marveled. The shadows of the tomb, which had been sealed up since 1884, still held the same crypt-cooled air of that year and two small, sealed iron sarcophagi that Mom mused distractedly could've been yellow-fever victims, since the date was about right and that was often a method of burial for the more affluent victims of the disease.

Over the next several months, the thought of Rebecca being interred with nineteenth-century yellow-fever victims nagged me, embellished my grief in a way I didn't understand. The metaphorical connection was not neat: yellow fever was an impersonal affliction while suicide was intensely personal. One had been more or less eradicated and the other probably never would be — timelessly, universally, connected to our condition. But both were associated with helplessness, a giving over to an invading force. And both were contingent on the communal, and thus could have devastating effects on the community.

One afternoon, still mired in grief, I remembered an old book about yellow fever I'd acquired at that cursed estate sale where I'd found *A Concise Dictionary of Existentialism* and searched for it around my apartment. At the time of Rebecca's death, I was renting a cheap, grand place on Felicity Street, in the Lower Garden District, one of those mansions divided up into apartments during the city's late-twentieth-century decline, with double parlors, tall ceilings and windows, tiny, squalid bathroom and kitchen, and a man I should have left long before. I finally found the cinder-block-sized book in a closet, hosting silverfish in a musty cardboard box. As I sat on the floor and carefully opened it, the book shed vestiges of leather spine. It was actually the *1882 Annual Report of the Louisiana Board of Health,* including brittle foldout charts, graphs, and maps detailing various public health issues, and also the latest medical research, statistics, speculation, correspondence, and quarantine efforts relating to diseases like smallpox and yellow fever. Apparently, sixty babies died from *teething* that year, while Mardi Gras travel from the North and West brought in smallpox, as did the booming cotton trade. The report blamed "the coloreds'" reluctance to get vaccinated for various diseases' persistence in the city, but who could blame them for not trusting white men with needles? The thousands of ships that came through the port were described as disease-breeding vessels importing microscopic threats from all over the globe.

The book and I soon moved from the floor by the closet to the airy front parlor, and settled onto the couch I'd bought with the live-in boyfriend and which I would leave behind a couple of years later, with most everything else, when I finally came to my senses. The annual report was from around the same time our Lafayette No. 1 tomb had last been used, and I focused on information regarding yellow fever in New Orleans. An extensive article by Dr. Joseph Jones, who spent twenty-seven years of his life studying the disease, began, "A pestilential fever of continuous and specific type, originally developed in tropical and insular America; confined to definite geographic limits and dependent in its origin and spread upon definite degrees of temperature and capable of transportation and propagation in ships and towns and cities." Dr. Jones cataloged its symptoms thus:

> intense pain in the head and back, injected eyes, rapid circulation, elevated temperatures...depression of the nervous and muscular forces, and of the general and capillary circulation, jaundice, urinary suppression, passive hemorrhages from the stomach and bowels, nares, tongue, gums, uterus, vagina, gall bladder and anus, and in extreme cases from the eyes, ears and skin; black vomit; convulsions, delirium and coma.

Lurid, hand-colored, full-page drawings depicted a young man in a collared nightshirt tucked under a lovely green blanket in various stages of yellow fever. First: flushed forehead and cheeks under dark, delicate curls and gray, stupefied, bloodshot eyes. Several pages later, the final stage: eyes yellow, brow deeply furrowed as if in distracted concentration, black vomit splotching all over his pillow, dressing gown, and sheets. The shadows on the pillow, cloudlike in the first drawing, are now more jagged and urgent. The angle of the shadows suggests a bedside lantern, one that must've lit the artist's sketchpad as he tried to get the capillaries, the curls, and the spring-green blanket's arabesques just right.

Dr. Jones wrote, "We have, in New Orleans, great variations in the severity and duration of the febrile stage." So true, I thought, slipping back into the metaphorical. At the same age Rebecca was when she died, I'd been caught up in my own aimless febrile stage. I lived in an old Creole house from the 1830s on Orleans Street in the French Quarter where leprous plaster fell in clumps from the ceiling, cracks spidered and split, ivy worked its way subcutaneously into the rooms. During that time I suffered a sort of fever, the kind that made you stay up all night and spend late mornings in a pained, lethargic struggle for your senses. A dislocation of days, a disorientation of hours. I worked as a cocktail waitress and later at the front desk of a hotel down the street. I usually had a bottle of Dewar's on my dresser, and every night was another opportunity for a hundred bad decisions. But eventually, incrementally, through luck and inchoate forward movement, I broke through all that, applied to grad school, started teaching (though I was still making bad romantic decisions). Why couldn't Rebecca have broken through her stretch of dark confusion? What resources did she not possess? So many unsuccessful suicides are grateful for that second chance that it's become part of conventional suicide-prevention wisdom: if vulnerable people can just make it through those dark moments, they'll be okay on the other side. But roughly one in a thousand of us can't or don't.

Why did I conflate yellow fever with Rebecca's suicide? If her fellow tenants in the tomb were indeed yellow-fever victims, why was I so preoccupied with the symptoms and grisly circumstances of their deaths? The images, the suffering? Was it an attempt to ground her death in something both historical and visceral, rescue her from the void? Metaphor can be good for attempted void rescuing. The satisfaction of connection, the sharpening of feeling. Even though I was having a hard time reading books during that first period of intense grief, out of my inner chaos literary patterns of arrangement were still forming, almost helplessly.

A similar thing would happen in the aftermath of Rachel's death, when I was once again thrust onto the Tragic Plane. At a springtime lunch at an outdoor café with my mother, both of us still very much in that raw, pained state, I saw within a cascade of jasmine vine a young tendril that had curved back up on itself and twisted into a perfect noose. I was so distracted by the noose I could barely participate in conversation. Even nature was conspiring to make sure the chosen method of both girls' deaths would always be present to me, always exist somewhere in the world. For a time after that lunch I began to see nooses and potential nooses everywhere, in oriental carpets, in belts, in necklaces, in cursive letters, electrical wires, a knot of twine in the junk drawer.

While the noose was a rather focused motif, the yellow-fever metaphor/preoccupation had been compounded by the appearance of bouquets of yellow roses at Rebecca's tomb every now and then for about a year after her death. It was presumably her ex, M., the large, blond, doughy, abusive strip-club owner. I had suspected he'd been abusing her, and it was confirmed one night at a party after she died, when an acquaintance began a conversation with condolences, but then suddenly revealed that he and his wife had briefly lived next door to Rebecca and M. and had often heard the unmistakable sound of my sister being beaten. Slaps, thuds, cries, etc. I turned stony inside and asked why he never called the cops or told anyone. He said he was afraid of M. and his two massive Rottweilers. I don't remember how the conversation ended, though I do remember leaving the party immediately, weighed down with disgust and sadness. Though M. had not been invited to the funeral and it would've been hard to find the right tomb in the labyrinthine cemetery, I assumed he was the one leaving the flowers because of a discovery my sisters and I made when we broke into his house a few days after Rebecca was interred.

The night we learned of Rebecca's death, Rachel and I drove from New Orleans across the Lake Pontchartrain Causeway through the first bands of Tropical Storm Frances (Rebecca died on September 10, in the height of hurricane season) to the house where Rebecca had been living with M. The Causeway, at twenty-four miles, is the longest bridge over water in the world. But Frances transformed it into a dark tunnel, the bridge's lights relentless little explosions against the windshield and harassing rain. We were riding inside of something terrible and terrifying on the way to something terrible and terrifying. I felt as though we could veer off the bridge and into the lake at any moment, be effortlessly absorbed into the tragic night.

Leaving the city for the suburbs had seemed like a bad move for Rebecca. She did not have a driver's license and would be completely dependent on M., becoming even more isolated from family and friends. I didn't have a license at the time either, so I was riding shotgun in Rachel's truck while she drove and cried and ranted, about Rebecca, about her shitty neighbors who were probably pilfering Rebecca's stuff at the house, about what an asshole M. was. About how earlier that afternoon during her waitressing shift, as she stood at a table to take an order, her throat suddenly felt tight and constricted, for no apparent reason. And then it stopped, but she felt uneasy until the minute she got the call.

The house Rebecca and M. shared was in a dismal subdivision with shoddy ranch houses and aristocratic, British-sounding street names like Westminster Road and Tottenham Place. They had lived there only a couple of months and I had never been. Parked in the driveway was a young sympathetic state cop, though I wasn't sure why. Rebecca's body had been taken away by the coroner's office hours before. The cop escorted us in and informed us that M.'s mother was inside, which was news to us. She was cleaning the house and barely spoke to us, busying herself in the living room. I wondered if this was part of some pattern, of her cleaning up after her son's messes. We looked around the open-plan living area: black leather couch, big television with black particleboard shelving on either side, lined with dozens of unmarked VHS tapes like a keyboard missing its ivories, all sharps and flats. In the dining area, a glass-topped table with black place mats. All of the windows were covered, but mostly with dark towels, not curtains. One was a souvenir beach towel from Biloxi, Mississippi. HAVE FUN IN BILOXI.

Rebecca was always making imperfect attempts at domesticity with the wrong men. Once I drove past the apartment she shared with a different wrong man, uptown on Marengo Street, and saw a crushed television on the grass next to the sidewalk and their busted living room window two floors above it. I had just given her an old mirror I wasn't using, because she was trying to decorate the place. Later, I tried to call but she didn't pick up, and I never learned the story of the smashed television in the grass.

M.'s mother obviously had not made it to the kitchen because there was a casual mess and an unfinished saucepan of safety-orange macaroni and cheese on the stove. Was that Rebecca's last meal?

Would've seemed fitting. Hasty, ill thought out. A chemically deceitful Kraft box nearby on the counter.

I don't remember exactly what Rachel was looking for, but I followed her to the bedroom, which was a wreck, its disarray sadly typical of Rebecca's life, her impulsivity. Clothes that still had tags on them were mixed with dirty laundry in a pile on a leopard-print settee. It was a dancer's wardrobe — most every article contained some high percentage of spandex, a degree of shimmer. Treacherous heels and patent leather boots spilled out of the closet. The young state trooper had also entered the bedroom and remarked that it was such a mess they couldn't tell whether it had been ransacked or if that was its regular state. At the moment I could envision both, Rebecca regularly ransacking her own room, her long lacquered nails tossing clothes off hangers in a panic or rage, all of her choices suddenly unacceptable.

The trooper must've sensed that his presence and commentary were intrusive and disappeared from the room, for which I was grateful. Especially depressing was the plastic storage container she was using as a bedside table, and even more so what was on it, half-used tubes of certain "intimate" products that I would never have left out in public view if I were planning to kill myself. Lord, that sibling impulse to judge and compare is so enduring. But did she not anticipate us seeing her life in all its sordidness? Was she thinking about us at all? Was she that lost to the world?

In the middle of the chaos was a video camera, angled toward the unmade bed. I instinctively looked through the finder and recoiled, not because of anything I saw, but because of the complicity of my gesture, of leaning down toward the lens like M. might have. Then I thought of all of the unlabeled videotapes back in the living room, and the darkness stretched farther out around me.

Sometime over those next few days, I told my other sisters about the camera and the videotapes. With little discussion about the video-tapes' implications, it was unanimously decided that we had to drive back across the lake and retrieve and destroy them all. Since M. had supposedly and suspiciously left town, some breaking and entering might be required.

When the day came, we actually weren't that nervous. We five remaining sisters felt armored by Rebecca's death, righteous and protected by grief. The Tragic Plane had given us permission. This time, it was a clear sunny day when we crossed the lake and drove the unfamiliar piney roads in Kristin's SUV to M.'s house. We parked out front, one of us lifting the unlocked garage door while the rest of us watched the quiet street of the subdivision, the replication of the same brick facing and vinyl bay windows and driveways and sloped curbs. M.'s lawn was looking shaggy, and two dead ferns dangled over the small concrete porch.

We all ducked inside the garage and quickly closed the door behind us. Inside was a crazy array of man-toys — an inflated army-green raft, a four-wheeler, miscellaneous sports equipment, a large empty animal cage. Kristin had brought a couple of screwdrivers in one of her baby's diaper bags, and she expertly removed the molding from around the door that led into the house.

"Shitty new construction," she murmured as she jimmied the lock open.

The house held a totally different sadness in the light of day. M.'s mother had cleaned it into a sort of stillness — most traces of domestic activity erased. Sliding patio doors I had not noticed the night I came with Rachel framed the white plastic chaise lounge where Rebecca might've sunned herself (she was always so perfectly tan) and a lawn mower stuck in the middle of the yard, defeated in the high grass. Our first order of business was to stuff all of the unmarked videotapes into my sister's diaper bags, in case we had to leave in a hurry. Then we did a tentative tour of the house. The bedroom had been cleaned and the camera was gone. Though the master bathroom had been tidied up, the laminate countertop was still dusted with the shiny mica residue of Rebecca's expensive and beloved cosmetics. A box of tampons left on the back of the toilet.

We paused for a moment in front of the bare, spare guest room where M. found her. The room was not giving up any of the despair and the horror that had so recently transpired there. It remained thoroughly unremarkable with its beige walls, single bed, and untroubled carpeting. We inspected the ceiling fan. Like the rest of the house, it seemed flimsy, installed up against the eight-foot ceiling. Rebecca was the smallest, thinnest of all of us children, but it seemed impossible that the fan could've sustained her weight. We all wondered, Why this room? Why not the bedroom? She did not leave a note. The hanging was the message and the room was the envelope.

For years, that ceiling fan would continue to sow doubt about her death. Given the abusive nature of her relationship with M., couldn't it just as well have been murder? M. had conveniently disappeared. No one ever heard from him again. Dad hired a private investigator, an ex–FBI agent he knew from the strike-force days, to look into him, but nothing came of it. Years later at a dinner party, the conversation somehow turned to a murder that was made to look like a suicide. As I was expressing an unusual amount of interest, someone at the table who happened to be a medical examiner explained to me that it's very difficult to fake a suicide by hanging. I confided the reason for my interest and the woman turned both firmly professional and compassionate, looked me full in the face. Most likely the coroner's determination was correct, she said. The cause of death that ended up in the obituary for both sisters was "undetermined causes," in collusion with the funeral home, the newspaper, the family, and society about the taboo of suicide. Nowadays when I scan the obituaries, it's the phrase "died at home" that tips me off.

We came to a room that must've been M.'s office, with not much more than a desk and a clunky IBM computer. One desk drawer was filled with bright hard candy. Another, a few Rolex watches, most likely knockoffs. For a moment, feeling even more criminal, I wanted to take one, but I shut the drawer instead. The walk-in closet appeared empty until I pulled the light chain. A blinding hundred-or-so-watt bulb illuminated a high shelf on the three walls of the closet. The shelf was lined with bouquet after bouquet of yellow roses in glass vases, in various states of desiccation. What was this? A vault of atonement? Of affection? Someone either needed to remember or needed to be reminded. (Yes, a few years later, the image in my father's office of the dead-flower arrangements did remind me of this discovery.) Whatever it was, it seemed central to the mystery of their relationship, and an expression of that mystery found its way to the tomb at Lafayette No. 1 every now and then for about a year after Rebecca's death. The bouquets' appearances at the tomb made me feel sick and bitter, knowing I had to allow M. his own grief, when all I wanted to do was throw the yellow roses in the trash, something neither he nor Rebecca could ever bring themselves to do.

After tapping the molding back into place and relocking the door that led to the garage, we went to lunch at a nearby Chinese restaurant, trying to make sense of that house and failing. We agreed to dispose of the diaper bag's cargo later that evening, planning to unspool the tapes and trash them over wine at Kristin's house. When the check came, we sat in the red padded booth, reluctant to open our fortune cookies. Gathered on the tray with the bill, they looked sinister in their cellophane wrappers, harboring tiny slips of the future, of wisdom, of nonsense, waiting to be crushed open.

A year and a half later, when Rachel died and we had to deal with her belongings, the Tragic and Trivial Planes collided again with great force. When we arrived at the house, four sisters now, wearily replaying a familiar scene, on the street were a discarded light fixture with a fussy Italian quality to it, painted metal flowers, and crystal pendants. It was what she'd tied her bathrobe sash to. In his derangement after having to cut her down, her new husband, D., had ripped it out of the ceiling that same day and thrown it on the curb.

Rachel's house was in a different type of disorder. She had just moved in with D., a fireman she'd married in Las Vegas a few weeks before, and his children, and was still unpacking boxes of kitchenware, CDs, art projects she'd worked on with her five-year-old son, including a particularly good one using recycled bottles and an old window frame. Some of it was detritus from her time on the Trivial Plane, but also what made her who she was, all of her tastes and choices. She'd started a new life, gone back to school, loved her young son as tremendously as any mother. We thought she had a chance.

We chose a few pieces of jewelry to give to Mom and shoved Rachel's clothes in trash bags to sort through later. Her style was much more conservative than Rebecca's, reflecting a young mother who liked to be comfortable but also look good. In the pocket of a rather dowdy cotton shirt, I found a drinking straw cut down to coke-sniffing size and a trace of white powder. Why had I thought that Rachel's destructive habits would die with Rebecca? Rebecca was often seen as the corrupting force, since she so outwardly embodied it, but the two of them obviously shared these impulses. I wondered if continuing to indulge in those impulses kept Rachel connected to Rebecca after she was gone.

Hanging on the closet doorknob was a simple black crocheted purse with a long strap. Not much was in it save Rachel's wallet and an unused, unopened eye-shadow case, wrapped in a receipt from

Rite Aid, which I scrutinized. (As well as being a farewell, suicide is an invitation, for people to study your stuff, a forensic rifling that can last for years.) It was purchased the day before she killed herself. *Who does that?* I thought. Buys an eight-color eye-shadow palette from the drugstore one day and then hangs herself with a bathrobe sash the next? It was probably a casual, pick-me-up impulsive purchase, meant to make you feel a little better, a little prettier, the kind that fuels a billion-dollar cosmetic industry.

I still have that CoverGirl eye-shadow case, an object that dovetails both commonly used definitions of vanity — the desire for admiration, especially in the sense of physical appearance — and that of Ecclesiastian futility. *All is vanity.* For well over a decade I've tried to throw that thing away, dislodge it from my own cluttered cabinet of vanities, but I can't, and I never use it. It's become both memento mori and cautionary talisman about putting too many eggs in the attractiveness basket, like Rebecca did, and sometimes Rachel, especially as I get older and the market competes so virulently to capitalize on my insecurity and degenerating cells. I truly believe that being beautiful contributed to the undermining of the twins' sense of self-worth, made them vulnerable to all kinds of bad situations, especially with men.

Here is the palette, purchased at the Rite Aid on Napoleon Avenue in mid-March of 2000, CoverGirl Professional Eye Enhancers Sonoma Sunset, or *Crépuscule Enchanté* (the packaging also includes the French translations of the different shades, which of course sound more glamorous and promising): Autumn Haze, Mink, Fresh Moss, Mint Green, Peach Nectar, Hazelnut, French Vanilla, and Champagne, half of them matte and half frost, a soft, aromatic confusion of nature and flavors. The tiny foam applicator is so old it's crumbled off its tiny blue plastic handle. I've held on to other objects that Rachel and Rebecca actually wore — pairs of jeans, shirts, some earrings — but this eye makeup was in some kind of pure, shrink-wrapped state of being desired but never used, purchased and then forgotten about, as all objects became useless and irrelevant when she let go of both planes, all objects except her bathrobe sash.

———————

In January 2012, when Dad died, the old wounds and older bricks were opened up to daylight again by the cemetery's mortar-splattered sextons. The marble slab engraved with the twins' names and dates had been removed from the tomb's entrance, as well as about a two-by-two-foot section of bricks, just enough space for my brother to reach through with Dad's urn and place it on the narrow shelf inside. The family closed in around it and a small crowd fanned out behind us, including a very emotional Chris in a tweed cap and jacket, the only nonfamily ECRG member who really knew Dad, as the priest blessed Dad's everlasting rest, reminding us that from dust we came and to dust we will return. A strong breeze knocked over one of the oversized arrangements of gladiolas flanking the tomb, and we joked that it was for Big Daddy, because he would erupt dramatically over spills at the dinner table, a near-nightly occurrence when we were growing up. We took turns tossing a flower into the tomb, and saying our silent good-byes. When it was my turn, I peered inside, looking for the twins' urns, which were matching but not quite identical, like the twins themselves, but I couldn't see them inside the dank opening. When we'd interred Rachel, Rebecca's urn was in plain sight inside the tomb and I laid my hand on its cold ceramic glazing and then on Rachel's, which was still warm with the March sun, but not for long.

It didn't matter that I couldn't see their urns. After all, it was part of the sextons' job to shuffle things around inside the tomb to make room for more dead. The mere act of gathering there at our personal Southern Gothic set piece — the molting magnolias, the grid of crumbling mausoleums, all that indifferent yet affirming statuary — reunited us all on the Tragic Plane. The twins' ghosts would begin reasserting themselves, and Dad's presence in my life would be augmented by his loss. When I'd drive by that bar in the mornings with my son, he was superimposed on those solitary guys in the threshold, residue from an old high school memory.

One early evening driving in slow traffic down St. Charles Avenue to pick up Rachel at a friend's house, I happened to see my dad in his lawyerly three-piece suit through the propped-open door of the Bamboo Lounge, lobby of sorts for the Audubon Hotel, known for all manner of transients. He was alone in this seedy bar, watching television. He looked both out of place and totally comfortable. It was almost dinnertime and I asked myself, why wasn't he home with his wife and eight kids? One of those questions that probably answer themselves. By then, he had earned his big house in an old-money neighborhood, but I guess he was craving a different kind of comfort, something that reminded him of the back alleys of South Beloit, where he'd court trouble as a kid, working at the Black Hawk Grocery. Who knows. It was a perfectly framed tableau illustrating what an utter stranger my father was and always would be to me. One afternoon a few years later, walking to work under the sheltering balconies of the French Quarter, I saw him playing video poker in a black leather jacket through the door of Harry's Corner, yet another stranger in another part of town. The aperture of the bar's doorway turned kaleidoscopic, and I wondered how many of my fathers were out there.

APRIL

The Last Suffer; or,
The Way of the Crisis (Via Dolorosa)

*F*or those of you who couldn't attend last month's ECRG, it was decided that since the date of our next gathering falls during the Christian Holy Week, in lieu of someone choosing a reading, we'd integrate secular and nonsecular ritual for our own attempt at shaping meaning and tradition. Someone brought up the Way of the Cross (also known as Stations of the Cross or Via Dolorosa) procession performed in the neighborhood during Holy Week, starting at the Blessed Francis Xavier Seelos Church on the corner, with prearranged stops commemorating certain events of the Passion of Christ, following Jesus's path from condemnation to crucifixion, a mini-pilgrimage of the faithful. Pilgrims have been visiting holy sites in Jerusalem since the reign of Constantine the Great, the first Christian Roman emperor, in the early fourth century. For those who could not make the long journey to the Holy Land, reproductions began to appear in Europe around the fifth century, when a monastery in Bologna built chapels arranged to mimic the progression through the sites. Some Via Dolorosa reproductionists tried to accurately measure the distances between sites by pacing them off in the Holy Land and recording and re-creating them, so the faithful in Europe could walk the same number of steps between stations, but the outcomes were wildly divergent. Over the years, the number of sites and events people thought it was necessary to venerate varied from about seven to thirty-one, with most settling between twelve and fourteen. (We will use the traditional fourteen stations.)

We also talked about Koestler's "Night Journey" archetype from that "Belly of the Whale" reading, when the hero undergoes a crisis that plunges him onto the Tragic Plane and he remerges transformed, purified. "[It] may take the form of a visit to the underworld (Orpheus, Odysseus); or the hero is cast to the bottom of a well (Joseph), buried in a grave (Jesus), swallowed by a fish (Jonah); or he retires alone into the desert, as Buddha, Mahomet, Christ, and other prophets and founders of religions did at the crucial turn in their lives." Koestler talked about how certain cultures symbolically re-create these journeys through ritual as a more communal way to "establish contact with the Tragic Plane."

Everyone drew a number from a hat, each number corresponding to a different Station of the Cross. We pulled numbers for those of you who weren't there and will send them along later. The plan is to reinterpret Jesus's Stations of the Cross in relation to our own Stations of the Crisis, to reflect some of the issues of existence we've been talking about over the last few months — personal, philosophical, or otherwise. The evening will be a sort of procession (not a spectacle — some were pretty adamant about that), with each of us choosing a location for our station, anywhere within the neighborhood's boundaries of Press Street and Poland Avenue, and from St. Claude Avenue to the river. At your station, you should offer up to the group a brief reading, a performance, a piece of art, anything, that speaks to your assigned station and how it relates to the Crisis. Then we'll end up back at the house for the Last Suffer. Or something. Wear comfortable shoes. See you soon.

*   *   *

When I was a kid, Holy Week was interminable. Days and days of Mass, kneeling, standing, sitting, kneeling, standing, sitting. The worst was Good Friday, which seemed the longest Mass of the year, the reading of the Passion Play, the congregation playing the role of the bloodthirsty crowd, murmuring such lines as "Crucify him! Crucify him!" without much conviction. Then, having to line up to kiss Jesus's feet, the crucifix taken down from the wall and laid out at the carpeted foot of the altar at Blessed Sacrament, I'd tremble and sweat, and suddenly I was leaning over the bloody spike, painted red rivulets slicking down the metatarsals and phalanges of his toes, the plaster so cold and terrifying, as my mind went white. The priest wiping the feet with a handkerchief after each kiss. It was both similar and worlds away from the sensation of dread and fear, years later, that I had when kissing Rebecca's forehead in the mahogany-paneled visitation room of the Lake Lawn Metairie Funeral Home. People have long referred to corpses' cold composure as marmoreal, but the shock that no harder element existed than a beautiful young woman's dead body seared my lips.

Participating in the Stations of the Cross during Holy Week wasn't really so bad, though. Among the stained glass and fluted columns and polished pews, the church even more theatrical than usual, a small group of us would shuffle behind the priest, who guided us through the story of Christ's Passion along the walls where the carved wooden stations were installed, toward something terrible and inevitable. Even though you knew exactly how the story ended, working toward it, communally, scene by scene, suffering by suffering, pausing and praying at each one, was still so emotional. The pacing and the events are already etched into you. As Kierkegaard said, "Repetition is the same movement as memory, but going the other way...repetition is memory carried forward." (*See also:* Hope.)

Weekly breakfasts with my mom began when Dad's hospital stays became more frequent, which coincided with Otto starting kindergarten nearby. Mom would often attend 7 a.m. Mass uptown and then meet me after I dropped Otto off. Taking care of Dad was a full-time job; being treated to breakfast, a brief reprieve embedded into her week. After Dad died, the breakfasts took on a different quality. Uncertainty opens up around a newly widowed person, especially one who's been married over twice as long as not. After she'd spent the first few weeks of dealing with the social and pragmatic obligations of death, her new life was starting to settle into an amorphous stage of distraction and discovery. With her days no longer centered on Dad's care, they slackened, but for the first time in her life, she was learning how to pay bills and use a debit card. One morning she told me how strange it was to have suddenly become a *widow*. It was the word, the label, that bewildered her. She said she had roughly the same reaction when she became a *wife*. In both cases instantly redefined in terms of her relationship to another person. As a new wife: defined by duty and possibility. But back then, just married, living in Washington, D.C., far from home and where she knew no one, with Dad in law school, she had no models to look to for advice and also no one to judge her, or the way she kept their small apartment in a Capitol Hill brownstone. She could make it up as she went along. As a new widow: defined by the tension between absence and possibility. Only now in the city she was born in, with friends she's had for sixty-plus years, some since kindergarten, generations of relationships and family, markers and milestones, births and burials, a rich and full life to renegotiate.

I was often concerned by the amount of regret Mom expressed during these breakfasts, and urged her to look ahead, even though she was confronted with the past and Dad's secretiveness at every turn, opening up surprising letters from the IRS about back taxes (*Why did I never ask about finances?*), returning calls from old friends from our brief few years in Washington (*Why did we ever move back to New Orleans?*), dealing with the repairs and bills for the beautiful center-hall house (*Why did we "downsize" to such a big place?*). She had been earnestly shocked when both the current and previous maître d's of the Rib Room showed up at the funeral to pay their respects. She had never been and had no idea how much time and money he spent there, what the place meant to him, or to us. (*Why wasn't I paying closer attention?*) These questioning regrets regarding her marriage often led her to the painful territory of the twins' deaths.

I asked her if it was harder to take part in the Via Dolorosa processions after Rebecca and Rachel died and she said absolutely, yes, it was. And Holy Week itself was more difficult. A couple of weeks after Rachel's death, she was supposed to be a lector on Good Friday, but for the first time, she just was not able to do it; her pain had merged too thoroughly with the intensity of those scriptures, with no immediate hope of resurrection or rebirth to temper it.

Surprisingly, at least to me, she very much approved of the ECRG's Stations of the Crisis, did not find the idea irreverent or sacrilegious at all. She thought it reflected the true spirit of the ritual, which is to embrace a personal interpretation of the trials and encounters leading to Jesus's death. When I brought up one supposed origin of the Way of the Cross, that of Jesus's mother, Mary, retracing the dusty steps of her son's suffering over and over throughout the rest of her life, a maternal expression of grief, she paused thoughtfully for a moment.

"Mary and the women were there to help take down Jesus's body," she said, "to clean and dress it and lay it in the tomb. Watch over it. But after the twins died, you kids took care of everything, dealt with the girls' belongings, with the funeral homes, the burials, wrote the obituaries.

Everyone always wanted to protect me, and I understand that. But in that sense, I missed the ritual part of dealing with their deaths."

It had never even occurred to me to ask if she wanted to be involved in any of those death chores; we *did* want to spare her. Following the lead of Dad, we grew up protective of her, the saintly earth mother who was so revered in the community that I once met the mother of a former special-needs student of hers who had literally erected an altar to Mom in their home. But our protection of her sometimes blurred into deceit, outright, self-serving deceit. After all, as siblings, our sins often overlapped.

I apologized to her. Somehow, I had never considered that we were denying her anything by concealing the messy, disturbing truth of the ends of Rachel's and Rebecca's lives. While they lived at home, she tried to stay on top of their problems with different schools, different counselors, even tough-love programs. But when they moved out, Rebecca around sixteen and Rachel around eighteen, they began disappearing into the excesses of adult culture in New Orleans. She lost track. We tried to keep tabs. Her point was that Mary was allowed to witness it all. The crowds, the falls, the succor, the nails and the spear. Mary's path might not have been easier, but it was clearer. We shielded Mom from as much as we could and years later she's still trying to determine her own Via Dolorosa. Did she know about Rachel's drug use in that last year? No. The toxicology reports just reflected a random night of partying to her. Did she know much about Rebecca's life as a dancer or her life with M.? No. But toward the end Mom didn't understand anything about Rebecca, and her life seemed hopelessly unreal, muddled and chaotic.

Well, she knows some things now. Telling her some of the details we encountered in our various cleanups did not seem like an act of cruelty, like it once might've, but rather one of atonement. And that morning, over coffee and too-rich grits, Mom did retrace some of the steps that led up to their deaths, like she has over many breakfasts and lunches and coffees and car rides over the years. None of these steps led to anywhere revelatory, only to the same places, same questions, and the same tears. Even Mary, whose son was resurrected and would live on in others indefinitely, changing the course of humankind, still maybe needed the Way of the Cross, the Via Dolorosa, to retrace his suffering, making the infinite pain of losing a child more finite.

Mom's Via Dolorosa leads as far back as the womb. When she is about three months pregnant with the twins, she begins having severe abdominal pain and is taken to the hospital, where they find an ovarian tumor the size of the proverbial grapefruit. Her mother happens to be in the room when the nurse enters and says, "You're the one who's expecting," and that's how my grandmother finds out Mom is pregnant. Mom usually would send Dad over to her parents' house to break the news about each new pregnancy, and once again, she'd been too scared to tell my grandmother about the twins, her seventh and eighth children. (Fear of communication apparently handed off wordlessly through generations.) Because she is pregnant, they don't give Mom general anesthesia when they remove the tumor, but the twilight variety. She doesn't feel pain, only tugging and things giving way. She listens to the nurse, a bride to be, complain about how difficult it is managing all of the little buttons on her wedding dress. When it's over, supine and numb, she asks the surgeon if she can see the tumor. He holds it up to her like a prize, a pearlescent globe. She can't believe the size, this aberration that had been growing alongside the twins, dwarfing them. Years later when problems with Rebecca and Rachel started cropping up, learning disabilities, lack of short-term memory, general behavioral trouble, she wonders if the anesthesia she'd been administered during the surgery had affected their tiny beginnings somehow.

Another station she brought up over breakfast: when the twins are in second grade, doing poorly academically and Rebecca in near-constant trouble — for disrespecting teachers, for convincing Rachel to switch the monogrammed shirts of their Catholic grade-school uniform to confuse the nuns, for threatening to burn the school down — Mom decides to separate them, put them in different schools. Rebecca is the dominant one, smarter, more talented, but sometimes cruel and envious of any attention or accomplishments Rachel earns. Mom wants to give Rachel a chance to grow outside of Rebecca's influence. Mom makes this decision (and many others) on her own, as Dad is always working, traveling. She will always second-guess it.

At breakfast, as always, I let Mom repeat these scenarios and questions, which have been churning through her for over fifteen years. The schools, the psychiatrists, the mental hospitals, the arrests, the interventions. The brief moments of stability and happiness, of hope. The boyfriends, the unsubstantiated rumors of abuse as adolescents, by a friend's father, by a worker at a state mental hospital. Police officers to psychiatrists would assure her — you have a nice family, everything will work out. During their short lives, neither twin would ever follow a solid trajectory. They tried to be separate from each other. Rachel became a single mother at nineteen, kept her hair short and practical, wore glasses, and kept trying to find the right man, the right job, the right house in which to raise her son. Rebecca became consumed by the dancing life, a world oppressively controlled by men and money, maintained long bleached hair and wore contacts, her days often spent recovering and preparing for the nights. They wound in and out of each other's lives, sometimes clashing, sometimes intensely close, but regardless, they called each other almost every night before they went to sleep.

The final stations of Mom's Via Dolorosa:

Mom is with a friend at an Uptown coffee shop and runs into

Rebecca. This will be the last time she sees Rebecca alive. She doesn't remember the conversation, just that she inwardly judges Rebecca for ordering two extra shots of espresso in her iced coffee, a wall thickening between them as Rebecca babbles about something that Mom neither believes nor understands. She just told so many stories. Mom never thought of them as lies, just stories. To her, Rebecca was still a little girl.

Mom buys Rachel a bathrobe for what would be her last birthday, her twenty-fifth. She wonders, if she hadn't bought Rachel that bathrobe as a gift, maybe she wouldn't have found its sash so handy, wouldn't have gone through with it at all.

This is when I will stare distractedly out the window of the café at those roots of the crepe myrtle tree, which boil over onto the pavement after years of confined growth in that carved-out hole along the curb. And at those errant shoots coming up from the base of the trunk that just needed to be lopped off to improve the shape of the tree.

How often has our conversation inevitably led to this moment? Or, even more often, started with this moment, in the way the suicides' final acts can come to define them, become the starting point of their lives' narratives, everything moving backwards from there. I asked Mom if she knew that centuries ago, the Stations of the Cross would begin with Christ's death and proceed toward his condemnation. She said she didn't, but she was just glad that Pope John Paul II added the fifteenth station — that of the Resurrection. After all, she said, that symbol of hopefulness is the whole reality of the religion. In my head I counted the stations we'd doled out to the ECRG, and the fifteenth, the Resurrection, wasn't one of them. Maybe we'd gotten it wrong after all. Ah, well.

But I told her I'd read that apparently, groups of pilgrims used to begin at Mount Calvary, the site of Christ's crucifixion, and then travel the route back toward the ruins of the Ecce Homo arch, where Pontius Pilate condemned Jesus and handed him over to the Jews with great ambivalence. Pilate was a governor, an imperial middle-man, manipulated by both Caesar and the people. As a child, I was always baffled by the figure of Pontius Pilate — he didn't seem evil but he didn't help either — but as I got older I recognized that he typified a certain dangerous species of adult, those who wield empty authority, the sorry-but-my-hands-are-tied bureaucrats. Pilate knew that Jesus was innocent but also that he had to give the people what they wanted at that moment, according to their custom and also the law of Caesar, since no one else could claim to be king, and he was being proclaimed the King of Jews.

In John's Gospel, the most poetic of the four, Pilate tries to under-stand where Jesus is coming from and save him. "Art thou king, then? Jesus answered, Thou sayest that I am king. To this end was I born, and for this cause came I into the world, that I should bear wit-ness unto the truth. Every one that is of the truth heareth my voice. Pilate saith unto him, What is truth?"

Pilate asks the key question, doesn't get an answer, and is unset-tled, tells the crowd he thinks Jesus is innocent. But they still clamor for his execution. After Jesus is beaten, dressed in purple robes, and bloodied by a crown of thorns, Pilate presents him to the crowd: "Behold the man!" *Ecce homo.* The whole beautiful, terrible point.

The night of our Stations of the Crisis, the person who'd chosen the first station, *Christ is condemned to death,* was out of town, as were a couple of others. (It was Easter break, after all.) Our Way of the Cri-sis would be imperfect and incomplete, like all Ways and all Crises, but we've already addressed that first station with Pilate anyway, and can start with the second:

The cross is laid upon him

Ellen showed up at the house looking tough and terrifying in a ribbed white tank top and tightly cinched man-pants. Heavy eye makeup streaked black down her cheeks, evoking a long night that had ended in wet, messy despair, but was actually more Shroud of Turin–esque in its studied application. She led the nine of us down our street toward St. Claude Avenue and the Saturn Bar, where the neighborhood gets a little dodgy. She took us down the dark side alley of a half-renovated house, the de facto aesthetic of much of that particular block, where people seem to run out of money or material or luck or will, and things don't get finished or fixed.

We were all quiet and a bit nervous, especially when she produced a key and let us into what might be considered a basement in other places, but in New Orleans was more like a dank, low-ceilinged enclosed garage beneath a raised unoccupied house. Crowded with boxes and a couch jammed up against them at such an angle that made clear it was being stored and not used. I remember a bare bulb hanging, though my memory has possibly superimposed it.

Then Ellen started yelling at us. " 'The first rule of Fight Club is: You do not talk about Fight Club. The second rule of Fight Club is: You do not talk about Fight Club.' "

She lowered her voice some. *This life is our cross. Here we are, together to engage and discuss, duke it out, support each other in our fight with this cross. Here we have gathered in our own Fight Club. Struggling with the classic existentialist questions like: pseudo life or authentic life? In the David Fincher film, based on the Chuck Palahniuk novel, protagonist Tyler Durden addresses life's cross through splitting his persona and creating an underground fighting club. "First you've gotta know, not fear, know, that someday you're gonna die."*

Though Ellen was kind of freaking us out as we huddled in the shadowy clutter, the place itself a way station for not immediately useful stuff, it made sense for her. She shouted more Tyler Durden at us. *"We're the middle children of history, man. No purpose or place. We have no Great War. No Great Depression. Our Great War is a spiritual war. Our Great Depression is our lives.'"* Ellen is a fighter, in conversation, in life, and mostly with herself, always tussling with her "black mind," as she calls it, but also clasping it to herself, like when exhausted boxers collapse into each other with something that almost seems like protective affection.

His first fall

Fragrant chain-smoking Christine took us down the street about a block from Ellen's station, closer to the river, where tasteful renovations by wealthy out-of-towners were just starting to tighten up pockets of the neighborhood, bringing buildings up to code, installing new weatherboards, filling Dumpsters with decades of decay and modest though funky home repairs. She brought us to a newly restored corner building housing an outfit of newcomers, designers and artists, who were purporting to be community organizers through an online platform that gathered "neighbors'" input about what changes and improvements were wanted for the neighborhood. They were never around, and no one really knew who they were. Through some investigation by Christine and others, we learned that they were working with real estate developers and hedge fund managers, riding the tide of "creative place-making" and padding their résumés with "community" design projects that required no more than stickers and posters and a slick website.

Christine proceeded with a lamp-lit, street-corner screed about the inequity between those with the tools and the connections and those without, and the exploitation of the community for professional gain. New Orleans has accrued centuries of street-level stoop culture, many Creole cottages and shotgun houses built right up to the sidewalk, neighbors communicating concern and sharing news through stoop sitting and "door popping." Besides the disconnect with local culture, and the reluctance to actually engage, what made this type of digital carpetbagging particularly noisome was that in the early days of the rebuilding, locals and thousands of volunteers from all over the country sweated and bled for the city, back when it was dangerous and difficult to be here. Made it safer for the "creative class" and "entrepreneurs" to swoop in for the tax credits and profit from the residual cachet of disaster glamour. Technology, while a huge boon to the rebuilding, also ensured that you didn't have to get your hands dirty, or even physically interact with the "community."

In hand-drawn opposition to this, Christine made a sign from the side of a cardboard box, using colorful markers and crayons, with lots of arrows and underlining, the old graphic methods of emphasis, and hung it with twine on the stop sign in front of these community organizers' door. "STOP SPEAKING FOR US." "A DIGITAL ECHO CHAMBER IS NOT A STOOP. A STOOP IS A STOOP IS A STOOP." "SPEAK TO YOUR NEIGHBORS. LISTEN TO YOUR NEIGHBORS." Why did Christine choose this for the first fall? A first failure for this new enterprise? Jesus was all about neighbors, about listening to and respecting each other as brethren, equals. Her sign stayed up for a few days, buffeted and twisted by the spring breeze. Sometimes the message faced the renovated storefront. Other times it faced the street.

He meets his blessed mother

At the time of the Way of the Crisis, Sara was working for an events coordinator who handled spectacles like bowl games, inaugurations, and the Blue Angels Air Show, and I'd sometimes picture her at work in headphones, clutching a walkie-talkie and making decisive hand signals. She always sat on the right side of my grandmother's

Duncan Phyfe couch in our living room and hardly said a word for the first three months of ECRG meetings but brought extravagant desserts with overpowering frosting that I would find distracting throughout the evening.

Sara had drawn the fourth station, where Jesus meets his mother. She led us several blocks away down Royal Street to Mickey Markey Park. Playgrounds are such strange places to be at night — empty swings, the metal slide catching the streetlight in a menacing way, the ghosts of living children — and also suited to nocturnal adult behavior that the temporarily abandoned play equipment and poor lighting maybe attract.

Sara, single, in her twenties and with no children, explained that she brought us there because Markey Park is where she sees women she knows from different contexts in their role as "mom" and thinks about them in relation to their kids. Sara talked about her sometimes-strained relationship with her own mother and read a selection from Vivian Gornick's memoir *Fierce Attachments,* which is about how Gornick's relationship with her rather intense mother evolved as their lives accumulated. The book shifts between the densely synthesized light and sound and people of Gornick's childhood in Queens to walks with her aging mother around Manhattan. In the passage Sara read, Gornick reflects on her and her mother's "mutual disability," while looking at a store's plate-glass window, how they appreciate good clothes but hate to shop, so end up with limited, haphazard wardrobes. "The clothes in the window make me feel we have both been confused the whole of our lives about who we are, and how to get there."

I don't think she knew this at the time, but as Sara talked she stood next to a concrete bench and small garden that were part of a memorial created by some neighbors and friends for a three-year-old child who'd died a few years before in an accident, the son of good friends of ours who'd moved away after Katrina. An impromptu visit to his grandma's, a broken window screen two stories up, the mother looks down to stir her yogurt, and her son is gone. The grief at the funeral, our friends' broken faces in the front pew. In his memory, we planted small sweet olive trees, African irises, cast-iron plants and monkey grass around the bench.

Beneath the uneven wash of the playground's floodlight, Sara also read a dark, questioning poem by Louise Glück called "Mother and Child," about the mysteries of birth and existence and family, which ends with the lines

Why do I suffer? Why am I ignorant?
Cells in a great darkness. Some machine made us;
it is your turn to address it, to go back asking
what am I for? What am I for?

Then, Sara handed out white blackboard chalk and asked everyone to write "What am I for?" (which, for some, became "What am I here for?") all over the playground. Some wrote on the pliant, rough safety surfacing beneath the equipment, some on the slings of the swings, others on the concrete memorial bench. Sara wrote it on a skateboard that some kid had left behind.

Simon of Cyrene is made to bear his cross

My station. We stayed in the park, gathered near the shadowy play equipment, and I talked about Simon's role in the Passion. Jesus's physical exhaustion was holding up the procession, so the Roman soldiers found someone in the crowd, most likely strong-looking and, possibly, as some believe, very dark-skinned to force the cross upon. In that time, living under the empire meant that if a Roman soldier asked you to do something you had to drop everything and do it. Simon had no choice. It would've been considered one of the worst indignities, humiliating, to be forced to carry a condemned man's cross for him through a crowd. Simon came to watch and suddenly he was part of the spectacle. What was Simon's reaction to being chosen? How long did the wood, this alien burden, cut into his shoulder? Did he say anything to Jesus as he hoisted it back to him? Did some sweaty, bloodied, exhausted intimacy pass between them? There's speculation that instead of the experience fomenting resentment in Simon, he was moved to follow Jesus's teaching, mainly because in Mark's Gospel, the names of his sons are mentioned, which is considered a great honor. Simon was the first to take up Jesus's cross, literally, and endure a segment of his suffering. When, through oppression or circumstance, we are forced to do something we might not have otherwise done, it must define us in some special, sharper way that spontaneous acts do not. You come up against the Roman spear and you react, outwardly and inwardly.

Forced or not, helping others is central to being a good human, maybe our only true calling as we engage in our brief activity here on earth (after all, wasn't that Jesus's main message?), and it should be celebrated, even if in a goofy and obvious way. Like with pies. The neighborhood was part of the theme for the night, and one nearby business down on Dauphine Street was Hubig's Pies, an industrial bakery that had been operating fragrantly among the shotguns and Creole cottages of the neighborhood for almost a hundred years, making fried, glazed single-serve pies that you could grab from cardboard trays next to cash registers all over town. I loved the peach. Its famous mascot on the wrappers and the sides of the white delivery vans was Simon the Pieman, aproned and corpulent, brandishing a big pie. I brought a bag full of Simon's pies to distribute, in case anyone needed a snack during our night journey. On each pie wrapper I'd written phrases in Sharpie that we utter throughout the day without even thinking, all these small gestures of burden lifting.

"Do you need a hand with that?" "Here, let me help." "I can get that for you." "Do you need to talk?"

A few months after the Way of the Crisis, Hubig's bakery burned down to the ground (tired graveyard-shift employee, unattended oil fire), causing an early-morning citywide rush on Hubig's pies as the news spread. The loss hurt, but we're used to it. New Orleans has such a penchant for losing its best. But the fire was months away, we were still at the playground after Sara's moving piece about mothers and meaning, eating pies, surrounded by the chalky questions we'd all written.

His second fall

Once, at a party at Michael's house, I was exploring his second-floor studio and came across an easel set up in front of a window. A sharply realistic sky occupied the canvas, contours of clouds, depths of light and blues all achingly rendered, and across the bottom, the slate roofline of the French Quarter building across the street. You could've held it up to his window and convincingly replaced the view, though the world would've immediately deepened with beauty and skill and attention. I remember looking at his tidy palette of oil paint and tiny brushes and thinking, *What's the cost of all that perfection?* Weeks before, on Mardi Gras afternoon, Ellen, Tristan, Brad, Kevin and his wife, and I ended up sprawled around Michael's kitchen in our costumes, drinking champagne that he had on ice in the downstairs bathtub and eating red beans and rice as the crazy day wound down. As he always brought a bottle of champagne to the ECRG (arriving late and leaving early to meet a date), I wondered if he kept a case of champagne in his bathtub year-round, as a kind of ballast to the wrenching intensity of the work in the studio upstairs.

Michael brought us to the railroad tracks at Royal Street and Press Street, the latter named for the old cotton press that operated there about 150 years ago. Homer Plessy was arrested there in 1892 for boarding a whites-only car, prompting the "separate but equal" *Plessy v. Ferguson* court ruling, a series of events considered by some to be the beginning of the civil rights movement. The intersection is both crossroads and no-man's-land — sidewalks, curbs, and streets all busted up from eighteen-wheelers loading and unloading from the warehouses, glittering with shards of broken bottles from kids drinking on the loading docks at night, a brutal mosaic we walk over daily, a puzzle that'll never quite come together.

Under the tepid streetlight, Michael unfolded a piece of paper from the back pocket of his khakis and read an account of Jesus's fall, from Jesus's exhausted, bewildered point of view. *Stumbling on the road's crude paving, bones crushing against stones, stone tearing skin, pain searing from knees to groin, blood on stone, dirt-sweat stinging eyes, blurring the road, the figures closing in, staring impassively...*

Michael never looked up from the page, and read hesitantly, with a self-deprecating pathos. *And all the while, he asks himself, "Why won't they help me?" and "Why am I doing this?"*

Later, Michael explained to me that, no, he wasn't a masochist, he was just remembering how painful it was as a kid when he'd fall off his bike, how helpless he felt, and he just took it from there.

His third fall

When you first pick it up, it's not that bad. You kind of feel like a hero, "Look at me! I am strong! I can do this — this thing that should be difficult is easy for me!" and then a minute goes by and another and after ten it is no longer fun. You are no longer the hero. You hurt. After about fifteen minutes you question how long you can do this. In thirty, you feel forgotten, you wonder if anyone has ever done this before. Here you are. In pain, dust at your feet, dust on your tongue. There is no one. You are alone. No wonder Christ is a curse word, like a blister or a burn.

But a cross can be a crossroads as well, not just a torture device, a spiritual barbecue grill, but a changing of course. An "I am no longer going down that road that I have mistakenly chosen. The road I thought the world to be when I was young and imagined it as I was, optimistic, full of wonder. If you give me beauty, I will do the same. Not court orders and medical bills." At a crossroads you can change your mind, change your course, find new things, perhaps something that means more to you than where you started. Perhaps something that you were meant to find.

This was Susan's station and this is what she wrote and read, also by the railroad tracks at Press Street and Royal. She had been living a very, very difficult stretch of adulthood involving disasters both natural and unnatural — a house flooded in Katrina, illness, divorce, death, her oldest child's drug addiction. The bureaucratic gauntlet she ran to reassemble her family's flooded-out life was soon followed by those of civil and criminal court and various medical institutions. It was the kind of stretch that constantly eviscerates you, making you question every decision you've made since adolescence. And then you have to wake up each morning and stuff your guts back in, like the Scarecrow in *The Wizard of Oz* after he's been torn apart by the flying monkeys, get up, and keep stumbling down the path arm in arm with your other damaged and determined companions. But suddenly it also became a time of artistic success and freedom for her, a widening out of her life that could only funnel in more hope and opportunity. At the site of her reading, she left behind an old metal funeral stand with a collage on it. It was so lovely, someone had claimed this gift by the next morning.

I used to have a pile of crowns. I was in a Dumpster and found a suitcase. I imagined severed limbs yet touched the clasp regardless. The suitcase was pale blue and dusty. When I opened it, I found several old Mardi Gras crowns with jewels made out of paste or glass. I kept them in a pile, on a piece of furniture that was my great-grandmother's. The doors of the cabinet looked like temple doors or tombs and have small glass knobs. Over time I gave the crowns away, one by one. They were precious only when shared.

He is stripped of his garments

In our neighborhood, there's a grand old manse turned club, built in the early nineteenth century, with a wide raised porch across the front where you can drink under ceiling fans at eye level with a tall bank of pink oleanders. There are airy, double parlors off the ample center hall, a bar in the back, and, outside, clothing-optional swimming that you have to pay extra for. Once I was waiting at the bar for someone, having a glass of wine, and down at the other end near the door to the pool was a completely naked woman, her slim body damp, receiving a drink from the bartender with both hands, one leg slightly raised behind her, for a moment like neoclassical statuary.

Nate brought us to the club to give a lecture based on Georges Bataille's *Erotism: Death and Sensuality,* how the erotic act involves the attempt to destroy one's personal, day-to-day identity (the state of discontinuous existence in which we all live) in order to become closer to death (which is when we reenter continuity). Disrobing is a key part of this. It helps destroy our individuality, because our clothes are part of the symbolic order by which we define ourselves.

When Rebecca first started dancing, around nineteen, we tried to dissuade and discourage her. But when it was obvious that the pull of the lifestyle was too strong, we would at least try to make sure she was okay. I checked up on her a few times at a few different clubs, always backstage. She would seem upbeat, say she was having fun, making money. But it was hard to tell, because she was probably high, and also because those places are purveyors of artificial expression, of transactional fantasy. At least the front of the house is. Back of the house, the fantasy evaporates. Once I was backstage with her in a "gentlemen's club" in Baton Rouge. It was too bright and a little run-down, with doorless bathroom stalls reflected in the mirrored wall in front of the counter where the dancers fixed their makeup, adjusted their outfits. As Rebecca and I sat at the counter, a girl came in after being onstage, squatted on a toilet with a three-inch wad of money strapped to her thigh, and did her business, her full reflection between Rebecca and me as we talked.

I never met any strippers like the ones profiled in "gentlemen's magazines," focused and empowered and putting themselves through business school, their dancing just a means to an end. I met ones like Rebecca, sweet or nice enough, who got caught up in the means and lost their way toward the ends. Maybe Rebecca would let some of the brash front-of-the-house fantasy cling to her for self-protection when I was there, because if anything, she always seemed so vulnerable, so eager to build up her identity through men. Getting naked might be a destruction of our day-to-day identity, but with stripping, as you disrobe you become cloaked in another identity, that of pure commodity. And what replaces the destroyed self? Drugs, impersonal desire, strobing lights and techno bass lines, heavily fingered dollars strapped to your thigh, many of which were paid back to the house.

A brutal and tawdry digression from Nate's and Bataille's intellectual treatment of eroticism and nudity, perhaps, but the manse where we gathered was known at the time not just for its robust gay scene, but also for its stripper scene, dancers lounging under the patio-bound palm trees and by the heavily chlorinated pool. Nate had wanted to deliver his lecture in the proximity of nakedness, but the guy working the door wouldn't let us back there without paying. Plus, when we tried to explain what we were doing (a mistake), they thought we were some religious group that might burst into protest, so Nate gave the lecture on the front porch by the oleanders, people walking by with towels rolled under their arms, shooting us curious glances.

Jesus is nailed to the cross

Our existential plumber, Kevin, walked us away from the river down Louisa Street and up Burgundy, back toward the railroad tracks and warehouses at Press Street. It was almost midnight, nearing Good Friday, the day the crucifixion is observed. He brought us to a spot across from Southern Coating and Waterproofing, which still had trailers in the fenced-in parking lot left over from post-Katrina days of widespread transient shelter, near Montegut Street, one of many in our neighborhood named for old riverfront plantations. Our gardens and our weeds thrive in this alluvial soil.

Kevin sat on a stump near the curb, so some of us had to stand in the street, and he took something out of the bag he'd been carrying all night, a piece of Katrina-salvaged scrap wood, with text written on it and a spike nailed into it. With his dark beard and dark eyes and measured, reassuring delivery regardless of content, Kevin looked as though he'd always belonged seated on that stump, semicircled by attentive followers. He explained that this was the place where he had been held up at gunpoint one night when returning home to his wife and toddler son after a bartending shift. The text on the wood was a page of Shel Silverstein's *Giving Tree,* about a tree and a boy who love each other. As the boy grows older and less interested in just playing in her shade and swinging in her branches, and develops more worldly desires, for money, for shelter, for escape, the tree gives and gives and the boy takes and takes. Kevin read aloud to us from the stump:

But the boy stayed away for a long time. And when he came back, the tree was so happy she could hardly speak.

"Come, Boy," she whispered, "come and play."

"I am too old and sad to play," said the boy. "I want a boat that will take me away from here. Can you give me a boat?"

94

"Cut down my trunk and make a boat," said the tree. "Then you can sail away and be happy."

And so the boy cut down her trunk and made a boat and sailed away.

And the tree was happy. But not really.

And after a long time the boy came back again.

"I am sorry, Boy," said the tree, "but I have nothing left to give you — My apples are gone."

"My teeth are too weak for apples," said the boy.

"My branches are gone," said the tree. "You cannot swing on them —"

"I am too old to swing on branches," said the boy.

"My trunk is gone," said the tree. "You cannot climb —"

"I am too tired to climb," said the boy.

"I am sorry," sighed the tree. "I wish that I could give you something…but I have nothing left. I am just an old stump. I am sorry…"

"I don't need very much now," said the boy. "Just a quiet place to sit and rest. I am very tired."

"Well," said the tree, straightening herself up as much as she could, "well, an old stump is good for sitting and resting. Come, Boy, sit down…and rest."

And the tree was happy.

Kevin told us that the tree, like Christ, willingly sacrificed for another, that the passage represented for him the point beyond which there is no return, the sacrifice moving toward completion. While a metaphor for giving completely and unconditionally and without judgment, the story can also be interpreted as an allegory of destructive codependency. Kevin said he chose it because it creates passionate and often-divergent interpretations. And it's true; as we walked back toward Clouet Street, those who knew the story had strong opinions about it — it was either inspiring or infuriating. For me, as a child, the story turned uncomfortably recognizable at "The tree was happy. But not really."

The next day at the Rib Room during our annual Good Friday lunch, my siblings and I drank Rusty Nails and ordered lamb, carrying on one of our father's more perverse traditions. Dad took Christianity seriously but was sometimes irreverent about its symbols. Sipping at our cloying drinks, more out of obligation than desire, Susan and I told Soren, whom my father had named for Kierkegaard, inserting a bit of philosophical measure into our roster of biblical names, about the Stations of the Crisis. When we got to the *Giving Tree*/crucifixion station, his face contorted dramatically. "God, I fucking *hate* that book," he said. "That's one of the most perverse pieces of children's literature ever. That boy was the worst thing that could've happened to that fucking tree."

Jesus is taken down from the cross

This was Brad's station. He led us from Burgundy Street back to the field in front of our house, where we had started. Earlier that day he had stashed an eight-foot ladder behind one of the overgrown trash trees. He retrieved it, set it beneath one of the limbs, and climbed up to where it looked as though two paper grocery bags were hanging by a rope. From the top of the ladder, he talked about how, according to John's Gospel, when the Roman soldiers went to take down Jesus's body, one of them pierced his side with a spear, and blood and water ran out. My husband tore away the paper bags to reveal two taut, clear plastic bags, like giant IVs, one full of red wine and the other full of water.

Then he took out a utility knife. (He works as a scenic painter for the movies, and I'm always finding utility knives in his pockets when

I'm doing laundry, their small specific heft weighing down his paint-splattered cargo pants, which are filled with the day's detritus, the blue rubber gloves, the cheap face masks that I fear aren't keeping enough of the chemicals he works with out of his lungs, lots of potato chip and candy wrappers. Show after show, year after year, always the same contents.) He told us to have our cups ready — we'd been carrying them around all evening, drinking out of backpacks — *but first,* he said, *let's spill a little on the ground and take a moment to think of people we've lost.* He stabbed first the wine bag, then the water bag, and we watched the thin streams from high up in the tree glint in the yellow glow of the security light across the street and trail to the ground.

It's gotten too easy to catalog the people we've lost. As the water and wine spattered the dirt, I acknowledged them in my heart — Dad, Rebecca, and Rachel — and then thought about the people I've gained through loss. When Brad's partner and the mother of his first son died nine months before I met him, their child, now ours, was three. He had been trying to figure out how to grieve and be a dad. "It's too soon!" people said to me when we first started dating. "Besides, he has a kid." While it was overwhelmingly and immediately obvious we should be together, it was still a difficult start to what would turn out to be the best relationship I could ever hope for, and I also leapfrogged into becoming a mother.

I was introduced to Chris at a rooftop party, my first social outing after Rachel died, when I was still feeling raw and fragile, self-conscious in my grief. His first words to me were "Oh, I just met your younger sister Rachel a couple of weeks ago, at a St. Patrick's Day party, God y'all look alike. Is she seeing anyone?" I walked away without a word as he continued to talk to me about her, and after I was out of earshot my friends filled him in as to what had happened. He'd met her, been attracted to her, hours before she killed herself. Was maybe one of the last people to see her alive. For a while I avoided him when I saw him out and would always think, *My God, there's that guy…* Years later, at a Halloween party, dressed as a ghoul with a slashed throat, I ran into Chris, in ripped jeans, a T-shirt, and bandana, brandishing a sign and a borrowed bullhorn, a protester protesting Halloween. We finally started talking about our first meeting, about Rachel. He told me that after he was told what had happened, he went and sat on the edge of the roof by himself, looking out at the night city, wanting to throw himself off the ledge. He would eventually become our younger son's godfather.

Now, let's all partake together, in communion. We tightened our circle beneath the improbable tree-fountain with our cups, eager though sheepish about how beautiful it was, catching wine and water streaming down in the night, some splashing onto our arms and hands. Brad came down from the ladder and joined us. It was rigged but it was miraculous.

After Jesus is taken down from the cross, his suffering is over, he can let go. We can all let go. The bags deflated in the tree, wine and water mingled in our cups and in the dirt and scraps of grass trying to grow in the tree's shade. We took our wine inside the house and talked some more, ate more cheese and bread and grapes and the insane cupcakes that Sara brought. Had a modest Last Suffer, because, really, it was the lightest of jokes, so light it practically dissolved as you spoke it. We played records, some new releases, some older things we'd been dragging around since high school and college, like Bob Dylan and Prince and the English Beat and Billy Idol, with chewed-up covers and no sleeves, but the vinyl still sounded great and clear, though the occasional hissing skip would jolt us into attention and one of us would get up to lift the turntable's arm.

MAY

The Dark Wood

The ruins of the old St. Claude Furniture Store had no roof, just a concrete floor with some tenacious scraps of red linoleum, two long, high brick walls, and no back. Memories from before the interior turned exterior. A few dirt mounds along the wall sprouted spiny, exotic-looking weeds and spent bottles of fortified wine, and we swept up a couple of used condoms as we readied the place for the event. It resembled a spare, centuries-old Central or South American fortress, with palm trees and mimosas crowning the tops of the walls. Susan decorated it with candles and votives and statuary she'd pulled out of the trash over the years, a lot of it from after Katrina, during the Great Disgorging — damaged possessions from hundreds of thousands of homes and businesses left to molder on curbs. She'd also painted a huge red carnival devil with a six-foot-tall gaping mouth on the building's ramshackle façade to serve as the entrance. But Tristan, ever the cautious carpenter, warned against taking a saw to the old plywood, pointing to the brick soffit above it leaning perilously over the sidewalk. He didn't want to nudge years of decay toward fresh catastrophe. The devil's mouth remained blocked. "We can just tell people to enter through the devil's ass," Tristan said as he packed up his unused Sawzall. So we directed people around the corner, to the backless back of the building. "The façade is unstable" was our unofficial theme for the night.

We had decided to have a sort of undercover ECRG meeting at a public event. I was already taking part in a reading organized by Nate, and what I read would constitute that month's text, secretly dedicated to the group, most of whom would be in attendance. I was reading with a hot young fiction writer who had just published a story in a fancy literary magazine and was getting a lot of buzz, and a writer from Mexico City who was nervous because he'd never read in English in public before and drank Jameson's from a shiny elegant flask, which flashed in the jury-rigged work lights whenever he tipped it back.

I was happy with the low-pressure middle slot that evening, facing about a hundred people in rows of white folding chairs, a few who'd ridden in on bikes through the devil's ass. A security light beyond the wall on a pole by the street kept turning off and on with a tiny low hiss, arbitrarily. About halfway through my reading, delicate Formosan termites arrived. They swarm and harass parts of the city every May around Mother's Day, a phenomenon that sounds like the opening of a Gabriel García Márquez novel. Their frail, collective power can swath streetlights and porch lights so intensely that sometimes you have to turn off all your lights, even televisions and computers, and sit in the Victorian dark to keep them away from your old wooden home. The Formosans began alighting on my pages and I had to brush them off the words as I read this fragment of a piece, "Condolences from Death Row." Over the past four months, the ECRG had become an essential part of grieving my father, a dependable rallying of supportive souls on the Tragic Plane. Last month's procession had solidified our commitment to the project, and buried in the piece I read was a message of gratitude to the ECRG, my fellow travelers through the dark wood.

The envelope was facedown on the living room floor under the mail slot, mixed in with glossy campaign propaganda, the usual meaningless slogans, endorsements, toothy family portraits. This was a real letter with real handwriting but then, as I picked it up, a moment of confused dread. Next to my name and address was rubberstamped DEATH ROW in black. The stamp's imprint had that singular aspect from pressure unevenly applied, the bottom of the letters dark and resolute but the tops ragged and noncommittal, ghost spots blanking the middle of TH RO. The penmanship on the envelope was careful, cursive, rounded, small. I'm in one of the few professions where one still encounters swaths of handwriting on a regular basis — education. My students come from a variety of demographics, and if I had to peg this writing's provenance, I would've said Uptown Catholic-school girl, maybe Academy of the Sacred Heart? Plaid skirts, loafers, the mindful tutelage of nuns.

The return address was the Louisiana State Penitentiary, Angola. I admired the elegant loops of the *L* and the *S*, something I never quite mastered myself. More specifically, it was from Death Row G, from my brother's pro bono client. Though I knew the name, I wasn't expecting a letter from him. The back was stamped NOT CENSORED, NOT RESPONSIBLE FOR CONTENTS, LOUISIANA STATE PENITENTIARY MARCH 20, 2012, LA. STATE PEN. AN ALL-MALE PENAL INSTITUTE. This letter had been fortified with some dark and insistent bureaucracy, or worse, by some guy only doing his job, but it wasn't sealed, just had a dainty piece of tape across the tip of the flap's *V.* The next evening at dinner, I showed my brother the letter and he said to himself, incredulously, "Where'd he get the tape?"

A few months before, in late December, I'd interviewed my father and brother about their pro bono capital-punishment cases, which they'd been handling for about ten years by then and which they always talked about with a different tone and intensity than their other legal business. At one point their clients had been in cells side by side and would compare notes about their Gisleson lawyers: the father, a seasoned ex–federal prosecutor, the son, at the time, a brand-new attorney who'd never tried a criminal case. One would recount his elder attorney's courtroom successes and the other would wonder why the apple hadn't fallen closer to the tree.

Actually it wasn't really an interview, it was drinks and lunch and a tape recorder at the Rib Room, at table 5, next to a high rounded window onto Royal Street, a proscenium framing cast-iron balconies, arched transoms, and hanging ferns, the kind of lovely amnesiac view cherished by tourists and locals alike, a French Quarter postcard tacked over the city's troubles.

That month my dad did what he'd been doing the past two years of living with leukemia, nose-diving into the desert of zero immunity and the ICU only to pull up at the last minute, leaving us all — family, nurses, doctors — dusting off our clothes and craning our necks at his ascent. He did it again! His nurses called him the rock star of the Touro Infirmary oncology ward — he'd invited them to our family Christmas party and they'd actually shown up. As he did with most things in his life, he litigated his illness, read all the pages of fine print that accompanied his medications, cross-examined his doctors, mapped out defensive strategies of his symptoms and treatments on legal pads. That afternoon at the Rib Room, a few days after Christmas, he was drinking wine and excited about his record-high platelet count and the possibility of going to MD Anderson for a bone-marrow transplant. He sounded good, though I had to discreetly push the tape recorder toward his weakened voice a few times as he talked about the death penalty, his legal career, the mysteries of the human personality.

Near the end of lunch, he mentioned that the next week he had four days of chemo lined up and then planned on going up to Angola, to Death Row, to see his client on the fifth day. Talk about "ineffective counsel," he joked. A genuine practitioner of gallows humor, he'd often say he was fighting to keep his client from lethal injection, but he was the one getting poison shot into his veins on a regular basis.

So the next week, after his round of chemo, with zero immunity, he took his long-cherished drive to Angola, visited his client, fell ill upon returning home, and died within days. It would be narratively convenient, powerful even, to say Death Row finally killed him, but honestly, we'll never know which handshake, countertop, doorknob, between New Orleans and West Feliciana Parish slipped him the enterococcus bacteria that finally did him in. Vulnerable as my dad was, the whole world was a threat, health care workers and children being more lethal to him than Death Row convicts, who lived pretty physically sterile lives, and I think he was more concerned that the associate he was driving up to Angola with had young kids and their empty car seats in the back were probably teeming with invisible peril. But since most narrative is part purpose, part accident, and the messiness of life always pulses up against the myth, I think we can claim it as a good ending for him anyway.

One of the things my dad appreciated about his adopted state, where he married a sixth-generation Louisianan, raised eight kids, and buried two, is its ability to create and maintain its own myths, for better or for worse. He loved that he could drive from his home in Algiers to Death Row in Angola and back in one day, traveling these overlapping colonial histories, highway sign to highway sign, continent to continent to continent, through the snares of exoticism laid by our forebears, who were endowed with that pioneer privilege of naming places, subjecting generations to their desires, their enterprises. Sometimes the names become merely cartographical curiosities. At other times, their legacies hold. Angola, known also as the Farm, bounded by the Mississippi River on three sides and the gentle Tunica Hills on the fourth, was originally a plantation owned by a slave trader notorious for breaking up families. It was eventually bought by the state and maintained as such a medieval prison that in the 1950s a couple of dozen prisoners cut their Achilles tendons in protest of the conditions there. If Louisiana were its own country, and some would posit that it kind of is, we would have the highest incarceration rate in the world. There are over five thousand men in Angola, in that tight bend of the river, in the country's largest maximum-security penitentiary, there because of bad luck, bad judgment, bad legal counsel, bad laws, or just fundamentally bad souls.

Honestly, that Death Row envelope sort of frightened me and I had a very quaint moment, having to sit down on the red velvet couch, a Duncan Phyfe inherited from the frozen tableau of my grandmother's front parlor, as my hands trembled with a piece of mail. But that was an interesting discovery — both fear and tenderness can be accommodated within the same instant. The letter was formal, deferential. He sent belated condolences for the loss of my father, whom he'd had the honor to meet. He talked about his warmth, charm, professionalism, said many of the same, particular things that people had said during the visitation line that snaked out past the brick walls of Saint Clare's Monastery and onto Henry Clay Avenue the morning of the funeral. And I appreciated that there was some continuity of perception between Angola's Death Row and Uptown New Orleans, and that my dad had been that vehicle.

In his letter, my brother's client was trying to set up a meeting with me, and needed a little more information for the required paperwork, "sensitive information" like my date of birth and Social Security number. During another dinner when my brother was explaining some arcane procedure of the capital-appeals process and I was pretending to follow what he was saying, he started talking about how tough it is to visit Death Row. If you're not related you can't just ask to visit someone and get access. "Unless you're from Hollywood," he explained. "Billy Bob Thornton or John Cusack or whoever. Those guys get access."

John Cusack, really? That name hit a lever in my brain and shifted something. Cusack and I had grown up together, he in John Hughes–type movies and I watching them in theaters that don't exist anymore. Now we're both aging, the skin under our eyes thinning, both taking on glum roles of middle-age discontent. About a year earlier, he'd become a sort of bête noire for me. One late night after watching *Hot Tub Time Machine,* I couldn't sleep, as my then-four-year-old had come into our bed, snoring like an old man and driving my husband out to sleep on the couch. In the movie, Cusack's character is transported back to the '80s, via a malfunctioning hot tub and a Russian energy drink. Recently, I'd come across my own portal back to the '80s, via an effusive evite for a high school reunion, to be played out on location in the French Quarter. Open bar, uncomfortable appraisals, balcony drama. Much of *Hot Tub*'s campy nostalgia and plotline seemed contrived so Cusack and his buddies could get busy with girls who were way too young for them. In the cascading credits was the name of Cusack's personal chef, which I found depressing for some reason, and I remembered a picture in the newspaper of Cusack when he was in town filming another movie, riding a bike, all protectively padded as though he were going jousting or something.

Now, it was about three in the morning, I still couldn't sleep, and I thought I heard some howling in the field across the street from my house, an empty lot that nature overtook when the city tore down a Section 8 apartment building, a little urban oasis littered with syringes, broken bottles, and plastic bags with suspect brown smears on them. The howling seemed alternately human and animal, and I got up to investigate, discovering nothing, just muddled shadows ringing the edges of the field. Wide awake now, I checked my email, which they tell you not to do when you can't sleep, and a one-sentence message from another lawyer brother was waiting: "Dad's doctor said he'll be dead by the Super Bowl." My dad and his oncologist were evidently combining the manias of cancer-death timelines and the possibility of a second world championship for the Saints. "Two dat?" my dad reportedly said. "Fuck dat!" I went back to bed, to the loud corrugated breathing of my little boy and the indeterminate howling. The ceiling fan needed dusting, my dad was dying, the '80s were reasserting themselves in my consciousness, and I kept picturing that funnel vortex rising out of the hot tub at the end of the movie, sort of like the tornado from *The Wizard of Oz*. But nothing swirled inside of it, no witches on bikes or farmhands. It was an empty, dark, expensive CGI spectacle, its team of creators buried deep in the credits, down below even John Cusack's personal chef. It was one of those middle-aged moments you sink way into, the past and future touching, the present crystallizing around you, tiny filaments in the air connecting icily to trap meaning.

But maybe "trapping meaning" is a little wrong, and after all, it's really only trapped in the fat rectangle of the previous paragraph. Its bars are palpable enough, though. Mortality, the parental conundrum, and also a certain anxiety of authenticity felt both generationally and personally, as a writer. What's real? What's manufactured narrative? What's the relationship between them? Where's all the noise coming from?

See, there are times in your life like that, in grief, in love, when you walk around like a live wire, with meaning sparking off of everything, and go through the day dazzled and hurting. Maybe I was being oversensitive about the Death Row letter, but lately I was back in that place, feeling like Dante, "midway in our life's journey," lost in the dark wood at the entrance of the Inferno and holding back furry demons of worldliness before Virgil shows up to guide him. Like Cusack in *Hot Tub Time Machine,* Dante ultimately sees much of the redemption for his midlife crisis in the fantasy of a too-young girl, Beatrice. I guess men have always been built to disappoint. Though I'm starting to think that the dark wood isn't really so bad. Sometimes you run into people you know, sometimes sympathetic strangers. There can be camaraderie there, like, Hey, we're here together in the dark wood, can I pour you some more of this bourbon, can you recommend a good book? Was the letter from Death Row another low branch across the path or was it the murky green light that filters in between branches? And what about your kids? They're happy enough, they're fine, you can hear them in the sunny clearing nearby and you can always go join them. Sometimes you think it would be nice if we could widen these paths, make it easier for our kids when it's their turn in the dark wood. But I think the best thing we can do is make sure they're equipped. They can bring their own machetes, their own bourbon.

In New Orleans, as in much of the country, we hadn't had much of a winter and we were enjoying a gentle glide into an early and perfect spring, the kind that blankets the city in a good mood. I read the letter a few more times, making myself late for work. The tall living room windows were filled with the bright flora of the improbable field across the street, trash trees holding their own alongside the sycamores, the busted light pole blooming yellow with a mess of cat's claw vine. The letter suddenly seemed like my most important possession, and like all real handwritten, postally delivered letters these days, an instant relic from a previous era, before time and space collapsed and we started sending messages to each other's pockets. Besides the thoughtful observations about my dad and the condolences, it was the letter's valediction that got me: "With gratitude & sincerity." Now I was really late. I set the house's burglar alarm and opened the door to a morning that was quickly turning to afternoon.

We hung out in our borrowed fortress for a few hours afterward, talking, listening to music, and waving away the papery swirls of termites if we stood too close to the lights. The writers slammed beers to recalibrate their nerves for conversation and exchanged cagey compliments. We never officially convened an ECRG, but throughout the evening Kevin, Ellen, Nate, Susan, Tristan, and Brad all acknowledged their recognition of the dark wood, though we didn't belabor it. Kevin said he was most struck by the "bourbon and machete" metaphor. Our sons have been best friends since they were about three, and the fear and pleasure of parenting constitute an ever-deepening element of our friendship. After the crowd strode and rode away through the devil's ass, the ECRG hung back and loaded up the trucks with the chairs and tables, podium and lights, unplugged extension cords, and abandoned the outpost to its quieter, more furtive uses.

———————

The week following the reading, I made the drive up to Angola with Soren to meet his client. I couldn't sleep the night before, and my stomach felt tight with nerves and dread the whole two-and-a-half-hour ride. As he drove, Soren talked about his client's case and his shoddy initial representation. When he was assigned the appeal, he was handed a thin three-ring binder, the sum total of the defense, unconscionable for a capital case. Soren said that his first trial ever as a young attorney had been for a dog bite, and there were boxes and boxes of evidence for that. In East Baton Rouge Parish, the public defender assigned to his Death Row client had no experience in criminal defense, had begged the judge to be taken off the case, but the judge kept him on — as a sort of punishment for some past misdeed, Soren believed.

Some of the long drive up I-10 is elevated over swamps thick with palmettos and miles of dying cypress groves, fuming refineries in the distance. Once past Baton Rouge, you turn down Highway 61 and its fields of soy and rust-bitten industrial plants. Entering West Feliciana Parish, 61 becomes the green Scenic Highway of oak alleys, Spanish moss, plantations turned bed-and-breakfasts (the disconcerting superimposition of genocide and *Southern Living*), gas stations stocked with excellent *boudin* and gumbo. Then you turn left at the Daiquiri Shack onto LA 66, drive the languorous, wooded two-lane road also known as Tunica Trace, which ends at the front gate of the belly of the whale, Angola.

There you are confronted by the blunt power of law enforcement. As an attorney, Soren was allowed to drive across the prison grounds to Death Row on his own after being questioned and having his car searched. He would wait until I was finished with my visit and then take care of business. As a regular visitor, you enter through Angola's nondescript processing center, are allowed only an ID, a single key, and paperwork, which an officer checks against the computer and then writes "DR" with a ballpoint flourish across the top. You're escorted to a plywood box with a fan at the top and a grate near the bottom, where a drug-sniffing German shepherd is stationed. When you enter the box, a guard turns on the fan, directing your scent down to the grate, and you can see a paw or a bit of snout through the metal slats.

After you exit the box, you're patted down, sent through a metal detector and into an area that looks like a rural bus station, which is almost entirely full of women of all ages and a few children, and you wait for your prisoner's name to be called. When it is, you board a Blue Bird school bus painted white, fear and anxiety now total throughout your body, and you register the lovely pastoral drive through the fields of beans and corn and squash, inmates in different shades of blue chambray shirts working those fields, the Tunica Hills artfully shading the perimeter. You note the carefully painted, expert signage on the buildings, the explosive murals of Native Americans on the water tanks, you make stops at fenced-in camps A, B, C, etc., to let off fellow riders, you glimpse, behind a stable eating some straw, a camel, a permanent resident and featured player in the annual Passion Play performed by inmates in the rodeo arena. Soon, you are the only person on the bus and the driver asks you if this is your first time visiting Death Row, *yes,* and you wonder what the giveaway is as you approach a lovely cattail-fringed pond, a waterfowl preserve that attracts herons, egrets, and roseate spoonbills, the kind of place John James Audubon would've set an easel in front of, which is yards away from the bus's final stop, the Death Row complex by the levee, its coils of razor wire topping rows of tall cyclone fencing.

Enjoy your visit. Once the guard tower buzzes you in the first gate you are trapped in the threshold until the next gate tag-teams your entry with another loud buzz. You walk the short path to the building, which looks like a pleasantly landscaped suburban dentist's office. Inside is just as banal, you could be in any office anywhere, dark wood-paneled furniture with tasteful molding, framed family pictures, good-natured office banter among the staff, thick-leaved plants in baskets that could be real or fake — hard to tell. At the reception desk, you sign in and are handed a menu.

I sat for a while in the visiting booth, waiting, my anxiety dispersing as I studied the photocopied list of options that was formatted like an order form, with boxes to check. Typical south Louisiana fare: shrimp and catfish platters, steak, hamburgers, sandwiches. Except I hadn't seen prices that low since about 1985. After twenty minutes or so, guards led to the door on the other side of the thick Plexiglas divider a man who looked uncertainly through the narrow security window, then smiled, almost in recognition, though we'd never met. He entered the room alone, shackled, and then bent down with his back against the door to allow the guards to unchain him through a slot. He was in his early forties, broad smile, blue chambray shirt, the lines from the laundry press sharp across his chest and arms. He was also wearing a watch. We sat on small stainless steel stools bolted on either side of the barrier. He thanked me for coming and I thanked him for having me. I asked him what he would like for lunch. He ordered a fried seafood platter and a Coke. Earlier Soren had recommended the catfish, but I ordered a grilled shrimp plate instead.

It was late morning and the window behind me created a glare that superimposed a reflection of myself and everything in the window onto my side of the divider; the only way I could clearly see him was to line up my reflection perfectly with his face to block out the glare, so we sat eye to eye, talking for almost two hours tethered to handheld phones. A fidgety and physically impatient person, I was forced to be still. For most of the visit, I could really see only his face and what was reflected from the window behind me, coils of razor wire along a wall and the occasional bird flying through the frame.

We talked easily and fluidly about his six children, my two, a Dan Brown book he was reading, his religious faith and initial fear that his epiphany about Jesus being his savior a couple of years into his incarceration was just jailhouse religion, not the real thing. But religion had stayed with him and fortified him over his sixteen years in prison. He asked if it was much of a hassle getting processed. I told him it was fine and remarked on the mostly female visitors on the bus. He said that sounded about right. All of his male friends and cousins had stopped visiting him after a couple of years, and now it was just his mother and sister and daughters who came.

What we could not talk about, for legal reasons, was his case, especially since everything was recorded in the visitation booth. I only knew the details from the Internet and from my brother. He had been convicted of murdering two employees of a restaurant in Baton Rouge where he'd previously worked as a dishwasher. He was reportedly witnessed riding up on his bicycle before the restaurant opened, greeting the bartender, then shooting him twice in the back as he entered. The bartender survived, but the manager who was calling 911 and begging for her life did not. The cook hiding in the freezer also begging for his life did not. Seven thousand dollars was stolen from the office. He was arrested soon after, with friends and former co-workers all testifying against him.

Our lunch arrived in Styrofoam containers. We awkwardly maintained the conversation, maneuvering the phones and plastic cutlery, the talking and eating. I kept losing him to the glare as he shifted focus to the seafood platter. Soren had long raved about the food they serve for visitation on Death Row. And he was right — it was really good. Fresh, well-seasoned, generous portions. The inmate who delivered the meal was wearing a chef's hat. My brother's client assured me that it was not what they were regularly served, that their diet is heavy on cabbage and light on protein, that he has to supplement it with tuna packets from the commissary. During their single daily hour out of their cells, some guys had figured out how to do a little improvisational cooking in the microwave they have access to. He walked me through a fellow inmate's recipe for Death Row pralines: a half-full jar of peanut butter, water, a microwave, a plastic spoon, and whatever preferred candy is available from the vending machine.

I understood that inmate's desire to attempt to re-create a praline. Just seeing them in the little baskets next to the register at the drugstore or hardware store or traffic court (a side enterprise for the cashier) evokes a convulsion of desire. The simplicity of the ingredients — sugar, butter, and pecans — yielding something almost too good to bear. I used to work across the street from Aunt Sally's praline factory near the Mississippi, and when their vats were bubbling and the coffee plant a few blocks away was roasting, the neighborhood smelled like the world's largest continental breakfast and I couldn't believe I had the good fortune to spend my days in such a place. But such concentrated delight has a particular relationship to heartbreak. Shortly after Hurricane Katrina, I befriended a Creole grandfather during drop-off at our kids' school. Many mornings he would talk to me about his praline business, which was just getting going before the storm, in a repetitive abstracted loop many older folks were stuck in during that time, struggling to move forward, the gears always slipping. He had just made some big deals with a few downtown hotels when his kitchen flooded and everything fell apart. One day he brought me a small, wilted, flattened box cheerily printed with his company's logo, never to be assembled and never to be filled with what he claimed were once the best pralines in the city. Did he present the box to me as evidence, as emblem? I wasn't sure. Later, I'd notice a drift of hundreds more empty packages in the back of his car, next to his grandbaby's car seat.

But my most cherished praline encounter occurred after Rachel died and I was on the ferry going to visit my sister Kristin in Algiers, in the middle of the Mississippi, in a low, deep funk, gazing into the fierce eddies churning off the stern. An older gentleman in a purple three-piece suit appeared before me bearing a tray full of pralines, actually the lid of a cardboard box, like an ambassador from the land of possibility. I bought two. They were a little crumbly in their plastic sandwich bags but so delicious that I snapped out of myself, surprised and grateful as I watched the man make a few more transactions among my fellow passengers.

My brother's client had more questions for me than I had for him. What kind of car I drove (he said what almost every man says when I say "Honda": *Keep oil in the engine and it'll run forever*), what kind of writing I did, if I went to church. He was fascinated by Brad's job as a scenic painter. They watch a lot of television and movies on Death Row, one TV for every two cells. I imagine this was a fresh way for him to scrutinize the most dynamic view of the outside world he had access to, give it another layer of interest. He asked what movie my husband was working on then and I told him the name of the director. He told me excitedly, "I've met him before! When they were filming up here." He named a few more actors and actresses he'd met while on Death Row.

"And there was that white dude with black hair, probably about our age but looks older, was in *Con Air* and a bunch of other stuff. *Runaway Jury*?"

I felt something like a warm benediction and relief pass through me and I smiled.

"John Cusack?" I asked.

"Yeah, him." I told him about the piece I'd read the week before, about how much his letter had meant to me. I hoped he was okay with it. He grinned and said he was.

He explained to me how that one meeting with Dad had transpired. A few years earlier, Soren and Dad had driven up together to visit their respective clients, visits that would often last several hours. At some point toward the end of the afternoon, they decided to switch visitation booths so they could meet each other's clients. He said Dad made such an immediate and lasting impression on him, so warm and cordial, but also kind of formidable in the way he presented himself. You could feel the force of his professionalism, and how much he cared about what he did. He looked for traces of Soren in him, just like he was looking for traces of Soren in me. *And?* He said Soren and I made the same gesture of sweeping our hair away from our face as we spoke. Funny to be scrutinized for observable familial bonds behind the Plexiglas in that little booth up in Angola, to be suddenly self-conscious of those tics and traits acquired over the years, often invisible to our own selves, that make us who we are to others.

He asked me about my summer plans and I couldn't bring myself to tell him I was going to Tokyo in a few weeks, that I'd been invited there to participate in a university symposium about cultural rebuilding in post-disaster communities. I was too embarrassed by my extravagant freedom. While during that week in Tokyo I would truly love the city's unfurling marvels of ultra-civilization, I also learned Japan has what's considered one of the more inhumane capital-punishment systems in the world. Its Death Row inmates have to sit more or less immobile, in silence, in solitary confinement. They are not informed as to when they'll be executed until the day arrives, so years and years can pass, sometimes decades, and suddenly a guard will show up to take them to their hanging. By that time, some executed inmates are elderly and insane. Families are not told about the execution until afterward.

I had come to Death Row loosely because of Dad, in a way retracing his last true gesture, his final statement to the world. I wanted to visit the place where his professional and moral life had taken on so much purpose. Of course, I'd done it in that oblique way in which large families sometimes operate — not meeting Dad's client (which I did not have permission to do), but my brother's. Throughout his life Dad was often driven by injustice within the justice system, and Angola is the physical reality of it, the consequences of it borne out in people's lives. You enter this bucolic, isolated realm suffused with a long history of brutality, with only your ID and a single key and cash for lunch, shedding the trappings of your life, your vulnerability amplified. In this manner, you confront human fallibility and our imperfect ways of managing it. I think this confrontation was part of the attraction of the place for Dad.

And Dad was nothing if not confrontational, impulsively so. As a litigator, a father, and a man out in the world. A few times he'd come home with a black eye or scuffed bloody nose, saying he'd been mugged, but nothing was ever taken, and he smelled like booze and smoke. As we got older we figured it was from bar fights. When I lived in the Quarter, in the crumbling Creole manse, the cops once showed up with him at my doorstep, a mess in his three-piece suit. They were deferential, almost gentle with him, as they asked me to take him in and keep him out of trouble. He crashed on the couch and was gone by the time I woke up. We never talked about it again.

Once he told of an argument with a Frenchman in an airport bar that eventually became amicable; when the man asked who he was, he replied, *"Je suis le Grand Asshole,"* and they became fast layover drinking buddies. "Asshole" is a word I always associate with my dad. The way he leaned on *ass,* stretched out the *o,* and barely acknowledged the *l.* Both epithet and banner. He loved being an asshole as much as calling them out. When I was in high school and meeting Dad one day at his office downtown before walking to lunch, he was on the phone with an adversary, discussing a lawsuit involving the Superdome. Dad began to relentlessly dig into the guy, cutting him off, raising his voice, having such a good time that he put him on speakerphone for my benefit. The more the guy pushed back, the more Dad enjoyed it. "No need to threaten and cajole, Eric," the man said plaintively, "no need to threaten and cajole." Delighted, Dad ended the call, telling the man he had to take his daughter to lunch. I was mortified for all three of us. Afterward, my brothers, sisters, and I, who were used to Dad's ferocious outbursts — over bills, losses by Notre Dame, frequent dinner-table spills, a vacuum cleaner left in the middle of a room — would sometimes refer to Dad's misdirected tirades as giving someone "the old T and C."

One thing I think I did discover was why my father kept going back to Angola so regularly, why it was so hard to hang up the phone in the visitation booth and rise from the stool — the guilt of privilege and freedom. The obvious tension girding the conversation was that when we said good-bye, my brother's client was going back to a tiny room where he would spend twenty-three hours a day, a cell block that he could leave only to go outside one hour a week, and I was heading back to the highway with my brother, through lovely and leafy West Feliciana Parish, to a gas station where I'd stock up on gumbo and crab bisque to bring back to my family and buy a huge Heineken for the road to pacify my despair while Soren drove and we later got caught in a traffic jam caused by a seemingly empty school bus hanging off the elevated highway over the swamp. When we arrived back in New Orleans, we hit the diviest dive bar we could find, ordered some bourbon to clear our heads. That bar happened to be next door to the ruins of the St. Claude Furniture Store near Elysian Fields Avenue, my sister's devil and its man-sized mouth still stretched down to the sidewalk, still boarded up, an empty invitation.

JUNE

Voices over Water

June in Louisiana is a threshold month. Nature's springtime sexual frenzy is burning itself out — the jasmine, gardenia, wisteria, that make the city's subtropical spring so glorious, so briefly, are browning and dropping on sidewalks and courtyards. Time to deadhead the flowers and put the garden into protective mode against the coming heat. But the heartier ones, like hibiscus, oleander, and passionflower, will treat us to hot pink and red and orange all summer, surprising us through the chain-link fence of a withering parking lot or brightening the crux of an overburdened power line. June also marks the start of hurricane season: a brief ruffling of the airwaves with stories about storm projections and disaster preparedness. It's always a relief when November arrives and we've dodged the meteorological bullet. For this year.

There's something about the New Orleans June heat slamming down that makes you vigilant about issues of will and momentum. It's crucial to keep the machinery churning so it doesn't rust in the humidity. So Susan's choice for this month's reading, John Cheever's story "The Swimmer," felt seasonally appropriate. Even the main character, Neddy Merrill, "might have been compared to a summer day, particularly the last hours of one." And of course there's the drinking.

I bought a bottle of claret, because "The Swimmer" begins:

It was one of those midsummer Sundays when everyone sits around saying, "I *drank* too much last night." You might have heard it whispered by the parishioners leaving church, heard it from the lips of the priest himself, struggling with his cassock in the *vestiarium,* heard it from the golf links and the tennis courts, heard it from the wildlife preserve where the leader of the Audubon group was suffering a terrible hangover. "I *drank* too much," said Donald Westerhazy. "We all *drank* too much," said Lucinda Merrill. "It must have been the wine," said Helen Westerhazy. "I *drank* too much of that claret."

Susan brought a bottle of gin because Neddy Merrill, husband of Lucinda, is introduced sitting poolside at the Westerhazys' "by the green water, one hand in it, one around a glass of gin." Neddy, who is feeling one of those moments of intense pleasure in life and circumstance, devises a plan to swim the eight miles from the Westerhazys' to his home in Bullet Park:

He seemed to see, with a cartographer's eye, that string of swimming pools, that quasi-subterranean stream that curved across the county. He had made a discovery, a contribution to modern geography; he would name the stream Lucinda after his wife. He was not a practical joker nor was he a fool but he was determinedly original and had a vague and modest idea of himself as a legendary figure. The day was beautiful and it seemed to him that a long swim might enlarge and celebrate its beauty.

Friends at the first few pools give him drinks and encouragement, and he feels an explorer's exhilaration of purpose. Soon, though,

Neddy's project meets its realities, both of the topography and of the true condition of his life. A storm comes, water from the sky, water beyond man's control, and he takes shelter in the Levys' gazebo. When he recommences his swim, things have shifted somewhat, the weather a little cool, his shoulders a little sore. He encounters the following: a dry pool that "disappointed him absurdly," the indignity of trying to cross a highway in a bathing suit, the discomforts of a public pool where he is "confronted by regimentation," some rich nudist-communists who allude to his misfortunes, a former mistress who scorns him, and, at a party where he is not welcome, social snubs by both the hostess and the caterer's bartender.

Neddy has been self-deluded, his life is no longer one of privilege, though the details of his fall aren't entirely clear — money lost overnight, some drunken humiliations. Time seems to speed up as if high summer is turning to late fall during his swim of the Lucinda River and his body starts to feel the fatigue. Neddy is so exposed, nearly naked in his swimming trunks, which become looser and looser on him as the day progresses, and he becomes more and more isolated from the people he encounters along the banks of the Lucinda River, the people who had given him meaning and shaped his identity — family, friends, strangers. In the beginning of his journey, he professes "an inexplicable contempt for men who did not hurl themselves into pools," and he always pulled himself out by the pool's curb. Now he finds himself achingly using the stairs and ladders. Even though he knows he can cut the whole thing short, exhausted and confused, he keeps going until he arrives at what turns out to be his former home, now for sale, the earlier thunderstorm heightening its state of disrepair. "He shouted, pounded on the door, tried to force it with his shoulder, and then, looking in at the windows, saw that the place was empty."

With a narrative like "The Swimmer," so rich on so many levels, some of the first things people grabbed for were the allusions and literary clues, like all the mythological references. Sara read to us from her iPhone that Lucinda is derived from the Latin word for "light," *lux,* and that in Roman mythology Lucina was the goddess of light and of childbirth. ("River of light!" I whispered to Brad as an aside. "The industrial jungle cruise on the Sumida." We'd just returned from Japan a week or so before, our minds still glazed and awed by the life-shifting trip.) Someone noted that in the beginning of the story Neddy slides down the banister and slaps the statue of Venus on the hall table on the backside.

Susan mentioned that Neddy wonders why he sees the autumn constellations of Andromeda, Cepheus, and Cassiopeia, a mythological family connected to vanity and water. Cassiopeia brags that her daughter Andromeda is the most beautiful girl in the universe, angering Poseidon, who has her chained to a rock, to be eaten by a sea monster, until she's saved by Perseus. One of the original tales of the consequences of hubris. Cheever's use of myth was so pervasive in his fiction that he was once called the Ovid of Ossining, the New York town where he lived the last couple of decades of his life, similar terrain to the Lucinda River, upscale midcentury suburbia cultivated around security, money, and privilege. But as Neddy swims the Lucinda River and his former world of privilege falls apart around him, his vulnerability overtakes him.

Kevin, legs crossed, balancing a wineglass on his knee, quietly, flatly, said that for him it was the most affecting of the readings we had done so far. He was going through a difficult time himself — job stress, the recent birth of a second child — and he was moved by Neddy's worn-down vulnerability, the relentlessness of its nature. Neddy is aging, Kevin said, drowning in his own psychological mythology, the seasons turning symbolically around him. And when he arrives home, locked out, all he can do is peer in at the remnants of his own destruction. For Kevin, the story was a great example of his belief that the less true something is, like Neddy's own mythology, the more powerful and potentially destructive it is.

The layers of myth in any family can be difficult to sort out. Living in the South, a few generations in, it's especially difficult. Our failure of the one test God put before us (as Walker Percy put it), that of not enslaving other humans, was converted to the grand collective lie of charmed southern living we white children of a certain demographic grew up with, one that is impervious to the most liberal of households, obscuring the monstrous reality of how and with whose blood our society was actually built and maintained. As a rangy midwesterner with heavy-framed Buddy Holly glasses, Dad came down to Louisiana to marry Mom, but had a difficult entry into the wary family, was called a vile epithet by my plantation-raised great-grandmother because of his civil rights work at the Department of Justice. So now, in addition to his own insecurities about his working-poor upbringing, his alcoholic father, and whatever other personal demons he harbored, he had something to prove to *these* people, though their myths and his overlapped in places, buttressing each other even as they competed. The successively larger houses and parties and extravagances became intertwined with his role as self-made man and patriarch, even as they were also gestures of competitive defiance to his in-laws, who had lost their big houses over the generations. He genuinely loved being a father, but helplessly cultivated a larger-than-life persona that seemed almost theatrical. When he became a grandfather, he chose to be called Big Daddy, a moniker taken from my mother's beloved grandfather.

Oddly, one of the first places Rebecca danced, when she was nineteen or so, was called Big Daddy's, one of the older, seedier joints on Bourbon Street. I could never get over the implied recrimination. Big Daddy's was famous for a pair of disembodied mannequin legs in fishnets and stilettos on a mechanical swing, a kitschy pendulum forever swaying out above passersby. Even more oddly, around this same time, years before I would ever meet Brad, when he was running with a crowd of musicians, artists, service-industry workers, and strippers, he went to a late-afternoon "band meeting" at Big Daddy's. When he showed up, a young woman in a black bob wig who was sitting on a friend's lap was introduced as Rebecca, whose sister worked with the friend's wife. In those first months of our relationship, during the insatiable biography swapping, we put it all together and discovered that it was indeed my sister, seven years dead by the time we met, and it was like he had encountered a pre-ghost in disguise, in that dank cave of a strip joint.

One night at Big Daddy's I had one of those backstage conversations with Rebecca that left me bewildered and depressed. I remember the dressing room as being narrow, with mottled mirrors and beadboard wainscoting thick and rippling with decades of sloppy paint jobs. I remember Rebecca as a blur: hot off the stage, flushed and transformed, shimmering and distracted. And probably coked up. She didn't even bother to cover herself, but then again we were sisters, and practically shared bodies. She said she was doing great, dancing was so great, so freeing. She had plenty of money and an apartment uptown.

When discussing the power of the lies we tell ourselves, Kevin had warned that the more people's delusions are threatened, the tighter they cling to them. He figured a person would rather remain deluded than admit she'd been lying, to herself, to others. Of course, Rebecca seemed to me anything but great, but the force of her conviction made me doubt myself. What was I even doing there? What did I hope to achieve, or worse, get out of it? What were the proportions of judgment to curiosity to concern that had brought me there? Was I projecting my values onto her? Was I the one being deluded about my motives, about her life?

Soon I'd learn from my mother that Rebecca had been diagnosed with borderline personality disorder a couple of years earlier, a condition so misleadingly named that Mom thought it meant that she didn't quite have a full-blown condition (this was before widespread Internet access, before we were all experts on everything). BPD actually treads along the dark borders of many other mental illnesses:

depression, anxiety, substance abuse, bipolar disorder. It's marked by delusions, risky behavior, low impulse control, paranoia, and suicidal ideation. Checks in all of those boxes for Rebecca, though surprisingly not for Rachel. BPD can also be notoriously difficult to treat, though my parents tried so many things — individual therapy, group therapy, institutionalization. In her last sketchy years, she seemed more and more detached from her family, but never from Rachel, who was locked into her orbit. In the end, it was the powerful myth of suicide, both as real and unreal as anything, that seduced both sisters.

Toward the end of the evening and the bottle of gin, when talk generally becomes both looser and more urgent, Sara brought up the letters of Cheever, edited by his son Benjamin — *you have to read the letters* — and talked about how she found them more affecting than his fiction. Later, when I finally did read them, after getting over my voyeuristic guilt (all those tendernesses and typos not intended for my eyes), it turned out Cheever was a man I recognized, had kind of grown up with. Funny, generous, perpetually and elegantly amused by life's absurdities, preoccupied with money, insecure and petty, alcoholic, manipulative of the truth for effect, the maintainer of a secretive life parallel to his family and public one, and largely unknowable to many around him. In love with life and with people, Cheever had lots of affairs, with both men and women, both carnally and emotionally. What I found most interesting about the letters was the clear vision of his refracted selves as seen through his correspondences. My favorite example was his two descriptions of a dinner held in his honor by his publisher in 1978. In a letter to a male lover (also apparently bisexual):

Dear _____,
    ...Last night was the gala dinner at Leutece and I sat between
Lauren Bacall and Maria Tucci and basked in that fragrance of

beaver we both so enjoy, but when I went out to take a piss between the 7th and 8th courses I thought deeply of you and how happy I had been eating French-fried onion rings at Admiral Woolsey's.

And to his daughter:

Dear Susie,

The most exciting part of the gala dinner came when they brought in the first course. This was a fish quish [sic] *shaped like an enormous pastry fish and decorated with a pastry frigate in full sail. I had Lauren Bacall on my right and Maria Tucci on my left and very much enjoyed myself.*

Amazing how we house all of these personas at once, flashing them to different people depending on expectations and desire. Maybe that's why it's so easy to deceive ourselves like Neddy does up until the end of the story. Just like the swimming pools are containers, people are containers of bits of our fluid selves. Several times throughout "The Swimmer," Cheever refers to the varying qualities of "voices over water" that Neddy hears as he approaches his next pool. "The water refracted the sound of voices and laughter and seemed to suspend it in midair," and as he leaves it he hears the "brilliant, watery sound of voices fade." Later, as he nears the public pool the voices become "the illusion of brilliance and suspense...but the sounds here were louder, harsher and more shrill," and then, heading back to his milieu, a party at the Biswangers', "from across the road, the lawns, the gardens, the woods, the fields, he heard again the brilliant noise of voices over water." His solo quest is dependent upon other people, and we learn about him through them and what they say; Neddy has been created through all these voices, even through the caterer's bartender. There's no continuous river of the self, it's just a construct, the

Lucinda River an illusion that Neddy is trying to chart through his force of will. Maybe the water is just bald, indifferent existence that we navigate and shape and dream through and ultimately all drown in. For many of us that June evening, "The Swimmer" was mostly about time and aging—the mind's and the body's adjustments to life-fatigue and the general disorientation of the self that can result. How time erodes around you as your body falls apart.

One afternoon my father, tethered to his oxygen tank in his brown leather, Mission-style recliner, with one of those vitamin drinks I'd buy him by the bag at Walgreens balancing on the armrest, said apropos of nothing, "It all just went too fast." "What did?" I asked. "My life." He wasn't ready for it to be over. I went cold. I was standing in the middle of the room, absently checking out what he was watching on the TV, on my way out the door to pick up my sons from school. Don't remember what I responded. It's always disconcerting to see a large man frail and frightened. He'd been a tall, intimidating person my whole life. He seemed slightly incredulous that one could spend so much effort moving things forward and making a big life for a big family and then suddenly it's done. When he looked at me, what did he see—a healthy woman with her own kids and own life, a by-product of his ascent and decline? For that matter, all of his children, dead and alive, what meanings did we hold for him? Had we just become his voices over water, coming at him from a wavering remove as he struggled toward his end?

For days that river metaphor and our discussion of it bobbed in my consciousness, as I tried to recall some echo of it from a recent reading. One day, passing the bookshelf en route to bed, I glimpsed Koestler's *Act of Creation,* that brick of a book we'd read an excerpt from back in March. I had been really taken with the excerpt from "The Belly of the Whale" and had ordered the book, a vast seven-hundred-page opus on the nature and purpose of creativity in life from scientific, psychological, and philosophical-literary vantage points. But when it arrived, I was so intimidated by its length and density and Koestler's genius that I skimmed through it and shelved it until retirement. The quote I'd been trying to remember turned out to be by one of Louis Pasteur's biographers and was on the last page in the section "Multiple Potentials," which I had flipped to, wondering how Koestler was going to finish this monster. In that section, he discusses the fluidity of genius, specifically regarding scientists and the role that accident and happenstance played in their paths toward major history-diverting discoveries. Apparently Pasteur's notebooks were full of projects and nascent discoveries that neither time nor circumstance allowed him to pursue. But had events or relationships or whims been differently aligned for Pasteur, suggests his biographer René Dubos, there might've been totally different outcomes for humanity.

It is often by a trivial, even an accidental decision that we direct our activities into a certain channel.... Usually, we know nothing of the ultimate orientation or of the outlet toward which we travel, and the stream sweeps us to a formula of life from which there is no returning. Every decision is like a murder, and our march forward is over the stillborn bodies of all our possible selves that will never be.

When I first read those lines, I couldn't help but laugh out loud, because they were so brutal and so true. As you get older all the bodies of your stillborn selves may pile up around you but every decision is also its own act of creation. That's one of the miracles of the self — that we keep creating ourselves amid the personal carnage.

The day before Dad's funeral, I sat in the kitchen in a hollow state of suspension, everyday life just bouncing dully off me, as I read the newspaper article about his life, an unreal exercise in language processing. When we were kids, he had warned us against believing everything we read in the paper, that there was no such thing as an objectively true story, that facts and circumstances ranged out far beyond the neat columns and the discreet authority of the byline. But reading his obituary engendered a different kind of disbelief. So did looking at the great picture of him, an unselfconscious side view sneakily snapped at a Christmas party, as he hated having his picture taken, smiling in his outdated glasses, the sweep of brown hair he compulsively combed and his big "lugan" nose whose forensic powers he warned us about every Saturday night before we went out. ("Lugan," a term he embraced, was a midwestern pejorative for anything Lithuanian, like his Kaunas-born maternal grandparents.) The biographical details, highlights of some of the more prominent cases he tried, even ones he would've considered disappointments, padded here and there with a little bullshit from our luncheon. The newspaper listed the children who survived him but not those who didn't, a sad erasure for the twins, especially since I suspect they were the last ones on his mind as he slipped away from us.

But it was the story to the left of my dad's, running exactly parallel on the page a mere centimeter from his, that kept distracting me as I read. INJURIES CITED IN DEATH AT OLD HOTEL. A decomposing body had been found at the bottom of an elevator shaft in an abandoned Howard Johnson out in the Katrina-ravaged but recovering New Orleans East. The coroner's office said that the individual had been dead about four to seven days before someone found him and that he'd died from internal bleeding from pelvic fractures. They had released a description to help ID him. "The man is white, between 20 and 30 years old, 5 feet 7 inches, 148 pounds, and has light brown hair, a full beard and a mustache.... The man also has a twisted right incisor in the right side of his mouth. He had several tattoos on his body, including 'Sublime' on his right inner forearm, a Cancer zodiac symbol on his left inner forearm and a cross on his right lower thigh with the letters 'AT' on one side and 'RM' on the other.... He wore a white shell necklace, a brown shirt and brown pants and brown boots." The coroner was awaiting toxicology reports.

Dad would've loved that juxtaposition because he thrived on contrast and connection. It doesn't matter who speaks for you after you're gone, your tattoos or your tipsy children, nor whether you died alone at the bottom of an elevator shaft, anonymous in darkness, undiscovered for days, or surrounded by your family uptown at the Touro Infirmary under excellent care. You ended up side by side on page B4 of the Metro section of the *Times-Picayune* on January 19, 2012.

At that same Rib Room lunch, sometime after hanging up with the reporter, my brother John said that Mom showed us the beauty of the world, took us, all eight, to plays, museums, to work at food banks, out to the country to nourish our city souls. Dad showed us its absurdity. Not a defeatist, nihilistic absurdity, but one you acknowledge and work with. Fun material that's part of who you are and not anything you ever have to reconcile with anything else.

But something about the man in the elevator shaft resonated with some deep strain within my dad. He often dressed monochromatically, too — in all black, part of his general rebelliousness, a shadow thrown from a tough youth marked by police trouble and car crashes. The intensity of the "Sublime" tattoo and the quirky ornament of the shell necklace. Dad was a loner with just a few loyal friends, loved cheesy holiday decorations and throwing big parties. He was self-isolating, drawn to the dark margins. Those black eyes and bloody lips and improbable excuses. Dad's ambitions and weaknesses could've led him anywhere. That man in brown at the bottom of the elevator shaft could've been one of Dad's possible selves, murdered and abandoned long ago, finally catching up to him in the stream.

JULY

The Least Dead Among All of Us

It occurred to me that I was the only woman in the room the night Jacques Brel filled the pull-down screen and charged the particles in the air with his existential Gallic virility. We were projecting him from the Internet, from the Olympia Theatre in Paris, 1966, in black-and-white, liberating him from the commercial scaffolding of YouTube via "full screen," so we could experience him in his unmediated and elemental glory. A dark suit, a spotlight, and a rapt, well-dressed audience. Singing seems an understatement — Brel was conjuring, in French, his ravenous sailors of the port of Amsterdam, ravenous for fish and *pommes frites* and drink and whores. In the beginning of Brel's "Amsterdam," sailors "die full of drama and beer at first light" but are also "born in the thick heat of the languid oceans." They "sleep like flags draped on the dark banks," "dance like spat-out suns...to a rancid accordion," and "blow their noses in the stars." The beautiful bodies and the *vertu* of young women are consumed by these men just like the piles of seafood dripping on the too-white tablecloths at the café. The port of Amsterdam is where human desire laps up against that constant in nature, sexual regeneration, exposing man's complicated, sullying place in it. Through the intensity of his delivery, his brown eyes fixed ardently on some space beyond the balcony, where maybe the firmament has cracked open to welcome these sailors home, the song climbs and climbs and never comes down. As Brel's performance crescendos toward the end, his face glazed with sweat and passion, he suddenly swirls away from the audience and disappears into the darkness behind the spotlight.

July is arguably the worst month of the summer in New Orleans and people generally leave town, hibernate in the air-conditioning, try really hard to be productive, or just give up. There's a sort of siege mentality that confines your plans and moods — *we can't do that, it's too hot; can't think about that, it's too hot.* Patience plummets, crime spikes. That night there were just five of us — me, my husband, Kevin, Chris, and Case, who had just returned from Europe and was making a special guest appearance at the ECRG. After their breakup in January, Case and Nina repaired to opposite sides of the planet: Nina to Taiwan to build floats, and Case to Belgium to help artists with marginal construction projects. Case had left the country lost, uncomprehending and bereft. He underwent his own night journey and came back a changed man, surging with ideas for new projects and inspirations. Among these inspirations was the Belgian *chansonnier* Jacques Brel, which Case shared with Brad one evening over drinks shortly after he returned stateside. Brad was deeply affected by Brel, by the raw power of his expression, which seemed so rock and roll, more dependent on the physicality of delivery than the words themselves. And when he came home that night, after hanging out with Case, he showed me the videos over and over, with English subtitles and without, both of us experiencing the slight bewilderment of discovering something incredible for the first time, something that millions of people had known about, and been moved by, since before we were born. So in turn, Brad wanted to share it with that month's ECRG, selecting "Amsterdam" and *"Ne me quitte pas,"* two of Brel's most famous songs. Besides, in midsummer, a listening seemed preferable to a reading.

"Ne me quitte pas" ("Don't Leave Me") is in some ways the opposite of "Amsterdam"; instead of the cosmic amplifying of the self, we get the wrenching diminishing of it, as a quietly desperate lover proclaims all of the things he'll do to keep his *amour* from leaving him. He begins with grand promises of bringing her pearls of rain from countries where it never rains, creating a new kingdom of love that she'll rule over, and inventing senseless words that only she can understand. Each sally is punctuated by the repetition of *"Ne me quitte pas."* In the film footage from the same performance, the phrase is sung through a forced grin, Brel's head shaking plaintively. He tries out a few desperate metaphors of hope, long-dead volcanoes unexpectedly erupting, scorched lands bearing wheat as if it were April. *"Ne me quitte pas. Ne me quitte pas."* His already shaky confidence breaks apart until he can barely utter the negating word *"pas,"* as if the syllable itself is too much to bear. Realizing the futility of his plight as he sings, he finally concedes that he'll weep no more, speak no more, just stand right here and watch her dance and laugh, become the shadow of her shadow, the shadow of her hand, the shadow of her dog. When he disappears into the dark of the stage at the end of that song, it doesn't feel triumphant as with "Amsterdam," in which Brel seems to connect with the black fabric of universal destiny. In *"Ne me quitte pas"* his disappearance is obliterating, the effacement that sometimes accompanies an overwhelming and unreciprocated love, the disappearance of all that you're willing to strip away from yourself just to be able to stick around. Which in the case of *"Ne me quitte pas"* is just about everything.

After we'd watched both videos a couple of times, acclimating to Brel's expressiveness and style, the natural question that evening was, What made Brel an existential figure? Born in 1929 in Brussels, he reached adulthood in existentially roiling postwar Europe. Raised Catholic and groomed for the family's corrugated cardboard business, he had the right things to rebel against and basically created his own self, his own "essence," apart from his upbringing. And though Sartre derided the *chanson realiste* as bourgeois fatalism, the genre did put expressive individuals, like Brel or Edith Piaf or Charles Aznavour, in opposition to the crowd, though ambivalently dependent upon it. Plus, the chanson's lyric intensity was grounded in realism, where humor and tragedy are often conjoined, as are death and sex, the elevated and the base, like in "Amsterdam." All of which made me think of the Simone de Beauvoir quote from *A Concise Dictionary of Existentialism,* "Man is both finite and infinite." (*See also:* Crowd; God; Self-Assertion; Women.) Which made Case impatient, for some reason.

"Do you think Brel got laid a lot?" he asked. "I bet he did!" he answered himself. The other guys seemed curious as well, except for my husband, who's not supposed to betray an interest in getting laid except as a specific, domestic phenomenon. But wanting some evidence, Case commandeered the laptop, which was connected to the projector, fed some words into the Google search slot, and summoned the Jacques Brel Wikipedia page onto the screen. This abrupt aesthetic shift in the dimly lit room, from evocative twentieth-century chiaroscuro to a bland, sans-serif, crowdsourced information platform was jarring. The five-foot-tall Wikipedia entry in our living room felt like a violation of the evening, an affront to the spread of food I'd laid out, the drinks I'd poured. The oversized puzzle-globe logo looming over us, with its earnest invitation to humanity to contribute to its project, was suddenly depressing. Thus I took my daily dose of ambivalence toward the great gifts of technology. We were given the stunning force of Brel transmitted through time and space, but, before full screening, had to put up with the kite string of comments below the video, the scraps and fragments of expression, barely worth the seconds it took to type them, but markings that people felt compelled to leave behind anyway, whether grubby, disgruntled prints or smudges of grateful enthusiasm. The grainy, black-and-white romanticism of man's plight in the universe was knifed right there in the living room because the guys had to know how much Jacques Brel got laid.

Case moved the cursor across blue linked words and citations, scrolled through the paragraphs of biography, each starting repetitively — "In January 1960," "In January 1961," "In March 1962" — to the bottom of 1967, the year Brel wound down his live singing career after an international farewell tour. "Look, I found it," he said. "Here's all the proof we need." He read aloud: " 'Toward the end of the year, with vague plans of sailing around the world, Brel purchased a yacht.' "

A couple of things occurred to me. The first was that the material chosen thus far for the ECRG, though our group was evenly split along gender, represented a male-dominated investigation (except for my reading in May, which, though female-generated was also male-dominated, featuring my father, my brother, and his client), most of the men we'd heard from being alcoholics and/or suicidal and/or misogynists. The second was that the need to investigate whether Brel got laid a lot seemed laughable. One of the most famous French-singing entertainers in the 1960s? I was sure he got chronically, epically, Europeanly laid. You didn't even need to read his only English-language biography, by Alan Clayson of the English band Clayson and the Argonauts, to figure that out, to be unsurprised that he sent his wife and three daughters back to Belgium after he got a little success, maintained a pied-à-terre in Paris, and had both dalliances and serious side relationships with gorgeous, sophisticated creative types, like Zizou, the temperamental chanteuse, and Sylvie, the green-eyed public-relations manager. Or that when he died of lung cancer, at forty-nine, his funeral was attended by both his wife of twenty-five years and his much younger mistress, with whom he had spent the last few years of his life in the Marquesas Islands of French Polynesia, near where Paul Gaugin had also moved to escape the "artificiality" of European culture.

I imagine I was experiencing Brel differently than the guys were, with admiration but also with caution. The longing and desire he pulled out of me like knotted scarves, his sharp suit and thin tie, his confidence that could turn to devastating vulnerability under the spotlight. He was the stuff of infatuation. I'd made the mistake of dating guys like him — charismatic performers who never knew when to stop performing — but luckily I didn't make the mistake of marrying one.

Another point of interest in the room was Brel's classy presentation. Wearing a simple dark suit and performing explosive, intimate numbers with just a spotlight concentrated the power into his words, voice, face, and hands, even his legs, with minimal distraction. In those clips, even his band was in darkness behind him, the disembodied accordion seeming both earthier and airier. Case, whose regular uniform was work pants, T-shirt, and tattoos, including one of a hammer drill on his forearm, was saying that he wanted to get himself one of those plain, black tailored suits, that it was time to step up his game. Brad, also an artist, had sometimes said the same thing — that when he was in art school he'd admired those Dadaists and surrealists from a hundred years ago who would create some of the most provocative, culture-shifting art the world had ever seen in their studios in a plain suit and tie. The suit also represented a workmanlike sense of containment, a uniform of duty or class, eschewing claims of sartorial individuality. Suit as cipher.

So many dads I know these days dress however they want and sport tattoos, their individuality conspicuously inked and illustrated, but I grew up associating dads with suits, the uniform of men with offices, secretaries, and salaries, part of the machinery of the Central Business District, which ground down for long lunches, especially on Fridays, when it nearly sputtered to a halt. Around noon, downtown filled up with simulacra of your dad, on Canal Street or Carondelet; you never knew where he might appear from the crowd of his doubles. Weekend leisure-wear seemed vaguely deceptive and awkward on him, legs too pale and hair too perfect.

But one day in high school I started associating the suit itself with part of a greater deception. I needed to get the car from him and went to his office to pick up the keys. His office was empty but his suit jacket was hanging on the back of the door, so I checked his pockets but instead of keys found a pack of Marlboros, which was a shock since he'd always been vehemently antismoking and we were forbidden to smoke under the threat of severe punishment. He admonished us that his lugan nose could sniff out the faintest trace on our clothes, so we better not even hang around with people who smoked. Both his parents had died of cancer, and I'd never ever seen him with a cigarette. As I smelled his jacket, it dawned on me — that musky, complicated boardroom/cologne/street exhaust man-smell also had a strain of cigarette smoke. Years later, I would understand how much parenting can sometimes be a performance, the much-discussed "modeling" and the united fronts presented to children at times being choreographed, with much of the negotiations, machinations, and messy behavior going on backstage.

But Brel didn't seem to believe much in backstage parenting. Clayson's account of Brel as father was as predictable as that of his love life. According to Clayson, he would drop into the family home in Brussels, sleep until eleven, hold court, issue judgment, recommend that the children read Camus, and generally dominate the house with his unruly temperament.

Domestic routine ruins everything. From my point of view, I insist absolutely on seeing my daughters from time to time and taking them with me, say, on tour, so that they can see a man who is fulfilling his proper function as a man because as soon as you take away that function, he's nothing but a ridiculous sight. Have you ever seen a great surgeon playing billiards? That interests no one — certainly not his children. It is much finer for them to look up to a surgeon at the operating table than a surgeon playing billiards. Children everywhere are being raised by surgeons who play billiards. The mother is above this sort of criticism because she is always playing billiards, metaphorically. The average father is only at home at a time of day when he's worth nothing and has nothing to give.

Most dads aren't surgeons or Belgian pop stars. Most do what they can to feed their families in rather unglamorous ways that don't lend themselves well to audiences. Brad's job, for instance, is to make his labors invisible to the audience. As a scenic painter, he's "below the line," as the industry calls it, creating the illusion of unity between real and fake. Working the surfaces, a scenic painter can make a naked piece of plywood resemble rusty sheet metal, Carrara marble, or speckled linoleum. To have your work noticed by a viewer is to fail. His job has ruined moviegoing for him, as he frequently gives the industry twelve- or fourteen-hour days and is loath to give it an extra ninety minutes during his off time. And when I do convince him to watch something, his eye moves to the artifice of the set or the location, his brain to the guts and the systems of movie magic, to the bureaucratic insanity that often drives these productions.

Sloppy decision making at the top means the bottom works weekends. Often it's someone in an office in L.A. deciding whether or not my husband makes it home for dinner. When he does make it home, he's either enervated or wearied by the absurd nature of his job, the crazy things he spends his days doing. Concocting fake bird shit to dribble on a fake pipe he's just rusted with fiberglass powder, aniline dyes, and shellac. Spray-painting the romantic lead's lawn to turn the grass a more desirous green. Soaking and staining piles of play money to look waterlogged, evidence for a post-Katrina cop to discover. Touching up William Burroughs's prop pot plants for a French production of *On the Road*. Lots of interrogation rooms and jail cells. The same cinder blocks carved from plaster, the same dado lines dividing the walls. The same requests to "make it dirty." He actually likes working on horror movies, the dripping walls and corroded torture chambers; you can experiment with materials, push the visual drama to the edge.

And his job is absurd in the existential sense of futility, too. While the image of what he creates ends up on the screen and in viewers' brains, the actual physical thing is dismantled, bulldozed, tossed in Dumpsters and landfills. Sometimes what he works on for weeks is annihilated without even ending up on-screen. For a western, he and a crew once spent over a month in a warehouse, sculpting and painting several tons of Styrofoam to make a realistically scaled cavern large enough for dusty outlaws to ride their horses through. The boys and I visited the set throughout its transformation — from a three-story-tall Arctic-white foam cavern to one with striated sandstone walls, conjured with about five hundred gallons of paint, dirt trucked in for the floor, and a stream running through it. The director changed his mind about the horses, and filmed one scene of the lead exploring the cavern with torches, discovering the mysterious cave paintings, the creation of which had been the source of tension among the scenic crew because it was a "hero shot" that the camera would linger on, one of the few times your work *is* singled out. In the end, they didn't use any of the footage at all in the movie, and the cavern was trashed.

When I take the boys to visit the sets or locations where Brad works, he'll explain whatever he's having to age or glaze and how he uses the different items from his scenic kit: paintbrushes, rags, shellac, Chapin sprayers called pumpies. The boys are usually quiet, a little disoriented. Already a line of reality has been breached — the line between what Dad does all day and their own days — and from there reality is tampered with even more: miles of cables, impossible lighting rigs, scissor lifts, ear-searing power tools, carpenters blasting classic rock, ad hoc paint shops, temporary structures within structures, and, on the other side of the noise and plywood, the Oval Office or a floating staircase to a witch's library or a perfectly outfitted morgue. Brad tries to detach himself from the craziness when he gets home, tries to be as fully present and engaged a father as he can — washes dishes, does laundry and bedtimes. Plays billiards, metaphorically.

Visiting my father at work was like entering the main chamber of his person. Messy piles of documents fringed the floor and covered his desk and shelves, though he insisted they had an organizational principle and that he could locate any piece of paper at any time. Given that his photographic memory was the envy of his children, none of whom had inherited it, I believed him. On the walls were a few family photographs, one in front of the house on State Street that he was so proud of, taken as a birthday surprise for him one Sunday morning when he and my mom were at Mass. The house looks perfect, its Victorian columns and wide gracious porch a reproach to the bleary, puffy-eyed gaggle of teenagers rousted out of bed and into dress clothes for an early photo shoot on the lawn. The walls also held citations from the Department of Justice, recognizing his beloved days as strike-force chief; a framed print of Daumier's *Don Quixote and Sancho Panza,* the knight a quivering miragelike figure with a spear, so elongated as to be almost skeletal, as if worn down by both the elements and dogged hope; and a panoramic window view of the city he loved and lived in for over forty years but never felt he could call home.

He resembled the Brel model of a patriarch, defined by his career, often absent. Once, over breakfast, when Mom was speculating about those absences, those long nights unaccounted for, she figured he was carving out some semblance of the freedom that he'd never had as a young man. He was engaged during his senior year of college, had three babies by the time he graduated Georgetown Law, followed by five more in quick succession, after which he had to feed and clothe them all while wary in-laws kept tabs. Mom also thought that Dad, as a child of an alcoholic, had some kind of hole that couldn't be filled, though she never reckoned with his own drinking. His larger-than-life presence in the house was marked by excesses — spending, anger, mood swings, an insistence on unconditional love, holiday parties, motionless marathons in his recliner. With eight kids, regimentation was sometimes key to domestic sanity, and he would line us all up before leaving the house for Sunday Mass to rake his black plastic man-comb through our hair with something like pride and resentment. When the comb would snag and pull out a knot, your scalp would sting for the whole walk to church.

Sometime after my father's death my mother gave each of us a copy of the same black-and-white photograph from the early '70s, taken at City Park on a slide at the long-gone playground among the oaks and Spanish moss, stocked with wonderful metal play equipment with chipped paint, treacherous bolts, minimal safety features, and thin eerie creaks and screeches that accompanied our play. Winter, we all were dressed in corduroy or plaid, in my case both. The slide's steps were parallel to its chute and we kids each occupied a step in descending order, oldest to youngest: John, Kristin, me, Susan, Soren. We're caught between poses, and it's not a particularly good photo of any one of us, with no one facing the camera. But all of us are looking at Dad and laughing. Six feet three, with mutton-chop sideburns and wide-cuffed checkered polyester pants, he has just slid down to the bottom and is laughing and crowding Mom, the only one who's looking away, smiling down at the youngest in her lap, my sister Amy. Rebecca and Rachel were not yet born so there were just six of us kids on that slide, an uncanny representation of both the past and the future. Soren is grabbing Dad's knee as he tries to steady himself, grinning so hard you can see the strain in his little jaw. Mom said she chose that picture because she wanted us to remember how much fun he had with us, his outbreaks of goofiness and play. How much fun we all had together.

It was an interesting gesture of my mother's, trying to manage our view of him, since he vigorously tried to manage our view of her. Dad would often refer to her as the "moral pillar" of the family, an image that gave her gentle earth-mother persona an architectural strength and rigidity. It also shifted the ethical weight off him some-what. If she was the moral pillar of the family, he got to be the shadowy eaves, dominating the atmosphere but slightly out of sight.

Watching Brel, and maybe because we were such a small group that night, made me conscious of everyone's roles in the room. Case: aggrieved lover, returned from the Continent bearing Brel and fresh ambitions. Kevin: professorial, still-waters type, never making a wasted or unprofound utterance. Chris: restless and brilliant, a true performer who also relished the backstage, constructing sets and wrangling props. Brad: a stable triumvirate of father, husband, artist. Me: facilitator, maternal snacks and drinks arranger, polite agitator.

All of us enthralled with this image of Brel, his music and his words, who through his own finite means played his role so well he was able to transcend time and space.

Though navigating the gaudy funhouse of celebrity identity, in Clayson's biography Brel also seemed like an ardent searcher for meaning, in life and in himself: "While endeavoring to remain true to his strange star, the swiftest show business lesson that Jacques Brel had learned and would pass on was that 'it's easier to be someone else than to be yourself.'" Maybe that's what kept driving him away from the crowds that he courted and cultivated. During his years of relentless touring, he became enamored of flight, bought and learned to fly a wooden-framed biplane, touring the great ruins of Greece, Italy, and the Near East from the air. And, yes, later he bought a yacht, with the intention of circumnavigating the world, but illness cut that plan short. Clayson claims that he took to the air and sea because land "disappointed him."

When, at thirty-eight, Brel did finally tire of the intense touring, the scattering of the self, he penned "quotable leaderettes" for the press in advance of the publicity blitz of his farewell tour, like: "The only luxury in life is being able to make mistakes. What irritates me most is being sensible." And most reassuringly: "People of fifty make love better than people of twenty, but they can't make love every day."

When he retired from his onstage singing career, he kept working — writing, directing, and acting in movies. Eventually, he removed himself from that life, too, and sailed to the Marquesas with his mistress, flying needed supplies and sometimes medical patients around the islands in his plane. Took up gardening. "Responsible for introducing the plum tomato to the island, Jacques was soothed by working with the soil," wrote Clayson. Maybe finally finding something nourishing in the land that had so disappointed him? Though ill and closer to death than he wanted to admit, he flew back to Europe, recorded one final record, his illness deepening his voice to a bass baritone. A year later, in 1978, he died in Paris, his music replacing regular radio programming throughout the day and *France-Soir* declaring, "Brel will always live. He is the least dead among all of us." But his remains were shipped back to the Marquesas and buried in Calvary Cemetery, near Atuona Bay.

Case clicked on the final link in the body of the Wikipedia entry on the screen, an image of that cemetery, where Gaugin is also buried, on a paradisiacal hillside overlooking neat white boats anchored in too-blue water. "Didn't Brando go native in Tahiti for a while, too?" Chris asked. "Yeah, that's right, he did!" we assented. Ah, the lush island beauty, the isolation, the mind-clearing sea buffering the disappointments of civilization, the women, the privilege of fleeing your domestic life for the fantasy. We finished the cheese and bread and overpriced Belgian beer I'd picked up while running errands around the hot city earlier in the day. I wondered what Brelian desires were swirling inside these men here in the living room, and how much they differed from my own.

AUGUST

The Metaphysical Hangover

My sister Susan takes copious, sprawling notes at each ECRG meeting in a standard black-and-white composition book. On the subject line of the cover, she's written: "He appears to be the bearer of an undecipherable message." She's an enthusiastic recorder of life — writes in her journal prodigiously, loads her camera's SD cards with thousands of pictures. Her swooping, idiosyncratic half-print, half-cursive style scrawls on month after month, skipping lines between the scraps of the discussion that seem important enough to snatch and capture. One steady thread from the last several months, stitched into the notebook's blue, wide-ruled lines by Susan's unruly handwriting, was the often-fraught relationship between the individual and the collective.

August's reading was an interesting tangle in that conversation. Nate, for whom drinking was still more sport than self-medication, had chosen the 1971 essay "The Hangover," from *Everyday Drinking*, a collection by Kingsley Amis (yet another brilliant alcoholic philanderer). He meant it to be a follow-up to June's "Swimmer" though we had to leapfrog over the hot, social sinkhole of July to land on it. Drinking, for better or for worse, was an integral aspect of the ECRG project. It marked our place in the several-thousand-year-long continuum of people sitting around together, sipping and gazing upon the navel of humanity. It's always interested me that for millennia humanity has contrived with nature to supply itself with never-ending and varied ways to take the edge off the condition and alter individual consciousness, to both connect more easily to others and hopelessly isolate ourselves.

Amis, whose vast, global knowledge of and experience with drinking was formidable, asserted that since "conversation, hilarity and drink are connected in a profoundly human, peculiarly intimate way...the collective social benefits of drinking altogether (on this evidence) outweigh the individual disasters it may precipitate." Everyone in the living room was familiar with the destructive powers of alcohol and everyone partook anyway, telling ourselves, like Epicurus, that excess is the enemy, while knowing full well that drink contains a cunning chemical underminer that subverts judgment. Funny, erudite, chummy, and biting, Amis's writing on drinking is a cocktail invitation to take issue with him, to enjoy the unresolvable argument that is humanity.

In the essay, Amis first gives advice on dealing with the Physical Hangover. According to Amis one should begin by making vigorous love to whomever you wake up next to, unless it's someone you're not supposed to be with, then abstain, because it will only compound your guilt and shame. And if you wake up alone, don't "take the matter into your own hands," for the same reason. Though this advice was disputed by at least one person in the room, who thought it was useful for getting the blood going after a rough night. Other possible remedies include alternating between hot-as-you-can-stand showers and baths, eating unsweetened grapefruit, and more drinking. He includes a few he had heard about but hadn't tried himself, like "Go down the mine on the early-morning shift at the coal-face," and also some "notable" breakfast recipes, my favorite being Samuel Taylor Coleridge's: "(Sundays only) 6 fried eggs, 1 glass laudanum and seltzer."

While people had lots of topical, animated things to say about the Physical Hangover, we soon had one of those moments of conversational gravity that unite the room when we moved on to Amis's description of the Metaphysical Hangover:

When that ineffable compound of depression, sadness (these two are not the same), anxiety, self-hatred, sense of failure and fear for the future begins to steal over you, start telling yourself that what you have is a hangover. You are not sickening for anything, you have not suffered a minor brain lesion, you are not all that bad at your job, your family and friends are not leagued in a conspiracy of barely maintained silence about what a shit you are, you have not come at last to see life as it really is, and there is no use crying over spilt milk. If this works, if you can convince yourself, you need do no more, as provided in the markedly philosophical

G.P. [general principle] 9: *He who truly believes he has a hangover has no hangover.*

Amis's cure for the Metaphysical Hangover is to make yourself feel worse before you can feel better. He proposes that you do some cultural wallowing by reading and listening to music that will take you down to the depths (John Milton's *Paradise Lost* or Solzhenitsyn's account of a Siberian labor camp; Tchaikovsky; Sibelius) and then work toward more bracing, affirming selections to give you hope for man. ("If you can stand vocal music, I strongly recommend Brahms's Alto Rhapsody — not an alto sax, you peasant, but a contralto voice, with men's choir and full orchestra.") I think this is something many of us do intuitively, giving our woes more texture and universality through art. And though I know exactly no one capable of so much heavy reading while hungover, it's nice to have someone lay out the course work for you.

The subject of hangovers in general brought out a tender, contemplative side of people. It might've had to do with the vulnerability of the condition, which is usually predicated upon a confounding combination of bad decisions, communal fun, and/or individual despair. A hangover is the visceral reality of a price being extracted. The uncomfortable grip of consequence. Many in the group seemed to agree that there's some opportunity to be found in the painful melancholy of the hangover:

"Everything shifts — the cadence of time, perception — when you're forced to confront this transformation, caused by your own self-poisoning."

"And all the self-questioning — what did I do last night? With whom?"

"Then there's the weirdly beautiful, empathetic state of the hangover — 'I am so miserable that I can clearly see the thread of misery running through other people's lives.' You're like, 'Oh my God, those people, they're waiting for a bus.' And you want to cry."

"But it's also such a personal space, how you're isolated in your experience."

"You don't move as quickly and must pay attention to every move you make. Kind of Zen, like, 'I must *cut* this onion.'"

"Best if you just embrace the misery of the hangover."

The general gist seemed to be that though intensely isolating, the wretched dissolution of the self can also make you more sensitive to those around you, lower your defenses, help weaken the barriers we put up between ourselves and others and between ourselves and our selves. Like Amis's description of the Metaphysical Hangover, so much anguish is connected to the things we work to create and maintain. Hangovers can exacerbate the thought that somehow we're not worthy of what we build up, including our relationships. After all, the existential definition of "anguish" is our deep recognition that our lives and decisions and choices are all connected to other people. When we fuck up, we fail humanity, too. (*See also:* Dread; Learning.)

That night, I do remember sharing at least one personal instance in which a hangover was inadvertently useful. One bright Saturday morning I found myself solo-parenting in a damaged state at my son Silas's middle-school fair, my husband at work on a set, probably at some plantation somewhere, artfully painting a layer of picturesque decay on top of the regular old decay. The night before, we'd happened upon Soren and his wife at a downtown bar, and instead of running the other way, as we should've, we allowed him to buy us shots of Chartreuse, aka "the Truth." Chartreuse is our family drink, maybe because things often end badly after spending some time with it.

Tickets, confetti eggs, kids in face paint, parents loitering behind barbecue grills and manning unambitious games of skill. After looking for a place to hide, I gratefully propped myself up on the inflatable base of one of those jumping tents/bouncy houses/space walks, which was rather stationary, the rest of its pillowy architecture lurching above me as my boys threw themselves at each other inside. The gentle, steady roar of the nearby generator felt stabilizing.

A former courthouse built in the 1850s, the school was one of the oldest public school buildings in the country, and looked it. I had actually gone there, back when it was a high school. Not sure how they'd gotten away with repurposing the old firetrap as a middle school, with its narrow hallways and canted floors, but I loved the place. Antebellum-high ceilings and crumbling plaster, walls impastoed with decades of institutional paint jobs, the "cafetorium" and portable buildings that were supposed to be temporary thirty years ago but were now being used by my son. I remember watching an Orleans Parish Prison detail in orange jumpsuits whitewash the huge, neoclassical columns across the façade while a deputy stood by with a shotgun. Outside my sophomore-English classroom window.

Different times, the '80s. I seemed to be having Time Hangover as well, dread washing over me in tepid, fading waves. I'd been in this town too long, a stick snagging the water while time surged past but the basic scenery stayed the same.

A woman I know came around the corner of one of the portable buildings, holding a toddler and looking distressed. A therapist, she's usually very well turned out, with carefully managed hair, makeup, and clothes, and the alert, gentle demeanor of someone who earns a living helping people with their problems. She makes me feel like an amateur human, always afraid I'll say something misguided or unhelpful.

"Hi," I said from the ground, squinting up at her, knowing the polite thing to do would be to stand up, but my body was temporarily indifferent to manners. "How's it going?"

She replied that she was really upset because the night before she'd gotten into a Facebook fight with her brother-in-law, who was kind of a right-wing jerk, and normally she doesn't engage but she'd had a couple of glasses of wine with dinner and now she was feeling so terrible about it, about antagonizing her husband's family, and she couldn't stop thinking about it.

She'd put her daughter down on the ground as she spoke, as though not wanting to sully her with all this adult tension. Inside the space walk, the kids kept hurling themselves against the net above me, which would catch and return them to the buoyant chaos of the interior over and over. Without pausing, or thinking, I said something like "Don't worry about it. Y'all are both adults and responsible for your own words. He can deal."

Impassively confident, definitive. This didn't even seem like me talking. The woman produced a rare, startled look of connection that you don't often see in casual social interactions. She said it was so great running into me and then chased after her little daughter, who was taking off her sandals in the hopes of joining the big kids in the inflatable Thunder Dome. The next time I saw the woman, she thanked me so much for being so helpful about her brother-in-law, what I had said was so true! In another state of mind my response to her problem might've been diluted by doubt, or overthinking, or impatience with Facebook, but bullshit is something that hangovers have little tolerance for. I thought to myself that she should've thanked the Chartreuse (but not Soren) instead.

A friend once described drinking Chartreuse as akin to having a thousand-year-old monk shove balsa wood down your throat. I've seen grown men, seasoned drinkers, tear up and run for the bathroom after a shot. It's become a tradition on Mardi Gras morning to serve it early, when people start arriving at the house around eight for breakfast, lining up shot glasses in the kitchen, everyone toasting the first big mistake of the day, which is drinking what I've put in front of them. Though pagan in origin, Mardi Gras is a thoroughly Catholic contrivance, one that allows me not to feel even a pinprick of guilt that I get to roll out of bed on a Tuesday and have a shot of bourbon before brushing my teeth. That's what Ash Wednesday is for, another Catholic ethical escape hatch, like confession.

My favorite job of Mardi Gras is manning the rented champagne fountain in the courtyard, shooting corks up in the air and seeding the garden with tangible future memories of carnival. All year long I find corks like truffles in the dirt whenever I'm planting or tending. As much as I enjoy Mardi Gras, I love Ash Wednesday possibly more. The pained hush over the penitent city: the Civic Hangover. Such a relief — the permission to stop all the nonsense and get back to work. The streets have been bathed and cleaned but still bear some traces of the big party: crushed plastic cups here or there, shiny worthless beads tangled in trees and overhead wires. Discarded, errant pieces of costumes that got too cumbersome or were too ambitious to begin with.

During our August meeting, Tristan brought up another kind of citywide hangover: the Rebuilding Hangover. Tristan reminded us how after the drama of Hurricane Katrina's destruction had subsided, we were left living in its heavy, burdensome aftermath, waking up every morning and remembering that impossible, awful thing that had just happened, that the city was still mostly destroyed, the National Guard was still patrolling our neighborhoods, the schools were still closed. Then we'd have to get out of bed and deal with it all over again, power through the endless work and headaches, the questioning and planning. Curse the forces that would slow the recovery — bureaucracy, crime, skepticism.

After a few years, the city's transformation that accompanied the Rebuilding Hangover was followed by the stubborn, natural, but rather American forgetting, a collective survival mechanism, a getting back to "normal." But I think that once you've seen firsthand what the wholesale destruction of your home looks like, the memory of it forms a substratum in your consciousness, alive and molten under the optimistic layers of the reconstruction, under the new foundations and drywall, new roads and schools.

In this sense, the Rebuilding Hangover resembles the Metaphysical Hangover that accompanies a death or a great loss. When the Metaphysical Hangover first hits with its full force, it's a disorienting overtaking of your person. Your days are pulled apart beneath the weight of it, you lose your sense of time, lose focus, lose desire. But gradually, over weeks or months, the world comes back to you, days regain their shape, it takes only a few seconds to remember what you are retrieving while standing in front of the open refrigerator, browsing online you see a pair of shoes and put them in your cart with a small sense of relief at actually wanting something again. Your relationships regain their normal contours, people their full dimensions. Each year lays down another fresh coat of paint over the trauma. Life gets easier, smoothed over. But something else happens simultaneously — buried beneath so many layers, the trauma becomes attached to your very structure, changing you in deep, imperceptible ways.

Someone once asked if it fucked me up having two sisters who committed suicide. I gave a wrongish, three-beers-in answer — "Yeah, when I think about it." But, wanting to cut that line of inquiry off, I didn't explain that I thought about it a few times an hour for the year and a half between their deaths and then for about another year after Rachel died. These continuous sucker punches to the gut wore me down in ways that weren't evident at the time, and maybe still aren't. Subsequent years were textured by the fragile, damaged quality of a Metaphysical Hangover. The roiling uneasiness of aftermath gives way to despair, then teases you with moments of relief and normalcy only to pull you under with another current of grief.

In those initial years, some of us siblings retreated more fully into careers, others into family life, extra scrutiny given to the next generation of children for any trace of the twins. Amy, the youngest once more after growing up a middle child, who was home with the twins during the worst years, felt the most immediate responsibility for them, took off for an extended sojourn in the grand consolation of the isolation of the Grand Canyon. Unmarried, insecure, and chronically confused, I became paralyzed in my personal life, unable to make good decisions to move things forward. Floundered creatively.

After Rebecca's death, Mom and Rachel attended Survivors of Suicide meetings together once a month. At the meetings, you were supposed to introduce yourself and talk about the person you'd lost. But Mom could never say Rebecca's name aloud. Could not physically speak it. (The transformative power death gives a name is formidable — it would take almost ten years for my parents to have the girls' names engraved on the tomb in Lafayette Cemetery No. 1, to carve their deaths in stone, so to speak. And when I visit the tomb to this day, the rigidity of the lettering is still impossible to reconcile with the vibrancy of their lives.) In addition to finding some kind of solace in connecting with other suicide survivors, Mom thought that Rachel, a mother herself, witnessing Mom's pain, hearing the stories of the damage and suffering caused in the aftermath of suicide, couldn't possibly follow Rebecca. Apparently, 50 percent of surviving twins die within two years of their sibling. It was Rachel who told Mom this symmetrically cruel statistic. Was it in warning, preparation, out of fear? I imagine the path becomes more tempting, as already a part of you has gone down it, cleared some of the brush. While we tried to be attentive and supportive (Susan called Rachel every night as a surrogate for Rebecca to temper the void), we couldn't have known the depth of the loss she was feeling, how thorough the destruction of this vital part of herself.

And for a short time, Rachel seemed to be doing well. Had a nice boyfriend she was so proud of. She liked to remind us he was getting his PhD, in sociology, her proxy in a family that valued education. He was a kind and thoughtful father to her son, and she was an involved and affectionate young mother. They lived in a sweet Arts and Crafts cottage in Mid-City with a porch and a dog. She'd gotten her GED and enrolled in community college. A picture of her I love from around that time was printed in the newspaper; she's flipping through a box of prints at a festival upriver at Destrehan Plantation, and her son, on her back, is looking over her shoulder, sharing a moment of appraisal, the sun backlighting them so that even in the flatness of the black-and-white newsprint, their pretty silhouettes, their wisps of short hair, are incandescent. Then, around the anniversary of Rebecca's death, some missteps, large and small, began to pile up. An affair, a breakup with the only real father her son had known, a quickie marriage in Vegas, a fender bender. I imagine the temptation was overwhelming, both to rid herself of the pain *and* to be reunited with Rebecca, so much so that perhaps she wasn't able to see that her desire to be made whole again would create an ever-expanding world of grief.

After hearing the news about Rachel, the family gravitated to my parents' house. The image from that afternoon, which recurs with great force and clarity, is the liminal moment of my parents telling her son his mother has died. They had wanted to tell him alone, so a few of us went outside and stood aimlessly on the walk leading up to the wide brick steps of their porch; none of us could bear to look at one another or say anything. I watched through a series of receding thresholds: between two white columns of the porch, through the floor-to-ceiling window frame, through the front parlor's pocket doors, to where my nephew sat on a couch between my parents. He listened to them and then made a movement forward and I felt all of me fall forward inside, and had to turn away.

Everyone was changed in that moment. Not only my nephew, who within seconds transformed from being a boy with a loving mother to being a boy with no mother, and worse, he would learn later, a mother who chose to leave him forever. But also my parents, because it was the moment they had to say those words to their grandson. I don't know why the pain felt compounded and not buffered by the house's architecture, but it did. I'd always had such wonderful memories of growing up there, days and evenings clustered around the hypnotic porch swing, the tar-coated balcony off the bedroom where we sunned ourselves until our minds went white and sparkly, the front alcove's perfect accommodation of the Christmas tree (but not the dozens of presents that materialized beneath it and spread toward the stairs), the front parlor for visiting, the second for lounging in front of the television, the dining room fireplace's intricately carved flora an absorbing distraction from the intensity of Sunday dinners that aimed to nourish ten mouths and ten minds. Even though I knew that it was all tenuously financed, and that the bottle of gin under the kitchen sink behind the 409 and Dad's explosive temper, both imperfect stress-management tools, were connected to that tenuousness, to me the house meant pride in my family. It meant the fun we had together, it meant Dad's hard-won status, it meant Mom somehow holding it all together with craft projects and family field trips and an abiding trust in us children to take care of one another.

Maybe in that moment, the house magnified the recognition that the twins' memories must have been so divergent from my own, the awareness that none of the positive things I associated with that house could have saved them. While we older siblings had known a series of modest houses that grew progressively larger and nicer, this was the only one the twins ever really knew. It was the house that helped make them, or was at least the vessel for their dynamic and disjointed selves.

Not that they hadn't had their own cherished memories. There was one Easter morning, when as a surprise for their little nieces and nephews who'd be coming over for brunch, they planted dozens of pinwheels on the front lawn. A spontaneous garden of exuberant, erratic whirling in a neighborhood landscaped with box hedges and azaleas. To this day family members sometimes leave pinwheels at their tomb as a more appropriate tribute than flowers.

Within a few years after the twins' deaths, Dad would sell the house that had symbolized so much compromised achievement to him, the same one that he'd mortgaged over and over to pay for our upbringing. Would try to escape the debt and those final difficult memories there. My parents also wanted to be closer to Kristin, my older sister, and her kids as they tried to raise Rachel's son. After she died, though my other siblings with young children had offered, almost insisted, my parents wanted to raise the son she'd given birth to at nineteen and whose father had never been in the picture.

Though mired in the difficult combination of being grieving parents and indulgent grandparents, they would do their best with him.

After Rachel's death, once again: the handling of the painfully transformed personal effects, the small excruciating funeral at Saint Clare's Monastery, the sextons at Lafayette No. 1 who had opened, then plastered over the tomb entrance only a year and a half before, busting open their handiwork to accommodate another sister and sealing it off again. Parents I couldn't look at. Siblings I found too painful to be with but who were the only people I wanted to be with. Extreme acts of generosity and support from friends and family; others who had no idea how to respond to a *second* suicide. And then the continuous, stubborn reevaluations of events that brought the girls, all of us, to that point. The counseling and hospitals, terrible boyfriends, nice boyfriends, phone calls, rumors, missed opportunities.

The compounding and the reverberations of the double deaths, how they informed each other, how they differed from each other, would preoccupy me for years. For example, their "viewings" at the funeral home were not symmetrical. Rebecca's was in a spacious dark-paneled parlor with fresh flowers and elegant settees. There was plenty of room for us to move around within our grief, gravitate toward one another, or just be alone next to her body, displayed on a ceremonial plinth. With a white sheet pulled up high over her neck, her blond hair brushed back, her makeup more demure than I'd seen it in years, she looked like one of those Pre-Raphaelite paintings of a lost luminous beauty, even more muselike in death. If Rebecca had had any romantic imaginings of how we would mourn her, this must've approximated them.

A year and a half later, that same funeral home was under construction. Rachel was put down a hall in a small room that only a few of us could fit into at a time, her body still on the gurney. Her makeup seemed haphazard and you could actually see the marks on her neck, which one of us covered before bringing her son in. The name of the hospital was printed across the top of the sheet. There were neither elegant acknowledgments nor any formal pretension for our grief. Down the hall, electrical saws and drills from the construction whined and seared the air. In the narrow hallway, the same funeral director, who'd been so deferential with Rebecca, sat in a chair, slightly bored, and said in an offhand way, "Seems like y'all were just here," and not much else. The next week, I wrote a letter detailing these disparities and indignities to the owner of the company, who responded with an apology and a generous donation to Rachel's son's school. I remember feeling surprised by his reply, a concrete response in an envelope, with a letterhead and a signature, my unreal grief and grievances having spawned a mundane business transaction.

I came across that letter while going through some of my father's personal papers after he died. Files and files of correspondences regarding the twins — with schools, mental hospitals, the police department, the D.A.'s office. The coroner's office. He applied the force of his legal apparatus to seek help and answers until the very end. There was even evidence of the old T and C in some of the grainy lawyer-faxing: *Eric, I understand why you were so upset on the phone yesterday but...* Apparently I had cc'd him on that letter to the funeral home. Though my name was on it, the document seemed foreign, forged. Yes, there was something familiar in the angry, strident, wounded tone, but it still seemed as though it was written by someone else.

Perhaps by this person:

A woman who one morning woke up deep in the blackest grief, in a lethargic strategizing about how she was going to get herself out of bed, and saw that the stack of books on her bedside table, Wallace Stevens and Virginia Woolf and William Faulkner, suddenly seemed like dry husks that had once held something vital for her but that she could no longer access. People often talked about seeking out books to cope with grief, but she found herself unable to connect with literature. She felt ashamed for spending so much of her life on its "pleasures" and then, when she should've found it the most helpful, should've needed it most, literature seemed useless to her. Sentences fell apart in front of her eyes. Little words and letters all lined up, attendant but inert. Language seemed a fraud, all this human striving for expression that couldn't approach the actual pain, could only dress it up, give it shape, and so what.

She wasn't just doubting language, but also the redemptive *power of the narrative*. Didion's proclamation "We tell ourselves stories in order to live" suddenly seemed like neurotic grandstanding. She reversed it, wondering what stories her sisters told themselves in order to die. This was a dank and webby rabbit hole to explore. Orchestrating your own ending would seem the ultimate control over your narrative, right? Did Rebecca tell herself that her soul was worthless, something that years of the commodification of her young body might have reinforced? The men, the transactions, the shame? That her suicide would be the ultimate punishment for M., for his infidelities and abuses? The ultimate punishment for all of those who didn't love her enough and who constantly judged her? That this was the best, most expedient ending for her suffering? Did Rachel have to tell herself that she was a terrible wife and mother and that everyone, including her son, would be better off without her? That she needed to join Rebecca, a tidy return to the womb, their beginnings? There at least was evidence of these stories of Rachel's in the notes she left, three of them, taped to her bedroom door — one for her new husband, one for her parents, and one for her son. Each with these explanations, each embellished with smiley faces. The woman later found out from a colleague whose husband, an Uptown financier who'd also drawn a smiley face on his suicide note before he shot himself, that this was not uncommon. The smiley faces were symptomatic of the profound disconnect that allows suicides to tie the noose, pull the trigger, down the pills.

How did the experiences they shaped into meaning, the stories they told themselves, match up with other stories of them? Of course, not very closely. Others believed they were loved unconditionally, the youngest, yes, troubled but full of hope and promise. But their older siblings were gone a lot, too, in college out of state, or in town but disappeared into their own young adulthood. Checking in with them when they could. What had they really known of them? Their stories?

For that woman at this time, a cold chaotic abyss always seemed to be on the other side of any worldly interaction.

Through both deaths, the woman was teaching high school, and one thing that helped pull her out of her nihilism was that she had to go in every day and convince teenagers that literature, stories, mattered. It was the task she was paid biweekly to do. And daily, through *Madame Bovary* and *Invisible Man* and British Modernism, through the tests, the papers, and the tentative revving of young brains in class discussions, she gradually reconvinced herself of literature's worth. She let time work its salve. Narratives survived all kinds of epic loss and tragedy, even if individuals did not. Even if the structures felt artificial and contrived, they still originated within an individual's consciousness. There was something hopeful in that. It was the collective human project her classes were dissecting and enjoying and suffering through. With her roll book and whiteboard, she was a kind of truss in the scaffolding, connecting the past to the future. By reading, everyone was involved in the project's endless construction. That involvement made life more tolerable. The woman conceded that maybe Didion was sort of right after all.

In "The Hangover" Amis discusses the paucity of literary treatments of hangovers, both literally and metaphorically. He makes a pithy, offhand case for Kafka's *Metamorphosis*. Starting "with the hero waking up one morning and finding he has turned into a man-sized cockroach," Amis claims, it is "the best literary treatment of all," and continues: "The central image could hardly be better chosen, and there is a telling touch in the nasty way everybody goes on at the chap. (I can find no information about Kafka's drinking history.)" Though some would dispute Amis's description of Gregor Samsa being man-sized and a cockroach, we know he woke up transformed into a large bug. As a human, Gregor was a traveling salesman, a hard worker who supported his middle-class family — his parents and sister. When he wakes up changed into something that is no longer useful for them, he conscientiously tries to minimize his family's fear and revulsion. As described by Kafka with heartbreaking particularity, Gregor negotiates his new state in his locked room, his world suddenly circumscribed by small objects and small desires. And even those are so terribly out of reach.

To complement the Amis, Nate had sent us the *The Metamorphosis* as well, a story that had been confounding me since high school. On this most recent reading, the confoundedness lessened as the tale progressed and the pathos for Gregor deepened. As Gregor becomes more animal, more detached from the machinations of civilization though still trapped by it, his longings and injuries and joys become more isolated and intensified. His movements are laborious and pained. Human mystery remains intact. The lovely woman in the picture with the fur muff he'd once torn from a magazine as a man and now inches toward as an insect; the apple lodged in the chitin of his back, launched by his own father; the beauty of his sister's violin playing that draws him out of his room.

Nate, whose mind magnetically connects phenomena, literary or otherwise, with systems, started a brief discussion about the buglike, scheming nature of Gregor's traveling-salesman job, Marxism, and the futility of most work. This led to a lively, exasperated detour with Brad, Chris, and Ellen, who sometimes land on the same scenic paint crews, about the transience of below-the-line movie work, long days in warehouses or on location, capricious art directors, gallons of paint and tedious brush technique, in service of cultural ephemera fated for Dumpsters and cable channels. Chris referred to the paint crew as "the Original Futilitarians."

But it was Tristan, standing and smoking in the doorway, who connected *The Metamorphosis* to shame and family: "We don't want to talk about the bugs in our family. We want to keep them locked away in the broom closet. Don't you think the Samsas are relieved when Gregor disappears?" And Ellen, eternally aggrieved youngest of seven children herself, agreed: "Gregor was a slave to the family, the family created that sad little monster. They made him possible and then they had to let him die." This discussion is something I've thought quite a lot about over the years: *Are we all creatures forged in the crucible of the family?*

Years ago, a friend visiting from college, an observant outsider, remarked after one of our big, lively family dinners that he didn't think we took the little twins very seriously when they talked. That we cut them off, or laughed at things they said when they weren't necessarily joking. In the bustle of older kids and larger personalities, they were overlooked and underestimated, he thought. Of course, I dismissed it — the rest of us were convinced that the twins were spoiled and that, as our parents got older and more worn down by parenting, they got away with stuff we never could have. I didn't think again about his comments until after Rebecca hanged herself and one of my other sisters remarked that she was surprised Rebecca even knew how to tie an effective knot. Underestimated indeed.

Rebecca once said she loved animals so much because they didn't judge her. She had been a junior zookeeper at the Audubon Zoo as a teenager, had lots of pets in her brief adulthood, including a sugar glider that slept in a tiny hammock and a Vietnamese potbellied pig that once got into her coke stash and cornered her for over an hour in her kitchen, crazed and wired. After she died, I ended up with one of her hairbrushes, grabbed from M.'s house, matted with her own long blond hair as well as that of her Siberian husky, Sasha, a dog totally ill suited to our climate. I'd picture them together on her black leather couch, Rebecca absently brushing Sasha's hair, then her own, not making any distinction between them.

I have a maroon velvet pouch where I keep locks of both twins' hair, cut by the mortician before cremation. Rebecca's hair had been bleached light blond, Rachel's dyed a deep russet, as if they were trying to distinguish themselves both from each other and from the family genetics. I feel kind of cheated that my one physical relic of them is artificially altered, but I guess it also represents a choice on their part, something they could actually control. Like in a lot of large families, our features were clustered into groups, and I share theirs — dark blond hair, brown eyes, slightly smaller frame than the others. At the funeral home, Rachel's new husband/new widower saw me in the corridor outside the viewing room and gasped that I looked so much like her, grabbed and hugged me too hard and for too long. Both times after the twins' obituaries and pictures appeared in the paper, people remarked on how alike we looked. Somewhere it's been absorbed into my person that I've seen death, kissed its face, and it looks a lot like me.

We helped make them; their deaths changed us. I harbor a terrible, guilty suspicion that the deaths of my sisters, their disappearance from the family structure, their removing themselves from it, made the rest of us who we are turning out to be, and maybe allowed us to do things we might not otherwise have ventured. "Strengthened" seems wrong, but it possibly drove us to prove things to ourselves, and to our parents. Since suicide is often viewed as the ultimate failure of everything, the surviving six became charged with the impossible task of trying to compensate, offering our accomplishments, trials won, children birthed, campaigns run, works published, art shown, communities helped, to them as evidence that, yes, they were good, loving parents and most of us were doing pretty well.

At the end of *The Metamorphosis* after poor Gregor has died, been swept up by the charwoman, and dumped out with the rubbish, the family takes a trip to the country to clear their heads, take a break together after everything they've been through. When Gregor had been earning for the family, they atrophied. But now, with him gone, they appear to thrive, or at least are going to try. On the tram, Gregor's family evaluates their newly unburdened circumstance. *The Metamorphosis* ends with this sentence: "And it was like a confirmation of their new dreams and excellent intentions that at the end of their journey their daughter sprang up to her feet and stretched her young body."

I've always appreciated the morning of the day after a bad hangover. Waking up full of gratitude for yet another second chance, remembering what feeling good is like. So much possibility and productivity lie before you, before the day locks in, starts its inexorable work toward sundown, when you can kind of use a drink. Luckily, for most of us, the hangover is just part of the cycle of good times, the hard fall, regeneration. For others, the fall is continuous and recovery is out of reach. When they finally succumb, their Metaphysical Hangovers are inherited by those around them. We survivors then struggle through it with all of our excellent intentions, negotiating the ebb and flow, the endless searches for something to get us to that new morning. The ECRG had reinforced that while searching, we should remind ourselves of the gifts of the hangover — the renewed sensitivity to the suffering of others and the tender generosity toward our own suffering. The extra necessity for kindness and patience. We hope, we know, that there's health and good feeling on the other side, we just have to get through this bad stretch, either alone, or with all the others out there willing to share their remedies.

SEPTEMBER

The Walled City

In an uncanny commemoration of the seventh anniversary of Katrina, another hurricane, Isaac, made landfall over the city. As we readied the house, putting away patio furniture and clearing our storm drains, we listened to weather updates on the radio and compulsively checked our weather apps. When I was growing up, hurricane tracking maps were printed on paper grocery bags and you could chart a storm's progression across the Gulf of Mexico by following the coordinates announced by a local weatherman wielding a big marker in front of an easel, or by listening for the Coast Guard's scratchy stats on the AM radio. All fun and scary reminders of our particular place on the planet. Now our personal technologies and social media collectively work people up about a storm's approach, a luminous, interconnected vigilance adding to the already-charged electricity in the air.

Logistical preparedness bolsters mental preparedness, and the basic mood in the city about Isaac was an industrious don't-worry-we-got-this calm, with some familiar anxiety fraying the edges. During crowded press conferences, the mayor touted the city's post-Katrina $14 billion improvements to the federal flood-protection system. One broadcast featured him breathless and adrenalized, just returned from helping the U.S. Army Corps of Engineers with the inaugural closing of "the Great Wall," a brand-new $1.1 billion, 1.8-mile, 26-foot-high wall protecting the city. Since there was no mandatory evacuation, most of us hunkered down, cooked off the food in our fridges, and hung around with our neighbors on the gusty sidewalk, trying to sort out a network of resources — who had the most food or booze or water or gas or guns.

Hurricane Isaac turned out to be a ponderous, lethargic Category 1, lashing the city with wind and rain for days. The federal levees around New Orleans did a good job of holding back the storm surge, our massive drainage system — which includes the largest pump in the world — did a good job of keeping up with the rainfall, and our old house did a good job of not falling down.

The big problem in the city was the loss of power that persisted for nearly a week while temperatures surpassed ninety degrees, a disappointment after the oft-touted new and improved post-Katrina mega grid. Schools and businesses closed. Ironically, Isaac's evacuations happened *after* the storm, to escape the insufferable heat and generally rank inconvenience of being in an energy-deprived subtropical city in late August or early September. Porches, front yards, sidewalks, and neutral grounds now served as living and dining areas, giving the city a communal air I hadn't felt since Katrina. Chris, who described the humidity as like living inside of someone's lung, would join us for drinks and gumbo on the porch that week, along with Ellen, who lived down the street and wandered the neighborhood in her fashionable rain boots, making social calls. We slept on the floor in the living room since it had the most ventilation, and then later at Soren's house, since his power was restored days before ours. I scrawled *total loss* on the calendar of the last week of August and the first week of September. All regular activity had been replaced by the tense days of preparing for the storm, Isaac's anticlimactic landfall, and then the misery of waiting for the electricity to be restored. In the shuffle of thousands of canceled or rescheduled meetings across the region, there would be no ECRG in September.

Besides, "existence" becomes less philosophical and more immediate in the face of natural disaster, as does "meaning." Disasters and evacuations are actually excellent exercises in life evaluation. It can be a healthy chore to have to decide what the most important things in life are and then flee your home to join your similarly burdened brethren on the clotted highways. Watching my husband, unprompted, gather our newly acquired wedding albums from the shelves and load them into the trunk while Katrina approached the coast and I pouted and procrastinated (I'd never evacuated in my life) reaffirmed that wonderful, central choice I'd made in marrying him.

After the danger of Hurricane Isaac passed, we put on shrimp boots and hats and took a walk with the boys in the waning bluster, the neighborhood a post-storm compendium of vulnerability and fortitude: blighted and neglected buildings that had finally given way, National Guardsmen in their desert-mottled Humvees and impressive gear, uprooted oaks revealing man-sized root systems. But mostly blocks and blocks of old shotgun houses and Creole cottages that had already withstood well over a hundred years of hurricanes, missing some siding and roofing shingles but pretty much fine. The more dramatic ravaging was still novel for our sons, but the familiar images of destruction gave me little spasms of post-traumatic stress disorder, as the seven intervening years between Katrina and Isaac collapsed for a few disorienting seconds.

Our sons' earliest years were spent in a world defined by epic loss and a communal obsession with rebuilding and protection. Silas — Brad's son, who had only just recently become *my* son when Katrina hit — was six when we evacuated to a Red Roof Inn in Houston. As we watched the same footage of the same broken levees over and over on CNN, it occurred to me with weird certainty that I might be pregnant. Later, walking back from the drugstore to the motel, where fellow evacuees sat on ice chests in the parking lot as their dogs relieved themselves in the harsh corporate landscaping, or stared at their useless cell phones in the lobby, I told Brad that if the test was negative, we were going back on birth control. New Orleans was still filling with water and we had no idea if we had jobs, a house, a city.

The day before, we had driven west along the I-20 corridor from Tuscaloosa, the first stop on our evacuation, swerving around downed trees, passing power-dead gas stations with lines of stranded cars, and watching caravans of linemen from all over the country exit south for New Orleans. The radio had rolling reports about which levees had given way and how it would be weeks before they could pump the water out. We kept losing the station, I kept trying to fish it out of the static with a tense hand on the tuner, and my new son was locked into an obsessive, repetitive loop about the Berenstain Bears, had not shut up about the Berenstain Bears since we'd crossed into Mississippi. Hungry for news, raw, and anxious, I had a selfish, unmotherly meltdown about whether or not I could handle this situation. After decades of being a self-involved single person, I didn't have a built-up reserve of maternal patience to draw from, did not feel ready. In the too-bright Red Roof Inn bathroom, the affirming pink lines appeared on the pregnancy test with surprising alacrity and conviction, bringing with them a whole new quality to my despair. Motherhood and Katrina hit me almost simultaneously.

As CNN churned out the unthinkable, Silas's sweet thin form asleep in the other double bed, I cried and Brad reminded me that we'd wanted this. That this was supposed to be a good thing? Remember? After the levees broke, many pre-Katrina desires and expectations had to be reconsidered, if not completely scuttled. But in this case, it was too late. We were facing a holdover from our recent Mexican honeymoon and the various Oaxacan mescals we'd discovered, and though we had just returned from that trip a few weeks earlier, now as we lay beneath the cheap, scratchy motel comforters and numbly aimed the remote control at the nightmare television, that trip seemed to belong to a previous, inconceivable life.

We could not return home, and unmoored from any sense of a domestic life, flush with FEMA money, we kept heading west, with me wanting to hit every Dairy Queen between Austin and Los Angeles. By early September, my body and instincts were no longer familiar to me, nor was my world. Normally, the changes in mood, taste, and basic biological purpose experienced during pregnancy are somewhat cushioned by the stability of the external circumstances of your life. But not this time. Suddenly, I couldn't stand the smell of coffee, couldn't drink alcohol while everyone else seemed to be steadily self-medicating, and my low-grade existential dread graduated to full-blown nausea. And suddenly, we were driving across lunar west Texas, thinking of nothing else but the inundation of our city and where we were going to sleep that night. My disorientation was total — geographical and molecular.

As we drove through the arid Southwest, marveling at how intact and solid this world was, the mesas and rocky deserts, and up through Los Angeles and San Francisco, wondering if they'd make good new homes, we visited and commiserated with other scattered evacuees and were warmly taken care of by friends. I began homeschooling Silas, a kindergartner, working through phonics and number patterns together in the backseat. When we returned in early October to New Orleans, which was wrecked beyond all our imaginings, we were undoubtedly a family, forged in the confines of travel (car, motel, highway), by the intensity of the moment, and the uncertainty of the future.

We were luckier than most. Living so close to the river, on the original high ground that the Native Americans had pointed out to the French as being a good place to settle, we were spared flooding. The water had stopped about a block and a half away. It was our downed pecan tree that kept us out of the house for about six more weeks, having ripped out the electrical box and caused some minor damage. We stayed with my sister Kristin's family across the river in Algiers, where most of my other siblings from flood-damaged areas had decamped to regroup and figure out what was going on and what to do next.

With some national questioning about whether or not New Orleans should even be saved, and many citizens evaluating what the city meant to them, whether to stay or leave, the city was facing a true existential crisis. And as we in the future ECRG would do, many turned to the literature of the past to help them articulate the culture, history, and meaning of the place and create arguments for its survival, from nineteenth-century journalist Lafcadio Hearn to the autobiography of Louis Armstrong. One oft-revived standby was "New Orleans Mon Amour," a 1968 magazine piece by Walker Percy, which tried to make the argument that New Orleans could somehow represent the salvation of the American city:

> If the French had kept the city, it would be today a Martinique, a Latin confection. If the Americans had got there first, we'd have Houston or Jackson sitting athwart the great American watershed. As it happened, there may have occurred just enough of a cultural standoff to give one room to turn around in, a public space which is delicately balanced between the Northern vacuum and the Southern pressure cooker.

Hard to say how much Katrina threw off that balance, with our gross racial and economic inequity laid so bare to the world, leaving many of us to question whether it had ever existed.

New Orleans was my home, and the only place I wanted to be, but it was no longer a nurturing environment, not for a pregnant woman. Being in a "delicate condition" didn't jibe with the new vernacular, where "gutting," "debris," "breach," and "curfew" got frequent play. Humvees rattled the pavement and razor wire coiled at certain corners. At work, my classroom was now a barracks for the National Guard's Task Force Raven, cots and M16s replacing the desks, a sergeant using my office as private quarters. Downtown, where we live, felt especially and overwhelmingly masculine. The military, along with contractors and relief workers, had taken over and put up tents, so that the neutral ground on Canal Street was jammed with huge trucks parked flank to flank.

We were staying with a college friend in L.A. on our evacuation when the front page of the *Los Angeles Times* featured a story about this influx of maleness into the city, focusing on the strip clubs that had hastily reopened to accommodate it. I wondered if Rebecca would've been part of that corps of first-responding dancers if she'd lived. We were still exiled in California on the seventh anniversary of her death, though with the events of the storm it seemed a whole lifetime had passed. Not being able to visit her tomb on that day compounding the disjointed helplessness of that moment.

In my first trimester in post-apocalyptic New Orleans, I was also endowed with a heightened sense of smell, a gift from nature to help pregnant women sense what to avoid eating, a bobbing gauge in the near-perfect machinery that is human reproduction. Without electricity, without human care, the city was rotting, and the sweet, oily smell of decay lay beneath everything. The refrigerator removals, the continual disgorging of businesses, the high tunnels of debris along the streets — the stench was amplified. As I shopped at one of the first grocery stores to reopen, though everything looked fine on the surface and they'd tried their best to disinfect it, the ghost of decomposition dogged me and I had to cover my mouth to keep from gagging while walking the aisles.

Soon after, I had what I thought was a classic pregnant woman's arbitrary public breakdown. In Schiro's, the one restaurant that had reopened in our neighborhood, cluttered amber fly strips dangling in the windows, the lone, weary waitress offered us the choice of "a cheeseburger, a cheeseburger, or a cheeseburger." So much for New Orleans's status as the cuisine capital of the country, we sighed. Between bites we waved the flies away from our hamburgers, like we'd done at so many seaside restaurants during our honeymoon on the Oaxacan coast. Then, over the restaurant's speakers, we heard the plaintive opening chords of Pink Floyd's "Wish You Were Here," which transported me so thoroughly back to high school, a time of unknowingness and anticipation, late–Cold War nihilism, analog desire — record players and backseats and levee mischief. We didn't know there'd be such sadness and loss ahead of us. We didn't know the apocalypse would feel so intimate. And now, inside of me, I was gestating more uncertainty, more potential for sadness and loss. *So, so you think you can tell / heaven from hell?* The force of all we couldn't know back then suddenly seemed altogether unbearable, and soon my face was experiencing that muscular confusion of trying to cry and chew at the same time.

But really, was it hormonal? How to separate it out? Everyone at the time seemed to be in that same raw emotional state, men as wide open and as liable as women to break down at any moment. And didn't most New Orleanians experience a kind of morning sickness, the Rebuilding Hangover, every day that fall when they opened their eyes, cleared their heads of the last shreds of sleep, and remembered, holy shit…

After my fifth month or so, as more people returned to the city, making it seem just a bit more normal, I embraced my new role as walking symbol for renewal. I was "God-bless"ed on the sidewalk and in sparsely occupied buses. With the proliferation of T-shirts admonishing people to DEFEND, RENEW, or SAVE the city, I made one that said REPOPULATE NEW ORLEANS curving over my belly. Our baby had almost become an abstraction, part of the drama of reconstruction. Since children were still so scarce, whenever Silas would clatter around the neighborhood on his scooter, people would peer from behind curtains when they heard him. In one science-fiction moment, a woman cautiously cracked her door open as we passed and stage-whispered, "Oh God, it's a child."

Eight months after the levees broke, I was in the Touro Infirmary, where most of my family was born, blind with pain and curled into a ball to receive the blessed epidural. The nurse holding my shoulders alternately admonished me to focus and recounted to the anesthesiologist, who had just moved back to town and was about to insert a needle between my vertebrae, that she'd gotten only $30,000 for her destroyed home in Bay St. Louis, and I realized that really no moment was sacred from the storm's narrative. Touro had lost some staff and had hired on staff who had lost their hospitals. Everyone who helped usher our baby into the world had suffered, was still suffering, but neither that, nor the nature of their profession, seemed to dampen their pleasure in aiding in the miracle. Over the next few days, I began compulsively asking the nurses for their hurricane stories, which were many and varied, usually mingled with advice on dealing with my newborn.

On the unnerving ride home from the hospital, past the still-shuttered former refugee horror show, the Convention Center, and the frayed crowns of the enormous new palms along Canal Street, I kept wanting to apologize to our tiny son about the state of the city, explain to him that it wasn't always like this and that we were working really hard to make it better. Then, when he was exactly a week old, I read on the front page of the paper about how the Army Corps of Engineers had botched the repair of the Industrial Canal, rebuilding the eastern wall two and a half feet higher than the unbreached western one, thus making our dry, unflooded neighborhood, which butts up against the canal, far more vulnerable than before. As I read in disbelief, that familiar rage ballooning in my chest, I kept glancing down at our beautiful son on my lap, his eyes closed, perfect lips pursed, hungry, and searching.

Aside from all the fear and damage, I came to believe that our sons were lucky kids, witnessing so much post-disaster transformation around town. They got to see buildings imploded, moved across neighborhoods, or elevated to accommodate new Army Corps of Engineers flood maps. They got to see dozens of cranes and bulldozers on construction sites, to ride their bikes on new sidewalks, to enjoy brand-new parks and schools. Yes, the five blocks of old warehouses on the wharves near our house burned down in Katrina's aftermath, shooting propane tanks like bombs all over the neighborhood, but now we had a lovely unobstructed river view to watch the boat traffic on the Mississippi. Besides, the apathy and stagnation of the town I'd grown up in had evaporated with the last of the floodwater. We were now a city in survival mode, a city imperfectly striving to be better.

The spectacle of rebuilding also served as a consistent reminder of the existential threats to our children's new New Orleans. As part of its coverage of Hurricane Isaac, the *Times-Picayune* published a map of existing and future levees in southeast Louisiana, showing where the storm's water went and how high. On the page, the wall around New Orleans seemed almost medieval, reinforcing the siege mentality we sometimes have regarding our own environment. Looking beyond the wall, you see the vast scope and cause of the threat — nature's indifference. Since the 1930s, the state has lost almost two thousand square miles of land, largely due to human activity — three hundred years of levee building, voracious oil and gas exploration and extraction, sea-level rise, and overdevelopment, to name a few — and it continues to lose another twenty-five to thirty-five square miles a year. Since our flood protection is only as healthy as the land that surrounds it, that map in the paper of our walled city starts to look like ramparts around a sand castle at high tide.

The year before Hurricane Isaac, we'd had another scare: the Great Mississippi River Flood of 2011. Like the *Deepwater Horizon* explosion the year before and the hurricanes before that, it had the trappings of a typical contemporary south Louisiana disaster: nature versus man, the Army Corps of Engineers versus nature, mass anticipation and catastrophic thinking among your friends that you politely tried to minimize. By late spring, the combination of snowmelt and record rainfall from major storm systems had saturated the river's watershed to crisis levels. Upriver, people had less time to prepare and react; lives and property were lost. All across the floodplain rippled the panicky checking of insurance policies and the re-remembering of the difference between "crest stage" and "flood stage." Another wearying opportunity to reacquaint ourselves with the power of our natural environment and the vulnerability of our built one, to test the walls.

Brad and I took the boys to the river, at its highest level in any of our lifetimes. While in "New Orleans Mon Amour" Percy wrote that "the River confers a peculiar dispensation upon the space of New Orleans... a sense both of easement and of unspecified possibilities," it can also carry with it a set of more alarming, specific possibilities. Climbing the grassy apron of the levee and reaching the top, I felt the apprehension of discovering a bathtub filled to its very lip, water still running, the lurching anticipation of the splash onto the tile floor. And also the urgent pull for somebody to do something, for chrissakes. General anxiety had gripped the city, compounding all other anxieties. Dad, who lived by the levee directly across the river from us, was in a serious but uncertain condition with his leukemia, and the vigilance our family felt toward him and our mother mirrored what many were feeling in this river crisis. Fear, cagey trust in the authorities and technology, disbelief that the worst could possibly happen.

During the highest point of the flood crisis, I was lucky enough to be invited by a photographer friend to take a private plane ride upriver. A privileged exercise in perspective — seeing at just the right distance and angle, detaching yourself from the anxiety on the ground and observing from the cool, meditative clarity of the sky, getting both a bird's-eye and bureaucratic view of the flooding, of the threatened and already-inundated "structures," of the engorged Atchafalaya and disappeared Mississippi River banks, of our myriad flood controls, like the Morganza Spillway, in action.

The pilot of the plane, a friend of my friend, somewhere in the middle of middle age with a soft, youthful voice, prematurely gray hair, a white linen shirt, and Ray-Bans, executed a smooth takeoff into bumpy weather, and we headed along Lake Pontchartrain to the nearby Bonnet Carré Spillway, several bays of which had been recently opened to divert water from the river to the lake. Cars glided along the top of the highway above the great gash in the river, water rushing beneath them, eddying whitely around the trees that usually have the spillway's floodplain to themselves, then blending in a muddy whorl with the slightly lighter tones of the lake.

The spillway was completed in 1931, a by-product of the movement away from the Army Corps of Engineers' previous "levees only" policy. The nineteenth-century push to build more and more levees, higher and higher, raised river levels, which raised flood levels, putting increased pressure onto the system, which resulted in the catastrophic flood of 1927 and caused a rethinking of this policy. Spillways added some flexibility, a compromise with the river's complex dynamics.

We left the forced juncture of river and lake and traveled just under the clouds on our way to the Gulf of Mexico. For a city dweller, it feels good to see unbroken miles of green, opens up a place of relief and hope inside your street-bound self. Behind us, the I-10 thinned to a pencil line, then disappeared into the spring foliage and deep chartreuse marshes.

My friend had been quiet and busy, aside from asking the pilot for this angle or that tilt of the wing. But as we approached the Atchafalaya Delta she excitedly mentioned that this was possibly the only place in south Louisiana that is actually accumulating land, not losing it. Beneath us were two main channels connecting the Atchafalaya to the Gulf — a natural winding one and a straight, man-made canal. The straight one was an Army Corps of Engineers diversion project called the Wax Lake Outlet, cut through in 1942 to reduce the flood stage at Morgan City. Back in the 1970s it was discovered that the Atchafalaya's fine sand and silt had been building up at the outlet's mouth, and now an accidental delta blossoms out at the end of the channel's stem.

And through the water you can actually see land forming in transparent layers, different shades of silt and soil around the edges of the splayed fingers of land; in other places lobes emerge like the blooming spores in a petri dish. This buildup is fast in geological terms, creating visual, tangible changes within our lifetime. Hope. There it was. Right below us. After some low circling and giddy speculating, we left the Wax Lake Outlet and followed the Atchafalaya upriver a couple of hundred miles to the suddenly popular Morganza Spillway.

Of course, opening the Morganza Spillway for the first time in

177

thirty-eight years, and for only the second time ever, meant the intentional and potentially catastrophic flooding of farms and rural communities west of the Mississippi along the Atchafalaya Basin, thus sparing the urban centers of New Orleans and Baton Rouge on the east bank. As a citizen of high-maintenance, narcissistic, though tax-revenue-generating New Orleans, I felt some guilt about this. What is our ethical responsibility to these communities that soon might be sacrificing so much for us? Then one morning in the newspaper in an article profiling the people and communities affected by the imminent flooding, I read the quote "I am a Morganza Spillway farmer." Speaking with a mixture of existential resolve and fatalism, the soybean farmer explained that he knew the land and the consequences of working that land. No recriminations, no resentment. Know your natural environment. Work with it. And be prepared to pay the costs. But in that same week, in the same paper, another quote from an Atchafalaya Basin resident: "Baton Rouge and New Orleans should be sending us help because we're saving their butts," she said. "Y'all pray for us. You can at least do that."

On the way to the Morganza Spillway, a large farming complex with fields, silos, and fenced-in buildings turned out to be Angola. I'd just read that the prisoners had already been evacuated to higher ground. In the not-too-distant future I'd be down there again, visiting my brother's client on Death Row, whose high, razor-wire-topped cyclone fences and towers are right next to the grassy wall of the levee, which prisoners helped build by hand over a hundred years before, and I'd get a firsthand account of their evacuation to the old Death Row facility farther inland. Learn how the inmates enjoyed the change of scenery, being back in the old place near the entrance to the prison, where they were able to lie down on real ground in the sun, telling one another to enjoy it while they could, because they might never ever feel grass again.

A massive mid-twentieth-century engineering project weathered to that same elephant gray of guardrails and bridges across the country, the Morganza Spillway apportioned the Mississippi into the Morganza Floodway and then eventually to the Atchafalaya Basin. With only a few of the 125 gates open, from the air it seemed merely a slow bleed from the river into the fields and trees below, enough to calm people's nerves back in the city, fulfilling its function as it has waited decades to do.

As we turned to head south, the Morganza Spillway became smaller and smaller, the river stretching for miles from either end of it, and I imagined the whole Mississippi from Itasca, Minnesota, to the Gulf, and all the controls and the other spillways, pinpricks in the side of a long garden hose left out on the lawn. I was impatient to get home, to tell the boys about everything I'd seen — all the destruction and possibility. The natural beauty and the works of man. Mostly I wanted to tell them the news of the Wax Lake Outlet, that we'd seen hope, blooming right beneath us.

For miles we'd been seeing the haze of fires in the east, controlled burns, narrow columns of smoke funneling up from patches of blackened farmland, and soon the smell was leaking into the cabin through the vents of the Cirrus. As we got closer we all marveled at this: smoky, crimson sunset, the river distorted and distended and burnished, peaks of a few swallowed buildings on the east bank and charred squares of land, bisected by thin lines of fire on the west, a sort of peaceful apocalypse. The darkness came suddenly, and with it a visual quietude, and we were all quiet, flying back toward the city, the unreal blackness crowding the smallness of the plane. Now night, it was the pattern and movement of light below us that showed the contours of the land, and the glimmering city in the distance, where our people were and where they were not.

For all of the upriver mayhem, the downriver levees would hold, the control systems would work, our families, New Orleans, would be safe. As soon as the Morganza Spillway opened and river levels dropped, the apprehension in the city dissipated with the threat. The flooding that ensued along the Atchafalaya and in the spillway floodplain wasn't as bad as anticipated, and the whole ordeal quickly left local consciousness as other news and other crises overtook our front pages and dinner tables.

OCTOBER

The Unwalled City

I don't know how we know these things, but that morning instead of just grabbing a coffee at the kiosk in the lobby of the Touro Infirmary and going directly up to Dad's room on the fifth-floor oncology ward, like I'd done every morning that week, something unexplainable pinned me downstairs. Maybe because it was the end of the week, maybe I needed a break in my routine, but that day I ordered a muffin, too, sat down on a lobby chair and looked at a newspaper someone had clumsily refolded and abandoned there. For the first time, I just really did not want to go up, and I lingered downstairs for about five or ten minutes longer than usual.

When I did make it to the fifth floor, with my coffee and muffin-greasy bag, his door was wide open, the room empty. It looked like a crime scene — his bed skewed, sheets trailing down, blood-splattered aspirator on the bedside table, sterilized wrappers for God knows what tossed all over the floor. Detritus of a fresh emergency. A nurse appeared behind me and explained that I'd just missed him. A few minutes before, things had gone critical, he'd crashed, blood had filled his lungs, and they'd taken him to the ICU. She told me to gather his things and head up there.

As I filled his overnight bag with his clothes, laptop, cell phone, charger, and glasses, I knew that this was it. On the too-loud television angled toward the scene came cheerful bantering from *Live! with Kelly*. For a vertiginous moment, I thought about how all manner of things, imaginable and not, were happening around the planet right then at that very moment. The cacophony of it. I don't know why that program was even on, as my dad only ever watched CNN and ESPN in the hospital, and please please please God don't let the *Live! with Kelly* show be the last thing my dad was conscious of on this earth.

The special saints of the ICU helped me with the bags I'd suddenly acquired and asked me to suit up and be patient while they stabilized him. The ICU kind of shorted me out. There, you feel the full force of modern medicine — the training, the technology, the money, the bureaucracy, but also the inevitable, glimpsed through the privacy curtains, in the frail, wired bodies. A week or so before, prepping for our first ECRG meeting, held the day before Dad went to Angola, I found an Epicurus quote: "Against other things it is possible to obtain security, but when it comes to death we human beings all live in an unwalled city." Yes, I thought, we try so hard to secure ourselves against the idea of death, the reality of death, but our mortal vulnerability connects us all. Over the next several months of the ECRG it would become clear that this was one of the main things that kept everyone coming back to our living room, huddling together in the bareness of our condition, with wine and food and fellowship and reading, acknowledging our defenselessness but seeking comfort in connection. But here at this moment, in the open floor plan of the ICU, watching people and machines work in nonstop, almost balletic accord, all I was feeling was the desperation of the species to stay alive, to spend just a few more minutes, hours, days, months, in the unwalled city.

All week my three sisters had been at the hospital with him most nights, and Soren, too, when his schedule allowed. Mom, who'd been his constant caretaker throughout his two-year illness, had a cold that week and couldn't come to the hospital. But here I was alone outside the sliding patio doors of his room, in my yellow-ducky sterilized gown, gloves, and mask, making greedy middle-child calculations. What parts of town my other siblings would be coming from, how much time I might have alone with my dad before the crowd arrived. After all, when you grew up in a large family, one-on-one time with a parent was a commodity. This was the rarest and luckiest of privileges.

Nurse Craig, steady and kind-voiced, around fifty, with the gray, closely cropped hair of a monk or an aging movie star, told me they knew about the DNR order. Those letters used in the concrete and not the abstract have a shocking, disorienting power — a wish becoming a command. He said they were making Dad as comfortable as possible. I was scared and asked whether he had been given enough morphine. He paused and said, "Honestly, we do that more for the families, not the patients."

Months later, by the time we read Tolstoy's *Death of Ivan Ilyich* for the October ECRG, Dad's loss had finally become real, the grief absorbed into my everyday melancholy, giving it a weightier, more defined quality. At the same time, the ECRG had also become integrated into my life, an indispensable occasion to focus my often-messy thoughts and feelings. I looked forward to the last Thursday of the month, a dedicated space in life's tumult in which to question and hash out big ideas, to expand your self while embracing the communal, evidenced in empty bottles lining the wall.

But there was something about the Tolstoy that destabilized the evening. For the first time, I thought our couch was in danger of having red wine spilled on it due to unwieldy, aggressive discourse. Tom, a newcomer to the group, a handsome, tattooed, older-than-he-looks psychology professor who works with Kevin, had suggested *The Death of Ivan Ilyich*. He'd begun the discussion by saying that it was the only book he'd ever thrown across the room upon finishing. And words flew across the room for the rest of the night, which was marked by posturing and challenging, rare at the ECRG. We disagreed all the time, but usually it was respectful and in the spirit of trying to understand the other person's viewpoint. The two youngest men in the room, Nate and the surprise guest he'd brought, another writer and blogger (the ones threatening our couch with careless grips on their wineglasses and sudden gestures), needled me about my use of the term "human condition," which they deemed a "meaningless phrase." At one point in the evening Tom, curious about the phenomenon of childbirth, earnestly asked the two mothers in the room about the experience. When I opened my mouth to respond, the young men rose from the couch and excused themselves to go smoke on the porch. I exchanged looks with Susan, the other mother in the room. Looks which meant *Oh, they'll get the "human condition" thing soon enough.*

That night I confessed that when I read Ronald Blythe's introduction to the book, I felt a creeping, cold recognition, and kept thinking about Dad's last hours in the ICU. Blythe was opining about modern culture's inadequacy in dealing with the individual's moment of death, claiming we didn't treat death with its deserved reverence until after the event was over for the person involved, and the focus shifted to the grieving and their ceremonies — the funeral, the outfits, the eulogies, the interment. Blythe describes how during the death watch over Tolstoy at the stationmaster's cottage in Astapovo, even Tolstoy's acolytes, whom he'd directed to ask him if his feelings toward life had changed as he neared the moment of death, were overcome and failed to follow through with his request.

Tolstoy had been death-obsessed and death-haunted nearly his whole life and the big moment had finally arrived, but, as Blythe says,

> the dying are in the hands of the living, who generally remain more loyal to deathbed conveniences than to deathbed revelations. It comforts them to know that the dead knew and felt nothing. "He felt nothing," they will later tell each other, forgetting that there are more things to feel than pain and fear.

Oh no, I thought, had I been more concerned with myself than my dad when I asked about the morphine? When later that night, curled up on one of the awful dorm couches in the family lounge after twelve hours at the hospital, I just wanted it to be over? Nurse Craig had planted the seed; Blythe and Tolstoy watered and fertilized it. But I honestly don't remember thinking much at all that day. That morning, alone with Dad, I told him what I wanted to tell him. He seemed unconscious but I thought I felt him squeeze my hand. The room was filled with late-morning sun. I don't know. I held his hand and tried not to think about how one might describe the sunlight on the IV bags, tried to stay "in the moment."

Years ago, at a Cape Cod junk store, I bought a 1906 copy of *Memoirs of My Dead Life,* a collection of essays by the Irish writer George Moore, for its great title, embossed white on a gray-blue spine, and a quick scan of the startling last page. Along with women, literary reputation, drinking, and "authenticity," Moore was also at times preoccupied with his inability to fully focus on the life happening in front him, to stay in the moment. In the book's final essay, "Resurgam," he's been informed by his brother via telegram that his mother is dying. On the journey from Paris to his ancestral home in Ireland, he hopes that his mother will die before he gets there, thus sparing him the pain of the ultimate mortal confrontation. He spends much of the time musing about his childhood, and thinking about how best to describe the scenery from his train carriage, like the morning light on a passing field ("soft as the breast-feathers of a dove"), or the nature of existence ("a fly climbing a glass dome… climbing and falling back, buzzing, and climbing again"). He can't help himself. "This sudden bow-wowing of the literary skeleton made me feel I wanted to kick myself." Even at the funeral itself (he was relieved that his mother had died hours before his arrival) his mind drifts, and he starts planning his own cosmic Irish burial and afterlife, replete with island pyres, dancing nymphs, and exploding planets.

Though regarding death Moore entertainingly evades and Tolstoy excruciatingly delves, both worried about turn-of-the-twentieth-century modern man losing touch with his true condition. What was "the real thing"? This question is what *The Death of Ivan Ilyich* labors so painfully toward. In the beginning of the novella, Ivan Il-yich, a forty-five-year-old examining magistrate, is already dead, as if Tolstoy is illustrating how absurd and false death rituals can be when the living are still so preoccupied with, well, living. Upon hearing the news of his death, his colleagues view it as some kind of profes-sional misstep, and everyone gauges it immediately in terms of his own self-interest, what it means for their position in the ministry — maybe someone will get a promotion, maybe someone's brother-in-law can be transferred to town to get his wife off his back. In the house of mourning, a card game is furtively planned for later that evening. The widow tries to find out if she can wrangle more money from the government through one of her dead husband's colleagues. During the exchange, her black shawl gets caught on some ostenta-tious furniture, and a broken, rebellious spring in the ottoman the man is sitting on creates bad feelings in the room.

"Ivan Ilyich's life had been most simple and commonplace — and most horrifying," begins Tolstoy's telling of his life story. A middle child born into a family of government bureaucrats, Ivan Ilyich was wedged between a "cold and punctilious" successful older brother and an embarrassing failure of a younger brother whom everyone tries to forget exists. Ivan Ilyich was an affable striver, a creature molded by his need for approval, whether regarding questions of morality or career or marriage or interior decorating. His decisions were compelled by what was considered "the right thing" by people in good social standing. This is what torments him so thoroughly when he falls ill after bumping his side while demonstrating to a draper how he wanted the curtains hung in his new home, which was purchased through a coveted promotion. Over three months, without a definitive diagnosis, he deteriorates quickly. His illness, manifesting in relentless pain, becomes intimate adversary, both part of him and detached from him, a gnawing animal, an "It" with "Its" own agenda, which even begins "Its own proceedings" against him during court sessions while Ivan Ilyich is still able to work.

Ilyich also fixates on the special, wary tension that sometimes exists between doctors treating lawyers, people used to their own spheres of authority, a tension maybe even more pronounced today, because when those professional spheres overlap, the outcome is usually damaging and expensive. Dad did the same things Ivan Ilyich did — researched different treatments, resented and mistrusted his own doctors, consulted others. Ivan Ilyich's doctors, stuck in their professional masks just like Ivan Ilyich had been stuck in his, can't be trusted, can't agree, and can't help. As his physical pain becomes intolerable and death seems the obvious outcome, he gets twisted up in a helix of hope and despair. But why is he suffering so much *moral* anguish in approaching the end when he'd done everything "right" in life?

*　　*　　*

The night before Dad crashed, we had our last, albeit brief, conversation as I fed him what I didn't realize would be his last solid food ever, horrible slippery canned peaches from one of the compartments on his plastic dinner tray, my other sisters in the room discussing what needed to be suctioned with the aspirator and how. He'd had a small stroke on the right side of his body and was talking with great effort and difficulty, an extreme frustration for someone who made his living with words, who'd often say that all he needed to do his job were a pen and a legal pad, who'd tell us over mandatory Sunday dinners–cum–cross-examinations that we had to be careful with our words because that's all we have to make ourselves. Haltingly, he told me he was sorry that he missed Silas's birthday dinner over the weekend, that he hoped our son understood that he wasn't feeling well. From the beginning, Dad had embraced Silas as one of his own blood tribe, fully and unequivocally, never as a stepgrandson. He even overindulged him, having a special affection for outsiders. That our last exchange was about him felt right and true.

After our younger sisters went home, Kristin and I had a drink at a bar across the street from the hospital that we referred to as the real "family lounge," since the one in the Touro Infirmary didn't serve drinks. Earlier that day, Kristin, a politician — though she would've said "public servant" — had met with a group called Resurrection After Exoneration, ex-prisoners who'd served time, were eventually found innocent, and were now dealing with the steep challenges of reentry into the society that had allowed their wrongful convictions. Formidable in her tailored suit and pumps, Kristin was worked up and distracted by the injustice of their plight, half with me at the bar, half mentally tapping her government-issued BlackBerry, conjuring up partnerships among city and state agencies that could help with the exonerees' particular problems of finding housing, of finding work, even with their years of ample, certified training. Their stories were amazing, she said. I was thinking the same thing. Of the many differences between us, that's one of the biggest — in situations like that, she sees potential solutions, I see potential material.

Then a thoughtful, inward look overtook her, the one that mirrored my other siblings' faces with increasing frequency in those days, that averting gaze searching for elsewhere in the room to land, the one that augured an attempt to assess the legacy and imminent death of our complicated dad. She said, "You know that's one thing that Dad did a really good job with, teaching us to get pissed off about injustice and not to trust authority." I reminded her, for fun, that she was now "the man." But I agreed it was true, that the Jeffersonian doctrine of healthy rebellion that Dad advocated, somewhat dangerously, to his teenage children was still pretty influential in our lives. As Jefferson said, "A little rebellion now and then is a good thing, and as necessary in the political world as storms in the physical."

On his deathbed, Ivan Ilyich finally begins to understand this, the necessity of questioning the status quo in order to connect with some sort of moral truth, when during his agonizing inner contortions he asked himself: "What if my entire life, my entire conscious life, simply was *not the real thing?*"

It occurred to him that what had seemed utterly inconceivable before — that he had not lived the kind of life he should have — might in fact be true. It occurred to him that those scarcely perceptible impulses of his to protest what people of high rank considered good, vague impulses which he had always suppressed, might have been precisely what mattered, and all the rest had not been the real thing. His official duties, his manner of life, his family, the values adhered to by people in society and in his profession — all these might not have been the real thing. He tried to come up with a defense of these things and suddenly became aware of the insubstantiality of them all. And there was nothing left to defend.

Of all of the things that might've tormented Dad on his deathbed — Rebecca's and Rachel's suicides, unresolved financial messes, certain professional aspirations never realized — a life of mute compliance with the status quo was not one of them. He was defiant and pissed off until the very end about anything he perceived as injustice. A week before he died, Dad wanted one last encounter with what he thought was possibly the greatest moral travesty in our country, capital punishment, and one last visit with the convicted murderer he'd grown to care about. When I asked Mom why Dad felt compelled to go up to Death Row in such a weakened state, after four days of chemo, she said he just wanted to be a lawyer. It was all he really wanted to do. She also said that he just couldn't let go of his client, Ronald.

The week before Dad's final trip to Angola, I'd had my last table 5 lunch with him and Soren at the Rib Room to talk about their death-penalty work. Dad ordered seafood gumbo; my brother and I split a gargantuan rare king-cut steak. For years, I'd been wanting to write about their work from the father-son angle, to find out what it was like. I also had a theory that since Dad had gotten his Death Row appointment around the time Rebecca and Rachel died, his pursuit was somehow driven by trying to save another life, by some kind of futile cosmic accounting, and I wanted to know what he thought of this theory.

They began the conversation by explaining how they were recruited into representing these inmates due to a burgeoning constitutional crisis on Louisiana's Death Row. Dad near the end of his career, Soren near the beginning of his, decades of experience separating them. A "sliver" of time existed at the state post-conviction stage (before federal habeas corpus) in which there was no statutory right to counsel for Death Row inmates in Louisiana, a procedural limbo that Soren tried to explain by arranging heavy cutlery on the space between our plates. The salad fork was the state trial, the dinner fork the post-conviction appeals, the knife the federal court, and the dessert spoon the Supreme Court. Between the dinner fork and the knife was the sliver where cases started piling up on Death Row with nearly half of the inmates lacking legal representation, an opportunity for overzealous prosecutors to start issuing death warrants.

Angola occupied a large region in my dad's psychic terrain, a moral proving ground for his abilities, intellect, principles. Soren's, too. They were both roughly six feet three, with full heads of brown hair, brown eyes, and large handsome features, and had both been athletic as young men, but were a little desk-softened now. I suspect that as litigators they let their physical stature do some of the work for them in the courtroom. They sat across from each other at table 5, volleying experiences, a kind of genetic ricochet I found fascinating and distracting as I sipped the cabernet and tried to keep up. My brother described at length his humiliations in court and inexperienced bungling. My father, his sure-footed confidence in moving his client's case through the system. Pumped up on wine and a conversation that ballooned with import as verbal paragraphs turned into whole chapters, Soren called Angola "the end of the end of the end. Where nobody gives a fuck about this last little tendril of humanity. These guys are the edge of the edge of the edge." Both of their Death Row clients' narratives had been absorbed into their own. They could walk you through their clients' childhoods, middle-school and (brief or nonexistent) high school careers, tour you through the scenes of the crimes for which they were convicted, a levee in

St. Martinville, a restaurant kitchen in East Baton Rouge. Both believed their clients could have been good, productive citizens if not for some drug-fueled mistakes, misfortunes of environment. Both were intimately, not just professionally, invested in these extremes of how people are made and unmade.

How people are made and unmade. Maybe that was the line of questioning we were all pursuing, the *belle chasse,* the beautiful hunt? This sliver, this moment of vulnerability in the vast, arcane legal procedure that brought these men into each other's lives, interested me, had metaphorical value. In the genteel vault of the Rib Room, at the height of its lunch rush, which never seemed like a rush, more like a slow swelling of the stage's backdrop, I imagined there were all kinds of slivers out there opening up, liminal, indeterminate gaps within our determined structures, places where you could get lost or make some soul-saving connection.

But it was not metaphor driving this conversation. It was the trajectories of lives gone wrong, lives destroyed, and society's attempt to reckon with it all. Ronald had confessed to the brutal stabbing death of an eighty-five-year-old Cajun patriarch while on a drug-crazed search for cash. As the man checked the water levels at the levee to report back to his crawfishermen sons, as he did ritualistically every afternoon, Ronald stabbed him fatally and took his money. He spent it on crack cocaine, then went to the house of a former landlady to try to get more. When she said no, he stabbed her as well, ran her over in his car in the driveway at the end of a cane field. When he returned to burn the house down, he attacked her with a tire iron. She survived.

Dad was clear-eyed about his client's guilt, the bloody, irreversible damage he'd caused, and the need for his incarceration. But Ronald's defense attorney had been beyond incompetent, Dad said. He called no expert witnesses to attest to any mitigating factors in Ronald's life, and though he pled guilty to first-degree murder, Ronald still received the death penalty, which had never happened in the history of the state. The same attorney was assigned to his direct appeal. Ronald began to study law and to seek help. He never claimed to be innocent, just poorly represented. A string of underqualified attorneys was assigned to him, and Ronald filed motions to dismiss each of them. Six years after Ronald's conviction, Dad stepped in to represent him.

Death Rows across the country are filled with stories like Ronald's, Dad said, devastating childhoods, poverty, truncated educations, addiction, the cul-de-sac of a system skewed against the poor. After nearly two hours of the technicalities, the anecdotes, Dad laid out the moral basis for his years of working on the case. He felt this administering of death to men by men, the ultimate judgment, defined hubris like no other issue. In this "Christian country" (his thick fingers gouging the air with emphatic quotes) you have a system rife with racial and economic inequity, waste, dysfunction, ineffective counsel, vindictive prosecutors, judges with political aspirations, grieving sundered families, and this system plays God.

"The commandment says 'Thou shalt not kill.' It doesn't say 'Thou shall not kill, except you assholes in Angola can kill anybody you want.' It doesn't say that."

And there was an even more basic rationale than morality. While the legal work was complicated, he explained, the motivation was simple. His client just wanted to live.

"Hey," he said, "I want to live, too. And the woman my client left for dead, mutilated in the cane field and who miraculously survived, she wanted to live, too. It's our natural imperative."

But then, whether it was illness or intractable injustice wearing him down, turning defiance to defeat, he slumped back a little in his chair, suit jacket bunching awkwardly around his shoulders, bluster dissipating. Buskers worked the curb across the street, a raggedy clarinet and a banjo duo sitting on overturned five-gallon buckets. We could barely hear the music, just some high reedy scratches and plinks through the muffled din of the Rib Room.

"So much futility, disappointment," he said. "A system as broken as this one will eventually win. You can only chase so many windmills." He was convinced that even after all these years of work his client would remain in the same place, same condition, as when he'd first gotten the case, something an attorney never wants to happen.

"So does it mean anything, Dad?" Soren asked, trying to wrap things up, sensing Dad's fatigue. "This crazy shit that we do? What is the lesson learned? In terms of the unquantifiable benefit. Being a man who stands up for what he believes in, does that mean anything?"

"Meaning? Only for the person who does it. I'm better for it because I thought I did something good. Attempted to do something good. Beyond that, no. You can affect people, but can't make meaning for them." Soren thought it was a great answer. I wasn't sure.

As Soren unspooled a long, animated story about recent, rather dramatic trouble with his teenage daughter, a kind of coda to the meal, and Dad listened, amused and sucking on a toothpick he'd gotten from the maître d' stand, I was conscious of time finally dislodging itself from the Rib Room, that stasis chamber for so many years. Forced into motion by the roiling generational activity of a big family, the waxing and waning of experience. Fresh young crises rising to the surface while the older, hoarier ones take root below. My brother's voice eclipsing my father's across table 5. The hand tapping the base of my wineglass becoming my mother's. All obvious, but our human place in time had suddenly taken on the material weight of inevitability.

After almost three hours of lunch, Dad was fading. Done with his kids for the day, he needed to retrieve his car from the valet and retreat to his leather recliner in Algiers. Call the doctor about refilling his pain meds. My brother picked up the check. My father let him.

Months later, listening to the tape, I realized just how unsatisfying that lunch had been. I was such a bad interviewer, lulled by the Rib Room back into my role as daughter, sister, diner, eating and casual conversing overtaking interrogation. I wasn't even brave enough to try out my big theory about the deaths of Rebecca and Rachel being catalysts for my father wanting to take on pro bono death-penalty work. I just couldn't pursue that line with him. Bringing up the twins was always a risk — you never knew how he'd respond. Which is why I never did and always just complied with his edict about not writing about their deaths. Just thinking about asking revived that nervous little-girl fear I still felt around him, even so close to his death. Fear of reprisal, fear of losing favor, fear of hurting him even more deeply than he already was. It never seemed worth it.

Contrary to Dad's enduring pessimism about Ronald's case, about six months after he died, Mom received a letter from one of his colleagues. Due to Dad's "tireless work," Ronald was being released from Death Row. To me, this seemed both a huge and cramped victory, Ronald's life widening out from a solitary eight-by-ten-foot cell, twenty-three hours a day, under the threat of lethal injection, to living with his guilt until his natural death in the general population of Angola. But for Ronald it was transformative. The letter went on to describe how not only was his life spared, but almost immediately he entered a training program to mentor younger offenders with the hopes of helping them avoid the mistakes he had made. Within the year, he would become a certified tutor, prepping other inmates for the GED, and begin working toward his longtime dream of becoming a minister, something unreachable to him on Death Row. He was accepted into the New Orleans Baptist Theological Seminary eighteen months after applying, a feat that takes most inmates years to achieve.

After Mom shared that letter, I started a correspondence with Ronald. As he was now in the general population, he could use a highly restrictive email system called JPay. In his first message, he apologized for taking so much of Dad's time near the end of his life, time that could've been spent with his family. Then he acknowledged that his crimes were against humanity, not just individuals and their families, and that he took full responsibility. As soon as he met Dad, he felt great relief. Finally, a good attorney and a man of compassion and conviction. He wrote that he'd come to regard Dad as his best friend.

Then one day, completely unsolicited, I received a message from Ronald. As usual, it was typed in all caps because it allowed him to write more quickly in the short amount of time given him at the JPay kiosk. Thus, his messages appeared on my screen with the urgency of a telegram, an important dispatch rushed to me over great distances. He wrote that Dad once told him that his own daughters had died with the same mixture of cocaine and alcohol in their systems that Ronald had in his when he'd committed his crimes. Dad knew the obliterating dangers of that combination. Maybe one more casualty could be prevented. I read it several times. My God, I'd been right.

I asked Mom and my brothers, who'd talked with Dad at length about the case, if he'd ever mentioned that connection between the twins' suicide and his dogged, decade-long defense of Ronald. No. Never. Was it too painful to talk to his own family about it? Just another wall he'd erected to make it possible for him to keep moving forward? Or was it for the same reason I could never ask him about the connection — fear?

Another telegram from Ronald, from the universe: when Dad arrived for what would be their final visit, they were both surprised to be escorted to a regular visitation room reserved for "contact visits," not a glass-partitioned booth. Ronald said that neither of them had requested a contact visit, which is rarely granted and usually reserved for family. Bureaucracy and procedures are so tight on Death Row that Ronald figured it was an act of God. The two men were able to hug for the first and last time instead of waving through a glass wall or shaking hands in open court.

Ronald had been surprised to see how much Dad had aged since they'd last seen each other.

As close as they were, Dad never told Ronald he was sick for those last years. That he was closer to dying than Ronald. Ronald was incredulous, devastated, to learn of his death shortly after the visit. Now it seemed even clearer to me why Dad made that trip to Angola before he died. Ronald knew him and his motivations like no one else did. It was a last chance to be known, not fully and deeply or even accurately, but in a way that was important for him. As best friend to a man condemned to death, as an attorney trying to save someone's life, as a lapsed Catholic still dedicated to defending God's word, as a father trying to account for the loss of his two youngest daughters. As a man who was not sick and not defined by his illness. And maybe Dad understood himself best in the intimacy of the visitation booth on Death Row, where life is distilled down to questions of law and survival, of sin and atonement, more chances to make things right, especially for those who need it most, the guilty.

Toward the very end of his struggle with death, Ivan Ilyich, like my dad, also finds meaning and connection in a man far outside of his own social circumstances. He feels his family, friends, and doctors have all but abandoned him, and he becomes peevish and difficult. His only comfort is in Gerasim, a healthy young peasant servant "with a light, vigorous step, exuding a pleasant smell of tar from his heavy boots and of fresh winter air . . . wearing a clean hemp apron and a clean cotton shirt with the sleeves rolled up over his strong arms." The only thing that provides him relief from the pain is to rest his legs on Gerasim's young shoulders, which he does for hours at a time, sometimes all through the night. Gerasim has a natural acceptance of the circumstances of life. He "was the only one who did not lie; everything he did showed that he alone understood what was happening, saw no need to conceal it, and simply pitied his feeble, wasted master. Once, as Ivan Ilyich was sending him away, he came right out and said: 'We all have to die someday, so why shouldn't I help you?'"

Though that night it was an otherwise-fractious ECRG meeting, with lots of smoking breaks and awkward exchanges — Tom imploring a disgusted Ellen to embrace the beauty of her middle age, Nate's young friend interrogating us individually about the ECRG's intentions — everyone rallied around Gerasim. Tristan spoke from a prone position on the floor. He'd hurt his back years before, falling two long floors down a service elevator shaft while helping move an armoire, someone having left the gate open. He once told me that as he stepped backwards into the darkness, he experienced an utterly lucid Wile E. Coyote recognition of the emptiness below him. "Gerasim is the character closest to nature, to the earth. Even the way he smells. So he's the one with the most natural relationship to death." I sometimes worry about Tristan. Living in his half-renovated Creole cottage on the edge of a gentrifying neighborhood, so sensitive to the world and alert to the needs of others; if it's not his back, it seems something else is always ailing him.

Even though Nate harped on the imbalance of power in the servant-master relationship, he admitted that Gerasim transcends his role as servant and deals with Ivan Ilyich as a fellow man.

"Just like Epicurus said, 'When it comes to death we human beings all live in an unwalled city,'" I noted from the floor next to Tristan, pleased to use one of my favorite quotes. "All equally vulnerable in our mortality. But Gerasim takes it one step further, suggests action. Since we're all defenseless against death, why not help each other out?"

"Exactly." Kevin stolidly anchored his end of the couch while the young men monopolized the rest of it with their agitation. "And it's through experiencing Gerasim's directness and generosity that Ilyich fears that maybe he got life all wrong, and that now there's no time to rectify his wrong, wasted life."

Ellen, as usual, corralled us back to the text by pointing a thin finger at her iPad, suggested we look at the ending.

When Ivan Ilyich's wife comes into the room "to congratulate him on taking the sacrament" of confession, "her clothes, her figure, the expression of her face, the sound of her voice — all these said to him: '*Not the real thing.* Everything you lived by and still live by is a lie, a deception that blinds you from the reality of life and death.'"

At this point, Ivan Ilyich begins to scream for three days. "'Oh! Oh! No!' he screamed in varying tones. He had begun by shouting: 'I don't want it! I don't!' and went on uttering screams with that 'O' sound." While his screaming is truly terrifying and torments everyone in the house, I've always been impressed by Ivan Ilyich's last-ditch marathon of defiance. He's right, of course, there's so much to scream about. Sometimes I feel like screaming now, to clear out the lungs and the soul, do an end run around any terrible deathbed realizations. Maybe making some noise now will help later?

But, in the end, at the last moment, Ivan Ilyich does seem to break through to the truth when he asks himself for the final time, "But what *is* the real thing?" At that moment, in his flailing, his hand lands on his crying son's head, and his son takes it and kisses it. Then he sees the pure grief on his wife's face, her unwiped tears. Having been so fixated on his own suffering, he hasn't made this very easy on them either, and finally he sees their suffering clearly, wants to make amends. There's still time. He wants to say "Forgive" but, enfeebled, mistakenly says "Forget." No matter. "And suddenly it became clear to him that what had been oppressing him and would not leave him suddenly was vanishing all at once — from two sides, ten sides, all sides. He felt sorry for them, had to do something to keep from hurting them." And that something, that one real thing that he can do for them in life, is to die. The light comes, the relief comes. "'Death is over,' he said to himself. 'There is no more death.'"

After leaving Kristin and the bar that night, I walked past the hospital's emergency-room entrance ramp to my car and I realized that Dad was probably going to die in the same building where Otto had been born. I still marveled at how moved the staff had seemed when he arrived. Birth was their job. They saw it every day. But just before midnight, as our wet, wriggling son emerged, their eyes softened above their surgical masks and the whole colossal mess of the city outside dissolved for a moment.

Several blocks down, on the same oak-lined street as the hospital, I drove past the white crumbling stucco walls of Lafayette Cemetery No. 1. If you look hard enough from the street, you can see the peaked roof of the twins' tomb. Sometimes I pass the cemetery and think about them with tenderness, other times with a cold calcification, almost bitterness. They took themselves out of the game, which became more interesting and richer than they could've imagined, and now are stuck behind the wall. But that night I was thinking about Dad and how much more time he had with us out here before he joined the twins in there.

Passing one of our famous walled cities of the dead within our walled city of the living that night, I was feeling the full effect of my citizenship in the unwalled city. The cemetery reminded me that the archaic bureaucracy of death that some families deal with in New Orleans was about to be set in motion. We'd have to find the yellowed, 150-year-old deed to the tomb, kept in the same Ziploc sandwich bag my grandmother kept it in, handwritten in beautiful nineteenth-century script, signed by my great-great-grandfather, present it to the city authorities (crazy that these relics still serve us), deal with the obituary, funeral home, cremation, and the near-criminal fees that accompany death in America. Cataloging the death chores and the dread and mystery of what lay on the other side of them propelled me through the dark city. Driving home, I stayed close to the river and the old neighborhoods and narrow streets, the tall buildings of the Central Business District rising up, sloping back down to the human scale of the downtown Creole neighborhoods, the intersections, the avenues, the red lights and the green lights, all our obstacles and permissions, and I wondered where all these other cars could be heading.

NOVEMBER

Nineveh

A poem focuses and quiets the room like no other reading, creates a white space of concentration around the talk as it does
around the words on the page. The poems Sara chose for November
called for small investigations of large questions; you could isolate a
line or group of lines and use them as a drawstring to gather everyone in. People seemed grateful for the careful packaging, the surprising gifts of these poems. The atmosphere that night was low-key but
engaged, in a pleasant, contained way.

This was in contrast to October's Tolstoyan provocation, and all the
generational and gender fissures it had aggravated. That night there
had also been grumblings that the readings for the year had been too
homogeneous; after all, white European men don't own the struggle.
Though on the shelves, in anthologies, philosophy departments, and
conversational references, they certainly monopolize it. The night of
the Tolstoy discussion, Sara was also being unusually assertive and
announced that she wanted to choose some poetry for November's
meeting. Though I was expecting her to present a full-on cadre of
women poets, she mixed it up, male and female, made them equals.

Each poem Sara chose held a quotidian Moment of Awareness, as
experienced with one's self or other people. The poems seemed like

attempts to pin the self down in the universe or, as in the lines from Elizabeth Bishop's "In the Waiting Room," which we read that night, "to stop / the sensation of falling off / the round, turning world / into cold, blue-black space." Poetry's combination of precision and mystery makes it the perfect genre for this task. It asks for a kind of thoughtful deference, and we indulged it.

We immediately pointed out that the poems Sara chose were all explicitly situated in different seasons, another way to locate ourselves in time, albeit transiently. Seasons afford concrete context but also can be obviously metaphorical, pointing out how life is experienced in stages and cycles. A reminder that the world is turning, orbiting, and time is passing in a more or less orderly, inexorable way, unless you live in a seasonally muddled and at times unpredictable place like subtropical south Louisiana. When I lived in Massachusetts during college, I marveled at the true seasonal distinctions, the predictability of them. Leaves blaze and fall, then the snow, then spring bursting through it with delicate little crocuses, and then real scorching summers. And it was interesting how people were communally affected and bound by the shifts in weather, how moods changed along with the seasonal gear hauled out of basements and attics.

For years, both early fall and early spring, the most pleasant and anticipated weather of the year in New Orleans, were tainted for me. Rebecca died in September and Rachel in March, and as soon as the temperature changed, I could feel the grief approach through the air, feel it on my skin, before I actually remembered their death dates. During that period, I remember thinking that those girls had managed to ruin both seasons for me. But time overtook that cycle, too, dulled the fine-tuned physicality of grieving to a less painful, more general *remembrance*. Now in spring, my body recalls being heavily pregnant with my younger son, can still conjure twinges of that amazing restless fear and apprehension mixed with the clean, vibrating blue of April. I imagine one day that sensation will also fade into mere recollection, but at least spring has been reclaimed for me within that ongoing dialogue in nature, like the line from Theodore Roethke's poem "Unfold! Unfold!": "What the grave says, / The nest denies." The nest gets the last word.

Though the nest is built into us all, maybe it doesn't get the last word for everyone. In the first poem we discussed, Stephen Dobyns's "Somewhere It Still Moves," spring in Sarajevo is connected to a conditional sort of hope. His Moment of Awareness occurs during a literary conference, a fun dinner in a centuries-old restaurant ("whitewashed walls, great black beams on the ceiling") that makes the speaker and his fellow American diners feel that they are in "the midst of history." Soon, however, the poem telescopes away from the conviviality of the table, the pantomiming waiter trying to make himself understood to his American customers, the lively clatter of the restaurant, to the city's war-ravaged near future, a time when Dobyns will see newspaper photographs confirming that "the restaurant, the entire block has been / transformed to rubble, so many rocks at a crossroads." During the dinner, Dobyns writes, "The waiter laughed with us." Now, seeing the photos of devastation, the speaker laments of the waiter: "He is probably dead now. / Killed by a sniper as he crossed a street or stood / by a window." Across time and space, the poem blasts us apart with war, reconnects us with love, but ultimately, remembering that night, the speaker lands on the impulse to destroy inherent in our species:

> On one particular evening
> the waiter brought his tray with a paper bag on a plate
> and we laughed. A fragment of that sound is still traveling
> so far out into the dark, an arrow perhaps glittering
> in the flicker of distant stars. Somewhere it still moves.

I must believe that. Otherwise, nothing else in the world is possible. We are the creatures that love and slaughter.

After we read the poem aloud, someone asked why Dobyns imagines the waiter "probably" dead by sniper fire in the future. Hadn't he already served the poem enough? Since we're all *definitely* dying, wouldn't that suffice? Maybe that was too much of a given. The walls and beams of the old restaurant gave the weighty illusion of permanence, of a continuum, but this moment of unity, with friends, with history, is blown apart, along with some of the diners — at least in Dobyns's imagination — and so the waiter needed to take a bullet, too. Earlier in the poem, Dobyns had mentioned the famed bronze footprints of Gavrilo Princip, near the Princip Bridge, and how the speaker and his friends "each placed our feet / into these bronze souvenirs." I wondered about Dobyns standing in those footprints, which indicate where Princip stood when he shot Archduke Franz Ferdinand and lit the fuse of the twentieth century. Had the footprints been placed there — in life, in the poem — for the vicarious thrill of the vantage point, or was their location a statement of ultimate existential contingency — all individuals are responsible for all human carnage? In other words, anyone can stand in the footprints of the assassin. Slaughter, the last word of Dobyns's poem, reverberates, but like stone hitting stone, not like that shimmering arrow of laughter in the stellar dark, the one that makes life possible for him.

In *A Concise Dictionary of Existentialism,* the only entries under *W* are "War," "Women," "Words," and "World." This is Kierkegaard's entry for "World":

One sticks one's finger in the soil to tell by the smell in what land one is: I stick my finger into existence — it smells of nothing. Where am I? Who am I? How came I here? What is this thing called the world? What does this word mean? Who is it that lured me into the thing, and now leaves me there?...Why was I not consulted, why not made acquainted with its manners and costumes but was thrust into the ranks as though I had been bought of a kidnapper, a dealer of souls? How did I obtain an interest in it? Is it not a voluntary concern? And if I am compelled to take part in it, where is the director?

(*See also:* Being; Reality; Time; Transcendence.)

Kierkegaard could also be describing the project of poetry, asking the questions that inhabit every line. For the season that provokes the most dread among the local citizenry, summer, Sara chose "Conversation with Myself at a Street Corner," by New Orleans poet Everette Maddox. Maddox's conversation with himself echoes Kierkegaard's wry confoundedness at being alive, at this preposterous situation we all find ourselves in.

I'm glad I caught myself
quivering here at the corner
trying to get across
the summer day to the branch
library. I wanted to ask me
a couple of questions, viz.:
Old Son, what interests
you about this or any
other moment of your or
anybody else's life? I mean,
I seem to detect a sort of
dull gleam running around
your general haggardness
like Scotchlite on a bike.

Well, ahem, since I ask,
I'd have to say
the impingement of Fate on
quotidian activity is
something I have always
kept abreast of, and I am
BEAT. And conversely,
the scampering of the quotidian
across the face of Fate
like squirrels in a yard.
I prefer that order.
My opinion of Heaven
is roughly Mark Twain's:
I won't even stay where *I'm*
singing. Why, fuck wings!
We got public transportation
down here! If I had my way,
my every thought would be
a stained-glass window
in a modest mansion, to which
I'd return each twilight
to my sweet baby — though
she's presently doubtless out
with some goddam brain surgeon.
But I'll have to excuse me:
the light is changing,
and I must be run over
by the shadow of a streetcar.

The land Maddox sticks his finger into in this poem is ours, the
alluvial soil of New Orleans, the anachronistic racket of the street-

car, our subtropical flora and fauna, the heat, the destructive shadows. His poems are filled with beauty and humor, booze and longing, are set in the streets and bars where we grew up. Maddox drank himself into the grave by the age of forty-five, in 1989, a few months before Stephen Dobyns was having his moment with history in Sarajevo, launching arrows of meaning into the cosmos. After his death Maddox achieved a local cult status — his stool at the Maple Leaf Bar turning pedestal, his ashes buried in the courtyard out back among the rangy ivy and cigarette butts, beneath the epitaph HE WAS A MESS. Turns out he was drinking himself to death at the same time and at the same bars where we were drinking our way to adulthood. Did I ever stand next to him, trying to get the barmaid's attention, as he composed love poems to her on a coaster, dissolving into his Cutty Sark? In one poem he even mentions oak-lined State Street, where our family lived in a "modest mansion" replete with stained glass windows on the landing of our front staircase that we eight kids threatened every day with our headlong running and jumping toward the beveled front doors. Dad used to shout that if any of us ever broke those windows to just "keep running and don't come back!" Maddox's description of thought as a stained glass window resonates with my chaotic upbringing: thought as precious, elevated, and constantly threatened by all the action.

Dad was so proud of that modest mansion on State Street, the white columns and high coved ceilings, but it fairly sagged under the weight of all of the mortgages he took out trying to provide for us the things we needed (food, clothes, education, psychiatric care) and the things we didn't (dinners at Delmonico's, Brooks Brothers, study-abroad programs). Like Maddox's modest mansion, our house on State Street was a projection of Dad's desires, one that we all lived in precariously, and that we all vacated when it was time for him to pay the bills. Once a month he would ceremoniously set up a paper grocery bag next to his recliner and spend a couple of hours opening envelopes and his checkbook, yelling and cursing, signing and paying. He'd pay and pay for his big house and his big family for a long time. Even after her death, Rebecca's psychiatric bills kept arriving, monthly reminders of that expensive failure, costly in every way. Mom figured there must've been a time when he became too angry and stopped paying them and they got sent to a collection agency, which just inflated the financial damage over time. He paid those bills until his own death. How did he feel every time he wrote out one of those checks? Signed his name in that dramatic, craggy signature. Certifying his sadness or anger. Some months in penance, others in resignation.

And then summer turns to fall, night into day. The time of day in a poem can figure as deeply in it as the time of year. The evening opens up the firmament and mystery, sex and danger, while the dawn opens up possibility and revelation, new opportunities to get things right and to mess things up. Matins are traditional prayers usually performed at dawn by certain monastic orders in Catholicism, ending a night of vigils, starting the day with supplication. The word comes from Matuta, the Latin name for the Greek goddess of the morning, Leucothea. Matins are also known for imparting various "lessons," about scripture and the lives of saints and martyrs, but Louise Glück bookends her poem "Matins" with questions, mimicking life. She begins:

You want to know how I spend my time?
I walk the front lawn, pretending
to be weeding.

But of course, she's not weeding, she's searching. Her search takes on the insistence and regularity and pose of prayer. Glück's questioning starts as personal, almost accusatory, and then softens a little as the nature of the search — for courage, for evidence — is revealed. Time passes, trees change color, "a few dark birds perform / their curfew of music," and eventually the voice seems more open and plaintive.

But it was a phrase from the middle of the poem — "summer is ending, already" — that I hung on. The "sick trees" and the "dark birds." Dad in his recliner with his vitamin drink and oxygen tank, telling me, "It all just went too fast." Dad at table 5 weeks before he died, telling me no one really knew him. All of us standing tombside with the small well-dressed crowd, empty-handed. I wish he would've opened up more, would've asked the right questions, freeing us to ask them, too. But what am I really asking for? The father's function isn't the same as the poet's function. The father (my father) is ensconced at the table, in the recliner, at work, in all his wounded, burdened authority. The poet is ensconced between wide margins, quivering at the corner and scrabbling on the ground, making pronouncements and beauty. At the end of the poem she asks:

You want to see my hands?
As empty now as at the first note.
Or was the point always
to continue without a sign?

There was some consensus among us that night at the ECRG that the answer to the final question was, most likely, yes.

In another poem, "How to Like It," it was fall, and Stephen Dobyns was still, again, questioning what makes life "possible." This other Dobyns poem seemed to be about midlife, a frequent topic at the ECRG, as that age bracket dominates the room with its throbbing ambivalence and urgent doubt, occupying the highest and most lavish

tower in the unwalled city. You can still make the stairs, the brocades
are still bright, the tapestries a little worn in the right places. Surrounded by the tapering beauty of all the seasons, you can enjoy the
panorama and the action in the streets and squares, even with the
encroaching knowledge you'll have to leave the city altogether one
day. It was a time Dobyns's speaker was well acquainted with:

These are the first days of fall. The wind
at evening smells of roads still to be traveled,
while the sound of leaves blowing across the lawns
is like an unsettled feeling in the blood,
the desire to get in a car and just keep driving.
A man and a dog descend their front steps.

Sara realized that the last three poems all featured lawns or yards,
like they were some kind of spiritual buffers between the domestic
world and the universe. Along with the squirrels frolicking on that
yard of fate, the dog was definitely an evening favorite. Everyone loved
the dog. As the poem's speaker, like so many of us, stands dreamily
suspended between youth and age, past and present, between thought
and action, the dog bounds around with crazy ideas:

The dog says, Let's pick up some girls and just
rip off their clothes. Let's dig holes everywhere.

So, we wondered, is the dog in the poem animal desire? Is the dog
our dynamic inner companion, promising action but out of sync
with our thinking self — the man — which is paralyzed by fear and
indecision, gazing at "wisps of cloud / crossing the face of the moon"
and fantasizing of escape? Is the dog the man, or is the dog the dog?
That dog wants to go *out!* His suggestions are at first energetic, reck-

less, sexual (to get "crazy drunk" and "tip over all the trash cans we can find," head to the diner to "sniff / people's legs" and "stuff ourselves on burgers"), and then become more manageable and domestic (to recline "by the fire and put our tails over our noses"). Instead of driving down the road all night to some new city or sniffing a stranger's legs at a diner, they go back up the walk to the front door as the man wonders, "How is it possible to want so many things / and still want nothing?"

Once again, it seemed to us, we are left with the inherent impossibility of desire. By the end, the man feels conflicted, but he still has an appetite and the dog proposes they make the biggest sandwich ever. Finally, the man's wife finds him in front of the refrigerator, gazing into it

as if into the place where the answers are kept —
the ones telling why you get up in the morning
and how it is possible to sleep at night,
answers to what comes next and how to like it.

As in the Glück poem, there are no answers to the questions, unless the poems themselves are the responses, as if to say all we can do in the face of life's mysteries is desire, give shape to that desiring, and through that shaping try to connect with others and lessen our collective isolation.

Finally, we arrived at the inevitable, winter and death. "Poetry holds the knowledge that we are alive and that we know we are going to die," said poet Marie Howe. "The most mysterious aspect of being alive might be that — and poetry knows that." Sara chose Howe's poem "What the Living Do" for winter. It's addressed to Howe's younger brother, Johnny, who died when he was twenty-eight. The loss of a sibling brings death up tight and close. That starkness leaves its mark. As an adult, when you're with your siblings, part of you is always a child, attached to childhood patterns of behavior and associations. All the jokes and gestures, affections and resentments. But losing a young sibling works similarly. You internalize their nagging unfulfillment forever.

Howe's brother died in 1989. Maddox died in 1989. Dobyns dined in 1989. I don't know what to make of the alignment of that year within these poems that Sara chose, all connected to this specific moment near the end of the twentieth century. In my mind they stitch an arrow pointing at my 1989, when I was living in an actual walled city, Siena, so young, lounging on the piazza, dating Italian paratroopers stationed nearby, and experiencing the exquisite crush of centuries of culture. I loved the stories of the warring medieval towns in central Italy, catapulting diseased donkeys over each other's walls, toppling their phallic towers as a sign of dominance, raiding the reliquaries of the town's patron saint. And the Berlin wall came down in 1989, contrasting historical imperatives regarding walls: which we want to preserve and which we need to destroy.

Also: in interrogating the year 1989, I remembered something I'd forgotten, or buried. It was the year Rachel first tried to commit suicide, albeit mildly, with Tylenol, news my mother shared when she visited me in Tuscany, on a *loggia* overlooking Florence's Piazza Santo Spirito. I was far from home, on another continent, living in a perfume commercial, all cobblestone and elegant arches, where even the paratroopers wore ascots on the weekends. Suddenly, all these years later, the accepted narrative of the twins seemed more complicated to me. Was Rachel the one who opened the door, and Rebecca the one who first walked through it? At the time, I dismissed Rachel's attempt as an adolescent bid for attention and it got lost in Rebecca's more dramatic descent. But eleven years later that ripple would crash to shore.

214

Howe's "What the Living Do" added personal loss to our discussion of people as seasonal beings, and the way we implicate seasons in our internal drama. She laments to Johnny about the clogged kitchen sink and the broken heater in her apartment, runs errands around chilly Cambridge, spills coffee and drops groceries. Buys a hairbrush. All these things that "the living do" are sharpened by Johnny's absence, by his inability to do them anymore, and the speaker feels the pressure of the Tragic Plane on the Trivial. Parking her car, she recalls what he had referred to as "that yearning": "We want the spring to come and the winter to pass. We want / whoever to call or not call, a letter, a kiss — we want more and more and then more of it."

Howe's poem describes the remarkable and unremarkable ways we experience our lives. Its long lines and its couplets seem to reflect the winding track of the mind, the inevitable track of our day. Caught between the frustrating breakdown of the material world (the clogging and dropping and falling and spilling) and the endless ratcheting of desire ("that yearning"), we can still be surprised by moments of acceptance of our imperfect selves, of our survival after deep loss.

> But there are moments, walking, when I catch a glimpse of
>   myself in the window glass,
> say, the window of the corner video store, and I'm gripped by a
>   cherishing so deep
>
> for my own blowing hair, chapped face, and unbuttoned coat
>   that I'm speechless:
> I am living. I remember you.

The attempt to know and be known seemed to be the dual purpose of each of the poems Sara had chosen for us. The restaurant, the intersection, the garden, the window of the video store — that night the ECRG talked about all the places we can meet ourselves, all of these unexpected encounters that help move us forward through our days. All of the poems look up — to stars, stained glass windows, birds, the moon, or, in "What the Living Do," the "headstrong blue" sky — while busily negotiating the ground, digging their fingers into existence, searching for something, memory or recognition, something. Maybe that movement is connected to the conversational tone of the poems, this need to both explain and engage, whether with a "you" or yourself. All these conversations, like the seasons, have the potential to keep us tethered to our tenuous place in the world, even as they acknowledge the bigness underneath everything. They do it by keeping us talking to our living and our dead.

At our weekly breakfast following the November ECRG, I told Mom about the poems Sara had selected, how helpful the seasons were in navigating them. It's not difficult to induce total delight in her, to make her forget the steaming huevos rancheros before her, as she brightens and talks about how much she loves the seasons, the thought of the year going round and round, the waiting and the expectation, the buildup to celebrations. And also, she added, how much she loves the beauty and order of the liturgical year. Advent and Ordinary Time and Lent.

Frenetic breakfast service buzzed around us: coffee refills, extra hot sauce produced out of aprons, checks laid down and money scooped up. I asked her if that structure of observance was how she reined in the chaos of the family all those years, since Dad was often gone working, how she provided us order and meaning, through Sunday Mass, lighting Advent candles, celebrating three Christmases — the Feast of Saint Nicholas, the twenty-fifth, and then the Feast of the Epiphany, which also kicked off carnival, which brought us to Lent and interminable Holy Week and glorious Easter. If it was one of the things that made it possible to bring up eight kids, largely on her own.

No, not really, or rather she'd never thought of it that way. She told me she knew early on that's what she wanted when she grew up.

"When I was a young girl in the fifties, I went to a friend's house on Father's Day and on the table in their dining room was a cake shaped like a necktie. I thought it was extraordinary. That cake left a big impression on me. That people would do that. I knew I wanted that, wanted to find ways to commemorate, to celebrate."

"Celebrate what?"

"Being alive."

One of the most formative revelations of her life involved a necktie cake? It wasn't even a spiritual epiphany. It was silly and secular. I could feel my face scrunch in disbelief as I moved the grits around my plate. She must've noted my expression.

"You know, growing up, our household was very staid, very… conservative." She was choosing her words carefully, searching for both accuracy and an inoffensive way to describe the dead. "There was no real celebrating. Just that one gesture, the cake, seemed so remarkable to me."

Then, in 1964, having graduated from college and gotten engaged to Dad, she volunteered for nine months in Anadarko, Oklahoma, tutoring and teaching kids from several different tribes, many of whose ancestors had come west on the Trail of Tears. Living in a large apartment with a rooftop for gazing across the Plains and starry nighttime talks with her roommate about the future, she had her first taste of true independence; she wouldn't have another until Dad died forty-eight years later. During this in-between time, of planning and the anticipation of married life, she found a book, *The Year and Our Children,* about various ways of celebrating the Catholic liturgical year and cultivating a "domestic spirituality." She and Dad were committed to Catholicism and had already decided they wanted a big family (a dozen kids!), and she knew she wanted to create a family culture of celebration, of ritual, of codifying joy into the calendar. Over the years, she'd try out different suggestions from the book, a Saint Nicholas puppet play, making yearly Advent wreaths, Epiphany dinners. Though she instigated all these, she credited Dad with keeping them going, insistently, year after year. She thinks he clung to their traditions out of a fear of change and that persistent void. "Everything to excess" was his motto, as he aggressively celebrated the holidays, overfilling Easter baskets and buying the biggest turkeys, seemingly more concerned with secular spectacle than spiritual observance.

Even if Catholicism didn't stick with me, celebratory ritual evidently did. I wondered if that desire to cultivate a domestic spirituality somehow informed the ECRG. By November, the monthly ECRG meetings were already a part of our sons' childhood household rhythm as well, though they experienced it on the periphery. When Mom started arranging cheese on a cutting board after work, the boys knew it was an ECRG night and got excited about raiding the table for Sara's decadent sweets as the adults talked and flipped through papers and opened wine bottles. Like our parents, we were shaping our family's experience through ritual and tradition. And as with that necktie cake, we could shape it into whatever we wanted.

After breakfast, Mom and I drove to Lafayette Cemetery No. 1, where unfortunately, too often, there was something to commemorate. We were bringing flowers for Rebecca's birthday. The twins were born on November 19 and 20, before and after midnight. They entered the world complicating things, already vying for their own space, with their two separate birth dates and celebrations. Mom said Rebecca was always envious that Rachel got her birthday breakfast in bed the day before she did. As much as they loved being twins, that tension to have your own separate life and identity persisted, with different schools and friends and haircuts and fashion sense. Though in the end, that twin connection won out over everything.

The day before, on Rachel's birthday, Otto had a doctor's appointment near Lafayette Cemetery No. 1, so we dropped by to pay our respects and, since I knew I'd be coming with Mom the next day, tidy up the tomb. It would need to be cleared of any dead or dying plants left over from All Saints' Day, observed a few weeks before. Formerly a citywide holiday to venerate the dead, it used to be a high social occasion, cemeteries crowded with vendors, the living leaving tributes of flowers and candles for their dead, and Masses said among the decorated and freshly whitewashed tombs. But in my lifetime that old Creole tradition has dissipated considerably, as many tombs have been abandoned for generations, the dead forgotten, the lineage of memory severed. All Saints' Day has been whittled down to a few votive candles and de rigueur chrysanthemums or bouquets of plastic flowers here and there, brightening the aging marble façades with fresh attention, a Mass or two, and maybe a few preservationists with trowels and buckets, trying to revive an old wreck of a crypt. For All Saints' Day, I'd taken Mom to a nursery to carefully select the chrysanthemum plants for our own dead — spiky purple blossoms for Rebecca, smaller but more prolific russet ones for Rachel, and for Dad, golden shaggy leonine flowers, exactly ten, one for each of us, Mom said.

Weeks later, on Rachel's birthday, the plants were spindly enough for Otto and me to toss into the dented metal garbage can over by the Prytania Street gate. While I brushed errant magnolia leaves from the tomb's base, he ran among the narrow avenues and between the crypts and larger mausoleums, looking at the dates, the exotic places where some inhabitants had been born, and the archaic names chiseled into the marble tablets. On a tomb in an adjacent row, he saw his own name leap out from among the nineteenth-century names. He was thrilled to see it, and I suggested we get some paper and a pencil from the car and do a rubbing. After Rebecca and Rachel died, my mother and I had wandered the cemetery with pencils and tracing paper to make rubbings of ornamentation that she liked and might want to use for our tomb's tablet whenever she finally got around to having the twins' names engraved. A weeping willow, a wreath, a draped urn, a lamb. All these archaic symbols, all meaning more or less the same thing. As I held the paper over the cold, slightly gritty marble (it was starting to "sugar," as old marble sometimes does), Otto gingerly rubbed the side of the pencil over it, and the heavy serifs and circles of his name materialized within the shadowy graphite cloud, his work a palimpsest of the engraver's almost two hundred years before. I wondered what he was thinking. What was I imprinting on him? What was this place, this family, imprinting on him?

For years, I'd referred to Rebecca and Rachel to our kids as "my sisters who died" or "your aunts who died," burdening us all with dread, and also mystery, since I'd always curtly replied to their inquiries that they had been very sick, or sometimes that they'd died from sadness. Telling myself that I was waiting for them to be old enough to understand seemed like misdirection. I knew that as soon as I told them the truth, I'd risk seeming like a different mother to them, more vulnerable and wounded, our family like a different family. I didn't want to introduce self-destruction into our shared history. A common fear among us surviving siblings was that some myth of the young, beautiful, gothically interred twins would be internalized by our own children, but not the realities of their lives, which were vibrant and loving and messy and so, so sad. But one day, in conversation with my boys, I happened to call the twins "my sisters you never met" and it felt like such a relief for us all. Just my referring to the twins differently freed us of the weight of focusing on their deaths, and spooled open their lived lives, the possibility that they could've been known. The twins will never be real to our children and they are becoming less real to us, but sometimes I'll see a photograph of them that I haven't seen in a while, some awkward, off-guard expression or gesture that captured the reality of their lives better than a camera-ready smile, and I'm jolted back into the fact of their existence. They were here. They were loved.

For the twins' birthdays, Mom had brought cut flowers for their personalized urns, positioned like sentries on either side of the tomb. As I distributed the lilies and alstroemeria between the two vases, Mom and I joked that they'd better be even. We took our usual graveside posture, heads bent, holding hands. Tears and deep sighs. Tried to block out the nearby presence of a shuffling tour group. We prayed the Our Father. Mom asked God for forgiveness for Rebecca and Rachel. Then she asked for forgiveness for all of us.

Over the years, forgiveness had become a dominant, guiding impulse for Mom, especially more recently, since Dad's death had raised so many questions for her, about their marriage, about what was kept from her and her own role in that. Once when I asked about his drinking, she said she never trusted herself to recognize the signs. She was so busy and focused on us kids and her teaching, she didn't have time to notice or to reflect. Not even the gin under the sink behind the 409? No, she laughed. She was a terrible housekeeper and had someone come in to help out or delegated chores to us kids. Besides, there was no time for real communication between them. She was isolated at home and he worked so much, traveled, volunteered at homeless shelters, rode his bike on the levee sometimes forty miles a weekend. It was a pattern set in place when they were first married. Think about it, she said, he graduated from college, got married, started law school, taking classes at night while clerking during the day, had eight kids and never stopped working for the family. She admired it, appreciated it, and gave him the space to have his own life. Forty-odd years later, at his funeral, not one but two maître d's from a restaurant she'd never been to showed up at his funeral to express how much he'd meant to them over the decades. How did he fill up the space she gave him? She'll never really know.

But her attachment to forgiveness crystallized for me when we drove up to Angola together to meet Ronald for the first time. Like me, Mom had been corresponding with him since his release from Death Row and into the general prison population. On the ride up, we talked a lot about Dad, about his attachment to Ronald, about how she worried that our children's generation might not be able to appreciate the wondrous mystery of human life, the miracle of our existence on this planet, because they spent so much time on their little screens. After enduring the gauntlet of security measures and boarding the bus with the other family and friends of inmates, we arrived at the main visitors' dining area. The place had a school-fair feel to it: handmade signs on poster board by different groups running the concessions, the Hispanic Club, the Literary Arts Club, the Asian Club, the Sober Club; wood and leather crafts, like chess sets and belts, for sale; a play area for kids; and a portrait-taking corner with a bucolic painted backdrop.

It was peak visiting hour. As we waited for Ronald, a man deep into a well-thumbed Koran, who was selling quilts to raise money for the prison hospice, helped us procure a table, and told us the wrong-place-at-the-wrong-time story of how he'd ended up in Angola, how hard he worked while inside to better himself, and his plans for after he was released, namely getting the heck out of Louisiana and back to his home in Texas. Though all of the inmates were wearing variations of blue chambray shirts, Ronald was easy to spot when he finally made it in through the holding area. His was a classic stocky Cajun build, but with pale hair and eyes, and a ruddy face. His wire-rimmed glasses and tucked-in collarless shirt gave him a ministerial air. A little nervous and anxious, he explained that we were the only visitors he'd had since he'd been off Death Row and he'd never even been inside this building before. As he looked around, taking it all in, Mom and I assured him that lunch was our treat, and arranged the Xeroxed menus from the different clubs in front of him.

Indecisive and reluctant to order, Ronald settled on one of the least expensive options, Convict Tacos from the Hispanic Club and a soft drink from the Literary Arts Club. But any self-consciousness as we tried to mesh our disparate worlds evaporated as Mom asked him about his studies at the seminary. From his correspondence, they seemed fairly rigorous, and he was eager to share. Mom had majored in Christian culture and before long they had somehow landed on the subject of Calvinism and predestination and whether or not God has a plan for us. Ronald thought yes, God does, a very specific plan for our individual persons and paths. Mom thought about it in more general terms, of God knowing humanity's potential for good and evil. Eventually I excused myself to acquire the tacos, navigating an elaborate system for ordering food devised so the inmates never touched the cash, tickets in triplicate and trips back and forth across the hall between the concessions and cashier's booth.

Since Ronald was immersed in Bible study, he asked what our favorite books were. I didn't have one but mentioned Ecclesiastes, and said that I'd read that there was some doubt about its provenance. Ronald paused thoughtfully and said the Bible was absolutely the true word of God passed down through the millennia. Another pause allowed us to accept his position. Unsurprisingly, his favorite was Job, and Mom said, "That was Dad's, too!" All three of us shared a polite, knowing laugh. Job's extravagant suffering — marauders killing his livestock and servants, all his children dying when a storm collapses the house where they're dining, skin overtaken by sores, unsympathetic friends giving him bad advice — is all just part of a game between God and Satan to test the durability of man's faith. There's an absurdity to the tragedy and the searching for answers and the disconnect between all parties involved. In the end Job seems to accept that man cannot know God, man cannot even know himself.

As we ate our Convict Tacos, Mom said that her favorite was Jonah, one of the shortest books in the Old Testament. God has tapped the good and pious Jonah to go tell the people of Nineveh that He is going to destroy them because of their sinful ways. Jonah tries to avoid God's request by taking a boat to Tarshish instead. Mom said that what happens next is what everyone associates with Jonah. God sends a storm to torment the boat, and since Jonah has told the crew he is fleeing God, they throw him overboard to save themselves. But God has also sent a huge sea creature to swallow Jonah, and he ends up in the belly of the whale, in total darkness and lyrical, biblical despair. *All thy billows and thy waves passed over me, compassed me about even to the soul, the depths closed me round, the weeds were wrapped about my head.* Jonah famously emerges after three days, transformed and resolute, and goes forth to Nineveh, where the king actually takes heed of his warning. In a sort of Pascal's Wager fashion, the king says *God may or may not smite us, but we shouldn't take chances,* and commands everyone to don sackcloths, rub ashes all over themselves and even their beasts, and start fasting. Jonah then leaves the city walls to camp out in a hut to watch what God will do next. When he realizes that, after all of his effort, God has forgiven the sinful denizens of Nineveh, he becomes angry.

This is the part Mom loves to retell, using her quietly excited teacher-voice and careful gestures. God sends down a gourd plant to grow over Jonah at night and give him comfort as he waits in the sun, for which Jonah is grateful. Then, the next night, God sends a tiny worm to destroy the plant, and Jonah gets angry all over again. The book ends with God telling Jonah, *You're upset about losing this little gourd plant that grew up overnight and yet you want me to wipe out a whole city of six score thousand repentant sinners? And their cattle?*

When I asked her if Jonah stopped being angry with God in the end and also forgave the people of Nineveh, she said that you never find out. The book just ends with God's question about the cattle, leaving room for the reader to think about how he or she would respond. Ronald nodded in agreement, giving meticulous attention to his unruly taco. It was the smallness of God's gesture that Mom loved, and the way the story showed God's sense of humor, the gentleness with which He teaches Jonah about forgiveness, admonishing us to look beyond ourselves, our anger at the world, at our foiled missions, at the injustices, real and perceived, and to recognize that everyone is deserving of forgiveness and salvation. The lesson arrives through the tiny, the finite, the gourd plant, the worm.

Mom has always exulted in the small. Over one spring breakfast soon after Dad died, she excitedly recounted the most fantastic thing that had happened over the past week. She was moving a chair on the front porch and felt something strange on the weave of its back. Inspecting, she found a chrysalis, which she knew housed a monarch because she used to grow them with students in her classroom. First thing every morning for a week, she'd check its progress on the back of the chair, feel it harden inside, and see the pupa's colors darken to a milky black and orange. One morning, the chrysalis was split open and empty, drops of blood on the concrete porch below the chair. She was so joyful, explaining that the butterfly shoots blood into its wings as they form. She didn't need to see the monarch, watch its tentative unfurling and first wobbly wing beats; it was enough to see the drops of blood. I realized that she truly lived in a poetic state of gratitude for the finite and awe of the infinite. It was the key to Mom's balance and spiritual happiness. I'd always envied her faith, the capacity for universal forgiveness. My fear is that I'm more like Dad, angry in his hut, in a disgruntled vigil over the city, aggrieved that things didn't turn out as he'd wanted them to. For Mom, though, we're all citizens of Nineveh, worthy of forgiveness, trying out our sackcloths, rubbing our beasts with ash, hoping we're right about God's mercy.

We finished up our Convict Tacos and Sprites, and I organized our Styrofoam containers to take over to the trash, by now overflowing with the remnants of hundreds of shared meals. All around us in the cafeteria, parents, children, siblings, friends, lovers, were winding down their visits in attitudes of almost unbearable intimacy, leaning across tables and holding hands, standing in prolonged hugs. We knew that many of these people were from New Orleans, as our city feeds much of the population of Angola. We knew that emanating from this place was another vast unknowable sphere of pain and loss that many of these men had caused or been victims of. Ronald wanted a picture of the three of us together, so we lined up with others in the waning minutes of visiting time to pose in front of the backdrop. It was a lovely painting, maybe eight feet by eight feet, a soft, nearly autumnal palette of bright green trees and warm gold grasses, a landscape in transition. Through the middle of it, a chalk-gray river faded into a haze of trees and winding banks. As we approached it together to pose and smile, I wondered if the painter, most likely an inmate, had done it from memory of a place he once knew, or if he'd created it entirely out of desire.

DECEMBER

Sharing Bread

We found ourselves at the bottom of the year, on the final page of our kitchen's Saturn Bar calendar, whose blunt utilitarian design has not changed for decades. Every year, the first week of January, I lay my two bucks down on the bar for my calendar and every year it looks exactly the same, the ringed planet remains slightly tilted though centered above the St. Claude Avenue address and phone number, the red border and blue lettering on the white field never vary. Only the days, years, centuries, have changed on it. December is the holdout month — all the others torn away, maybe a bit of March or August snagged beneath the grip of the staples. Tucked between the calendar and wall was Chris's portentous New Year's postcard with the Mayan calendar that we kept up all year long. Dad had died shortly after we received it.

Next to Chris's year-old postcard was a recent Christmas card from my brother's client in a chartreuse envelope, stamped DEATH ROW with the same wavering ink across the tops of the letters. He wished *Love, Peace and the Joy of Jesus to fill our hearts and homes.* His case, like most death-penalty cases, would continue to grind through the system. Ronald had been lucky, the dedication of Dad and his colleagues had paid off.

With Dad gone, the holidays were fraught. He had been a true patriarch, which meant that his absence created some fraying of relationships and shifting of roles within the family. Growing up in a crowd, you sometimes forget how thick the attachments can become and how they work on you in ways you don't even realize. In an effort to stabilize, we were spending too much time together, permissive holiday drinking taking on an extra dimension. As middle-aged siblings, our problems were becoming more baroque, and our children's problems more complex. And now here was December, so dense with familial and social obligation, all the scheduled giving and the annual rituals, much of which I do love, especially now that I have children of my own. Plus I just missed my dad. He loved Christmas, a sanctioned time to indulge his love of excess and family, his outsized generosity.

Because of the way the civil and Catholic liturgical calendars align, we end the year celebrating the same event we celebrated back in January with the Epiphany: the birth of Christ. But in December, the focus is still pretty much on the human miracle of birth (save the virgin-mother angle), like every other human miracle of birth. Each Christmas morning since we were children, my mother has read us, and now reads to our children, too, the story of the Nativity. Before the presents, before the too-huge breakfast and a day spent recovering from our bounty, selves overextended in so many ways, she focuses us on that one moment, on the humble birth of possibility, of redemption through love and forgiveness, in a straw-strewn stable, animals and angels in attendance. As you got older, that moment was made even more precious because you had to protect it in your heart against what you learned soon followed the birth — thousands of years of bloodshed and intolerance in that babe's name. But still, the year is bookended with good news, even if suffering is unavoidably sandwiched in between.

December's ECRG reading felt like a true holiday offering from

Michael L., newish to the group, early thirties, a writer and singer for a band whose music is all dark sustained tension and no release. We taught together in the same department, and with his uniform of black T-shirt and jeans, and a heavy curriculum of Eastern European literature, I'd been surprised to learn he was from San Jose, California. Michael L. had chosen a selection of Brazilian author Clarice Lispector's *crônicas,* published during the late 1960s and early '70s. The crônica is a literary form unique to Brazilian journalism, like a regular newspaper or magazine column, but short or long, topical or philosophical, produced by some of the most prominent writers of the day, who were given unimaginable freedom of style and content. To American consumers of newspapers, it might seem crazy that Lispector's intimate, strange pieces appeared in a daily paper. Hard to imagine waking up in the morning, mind fresh and receptive to the new day, reading about local politics, soccer scores, sales on shoes, and then coming across this:

I wake up in a rage. I am thoroughly dissatisfied with this life. Most people are dead without realizing it or they live like charlatans. And instead of giving, love makes demands. Those who show us affection expect us at least to satisfy some of their needs. Telling lies brings remorse. And not to lie is a gift the world does not deserve. And I am not even capable of smashing crockery like the semi-paralysed little girl when she took her revenge. I am not semi-paralysed. Although something deep down tells me we are all semi-paralysed. And we die without so much as an explanation. And worst of all — we live without so much as an explanation.

That Lispector crônica, called *"Dies Irae"* ("Day of Wrath"), read by Brazilians at cafés, bus stops, and kitchen tables on October 14,

1967, goes on from there for about a thousand more words, scorches through the papery layers of the quotidian straight to the bloody heart of the day as you sip your coffee.

Lispector, considered one of the greatest Brazilian writers of the twentieth century, is a literary figure whose biography sometimes overshadows her writing, because it's just too interesting and instructive, in a painful sort of way. Her Jewish parents escaped war-ravaged Ukraine months after her birth there, in 1920, after an arduous, years-long journey of privation and anti-Semitic persecution, during which time her mother was gang-raped by Russian soldiers, contracting syphilis, which eventually rendered her "semi-paralysed." The family ended up in the northeastern Brazilian city of Recife, her brilliant father struggling as a street peddler, her ailing mother reduced to sad statuary in a rocker on their balcony, until she died when Clarice was nine. Lispector never saw her birthplace again, and Portuguese was always her "native" language. From these dramatically muddled geographical origins, identity and belonging were themes that became central to her work. Lispector often claimed that she "belonged to Brazil" while asserting her transcendent "otherness," which many critics connect to a tradition of Eastern European Jewish mysticism. She seemed to live and write both the tension of the border and the full-feeling of the universal. Identity was one border she tried to dissolve to achieve a kind of divinity or understanding, but of course, it's also one we need, as people, for our sanity and humanity. So, which borders do we embrace, as individuals? Which do we transcend, as a species?

Lispector's first novel, *Near to the Wild Heart*, about a young woman struggling spiritually with the conformist demands of marriage, was published when she was in her early twenties, shortly before her own marriage to a diplomat. It was immediately pronounced one of the most important works of modern Brazilian literature, unleashing a cascade of literary comparisons, as such pronouncements do. When she was likened to Sartre, Lispector countered, "My nausea is different from Sartre's because when I was a child I couldn't stand milk, and almost vomited it back up when I was forced to drink it. They dripped lemon juice into my mouth. I mean, I know what nausea is, in my entire body, in my entire soul. It's not Sartrean." For her, "existence" did not precede "essence." There was no need to create meaning through our actions, because we *were* meaning, naturally, bodily. As Lispector biographer Benjamin Moser points out, her philosophical leanings were far more influenced by Spinoza, who believed that as creatures of nature, which is itself part of God, we are all bound to everything by divinity. Living is the navigation of that divinity.

When Lispector was compared to Virginia Woolf she rejected that, too, not on literary or philosophical but on moral grounds. She didn't want to forgive Woolf for killing herself, saying, "The terrible duty is to go to the end." Though born of suffering, and suffering greatly herself, in another of her crônicas Lispector said she "valued life much too dearly" to kill herself.

Her love of life would become increasingly challenging. As what tethered her to the Trivial Plane fell away — her structured life as a diplomat's wife after her divorce, the magnetizing beauty of her youth as she aged — she increasingly occupied the Tragic Plane. Her personal eccentricity became more pronounced, as if she were giving herself over to the strangeness and difficulty that her creative work was known for. Theatrical makeup, hostess-distressing social anxiety, insomnia, middle-of-the-night phone calls to friends. Her two addictions, cigarettes and sleeping pills, led to a terrible fire one night in her apartment, causing her nightgown to melt to her legs, leaving her with excruciating burns over much of her body and a permanently disfigured writing hand, though her face was spared.

Months of hospital convalescence followed. As they removed the stitches from between her fingers, she did not miss the opportunity to scream, loud and hard and long, not only from the pain, but "for the past the present and even the future." This wasn't Ivan Ilyich's wrenching deathbed-revelation scream, but a scream for the knowledge that she seemed to have been born with.

For someone deeply concerned with the eternal, the mystical, Lispector was also so vain about her looks that toward the end of her life she hired a professional makeup artist to come to her home monthly and apply semi-permanent cosmetics. The power of female vanity should never be underestimated — he was instructed to do the job even if she was passed out from the sleeping pills. He complained that the mascara was the hardest to do when she was in that state. Makeup is one of the most common of identity borders, an acknowledgment of the temporal, the material, the reflexivity of the social self. A beautiful friend in her fifties once told me that one of the worst things about aging was that no one looks at you anymore. You spend half a lifetime taking in the gaze, building part of your identity around it, and then the gaze, tenuous to begin with, disappears, and you're removed from the larger network of physical desire.

Years ago, on an uncommonly breezy summer afternoon in the French Quarter, I was having drinks at the Chart Room, doors open to the street so tables and air-conditioning straddled the hot sidewalk. Short skirts and sundresses were being whipped up before hands could subdue them, creating an almost comic, helpless concatenation of male whiplash. Something so animal was igniting up and down Chartres Street, among all types of people, flashing flesh and naked glancing. It occurred to me that whether you find it threatening or affirming when your face, breasts, and ass are checked out on the street by men, you're just one of millions being fleetingly appraised on the sidewalks of the world, a world perpetually replenished with younger women, more beautiful women, who will themselves age, because one day each of us will gray into anonymity on the gray sidewalks of the world and then what? Lispector's Spinozan exaltation of the natural must have been complicated by her being so abundantly gifted with physical beauty, only to endure the treachery of nature, indifferently taking it all away. Then again, another friend, on her fifty-first birthday, told me that that's one of the most liberating things about aging. Not worrying about the gaze anymore, you have more energy to focus on yourself.

The crônicas appeared toward the end of Lispector's relatively short life (she died on the eve of her fifty-seventh birthday), some of them dictated from her hospital bed. They were written with the open and fearless vulnerability of someone who has let go of a great deal of worldliness. While she was famous for her ambitious, abstruse novels and short stories, some of which she herself claimed not to understand, many readers connected more readily to the democratic, accessible format of her crônicas, these personal missives to the public: short narratives, memories, anecdotes, philosophical fragments. Some of the pieces Michael L. had selected were only a couple of sentences long, like "The Gift":

Perhaps love is to give one's own solitude to others? For it is the very last thing we have to offer.

Or "Searching":

A cat did so much wailing during the night that I have rarely felt such compassion for the living. It sounded like grief, and in human and animal terms that is what it was. But could it have been sorrow, or was it "searching," that is to say "searching for"? For everything alive is searching for something or someone.

The search. There it was again. At every ECRG meeting wine bottles are uncorked, quotes on pages located, reading glasses adjusted, and *the search* reasserts itself. Preacher-kings, philosophers, scientists, suicides, swimmers, lawyers, *chanteurs,* traveling salesmen, poets. All searchers. As Lispector points out, searching is a natural state for us animals. In a world that's constantly endangering our natural state, the search is made more difficult, even as searching has become such a routine function of our daily lives. We now have "search engines" prowling a vast conglomeration of human knowledge and information, but those same technologies, while helpful and world-expanding, are also vastly exploited to sell us stuff and dazzle us with our own self-fascination. The real search gets shut down.

But what is the "real search"? Every few meetings someone inevitably asks, with varying levels of exasperation, either mock or gentle or intense, "What's the point?" What were we trying to achieve? That night in December when the question lanced the discussion, the room quieted as responses pooled at the surface of our thoughts.

Well, Michael L. finally said, all he knew was that he's happiest when he's having these types of discussions about art or literature, or having sex. I totally understood. That was all part of the search, animal and human. If done properly, with the right people, both are ways of connecting with others, a sort of enacting what we're here for in a larger sense, of contributing to the elevation of the self through the dissolution of the self. I'd add spending time with my kids and family to Michael L.'s happiness equation.

Lispector claimed that she had "three experiences" in life: "I was born to love others, I was born to write, and I was born to raise children." For her, being a mother trumped the other two experiences, though it was the most fraught and difficult, the one that you have the least control over and that has the deepest moral resonance. "With the birth of a child every woman puts her hand to her throat and knows her child will have to fall as Jesus did, bear the cross and fall under the weight of it."

Since this is a feeling I experience with such abiding dread sometimes, I wrote that quote in my daily planner, alongside chores and household projects and reminders. When Mom and I were driving up to Angola to visit Ronald, riding through ghostly winter swamps and fallow farmland, the refineries enervating every horizon with their confounding systems, I took advantage of those captive highway hours to ask her the questions that pile up between visits, ones I'm always forgetting to ask at breakfast. I read her that Lispector quote and asked her if she'd ever felt that same nagging apprehension of having given birth to a being that is going to suffer and die. Eight of them, actually.

She'd insisted on driving up, and watching her face in profile, I immediately felt bad for asking. She said no, never. She remembered so clearly that when she took Rebecca and Rachel for their first checkup, she walked through the examination room doors with the babies and our pediatrician said, "Those are your jewels you're holding." Mom teared up, and paused, hands even on the steering wheel. "And I always felt so positive about you all and never dwelt on the negative. Children must all be loved, fully, not knowing what they become. Like when God puts us out in the world, knowing that some of us will fall greatly. He loves us all equally."

We had turned onto Highway 66, the final, most bucolic stretch of the ride to Angola, cinematic pastures with wide-chinked, canted sheds and tractors rust-frozen somewhere in the last century. Mom seemed to have moved on from the conversation, and ruefully pointed out the sign for Solitude Road, and another for the Cat Island Wildlife Refuge, home to colossal thousand-year-old bald cypresses, which we absolutely had to visit the next time we were here. I was still mulling. Why hadn't I inherited Mom's positivity? Could I will it into me? Why did my mind seek out the trouble, the problem, the threat? And even though unconditional love couldn't save her two youngest, her faith in it never wavered — she still reaches back through all of those harrowing, difficult years to her two jewels. When we arrived at Angola's visitors' building, Mom, the most motherly mom I've ever encountered, remained chatty and cheerful as she was processed with so many other mothers who'd traveled long distances, some of whom knew their sons would die in Angola, chatty and cheerful as she was closed into the plywood box and sniffed by a drug dog, guided through metal detectors, sent back to the car to put on a sweater because her white long-sleeved cotton shirt was too sheer, patted down by guards and paperwork-checked, as suspect as any of us.

But Mom's positivity is not without pain. She does share the same knowledge as Lispector — that of the inevitable fall. Lispector's first-born son was schizophrenic, and she helplessly watched his decline from brilliant precociousness to screeching madness. Having witnessed Susan's struggle with her firstborn's addiction and Mom and Dad's decade-long grappling with the twins, I approached motherhood with caution, knowing that no matter how hard you try, sometimes genetics or chemistry or evolution works against your maternal love. You can only love your hardest and do your best. Since I associate my own experience of childbirth with the wholesale destruction of Hurricane Katrina, the bureaucratic language of disaster response came naturally to my attitude toward child rearing, akin to an Army Corps of Engineers spokesperson at a press conference: "managing expectations" and "mitigating hazards."

This idea of life as a series of mitigations and mediations was something Sara had been especially interested in the month before when she chose those seasonal poems for us to read, particularly Elizabeth Bishop's wintry "In the Waiting Room." The soon-to-be-seven-year-old speaker has an epiphany about selfhood, that she was a human, a female, living on this earth like other human females, different, but also one of them. She is in the waiting room of a dentist's office surrounded by "arctics and overcoats, lamps and magazines." For Sara, that line in particular and the poem in general were about a moment of breaking through the mediating elements that keep us from experiencing the metaphysical, the natural world. Months after that meeting, Sara said she almost got that Bishop line tattooed on her wrist but she couldn't commit to a font. Bishop lived in Brazil, briefly befriended Lispector, a notoriously difficult task, and translated some of her short stories, though she wrote exasperatedly to Robert Lowell that the combination of Lispector's "Russian massive inertia and Brazilian does pile up."

The Lispector crônica we spent a lot of time discussing at the December ECRG, "Sharing Bread," was also about an unexpected moment of unmediated existence, and was my personal favorite of the evening:

It was Saturday and we had been forced into accepting an invitation to dinner. But each of us valued our Saturday evening far too much to waste it on a couple whom we found rather boring. Each of us had experienced happiness at some time or another and had been left with the mark of desire. As for me, I desired everything.

For a couple of paragraphs Lispector goes on about how much she and the other guests do not want to be there, languishing in the living room without hunger or anticipation. "Waiting for dinner to be served, we drank dispiritedly, toasting resentment." Then they are led to the dining room, where they are stunned:

The table was covered with solemn abundance. Sheaves of corn had been piled up on the white tablecloth. And there were red apples, enormous yellow carrots, round tomatoes with skins ready to burst, juicy green courgettes, pineapples of a malign ferocity, tranquil, golden oranges, gherkins bristling like porcupines, cucumbers stretched tight over watery flesh, hollow red peppers that made our eyes smart — were all entangled in moist whiskers of maize, tinged with crimson like outlined lips. And bunches of grapes. The purplest of black grapes anxiously awaiting the moment to be crushed. Nor did they mind who should crush them — like the mistress of the household in times gone by. The tomatoes were not round for anyone: for the atmosphere, the circular atmosphere. Saturday was for anyone who might turn up. And the orange would sweeten the tongues of the first to arrive. Beside the plate of each unwanted guest, the woman who washed the feet of strangers had placed — without choosing or loving us — a sheaf of wheat, a bunch of fiery radishes or a red slice of watermelon with its glossy seeds. All broken up by the Spanish acidity of green lemons. In the earthenware jugs there was milk, as if it had been transported across a rocky desert with the goats. Wine that was almost black after all of the pressing, shuddered in earthenware bowls. Everything cleansed of perverse human desire. Everything as it is and not as we wished it would be. Simply existing and intact. Just as a field exists. Just as mountains exist. Just as men and women exist, but not us with our greed. Just as Saturday exists. Simply existing. It exists.

After I read that passage aloud (I couldn't help myself), Michael L. said one of the reasons he chose this crônica was that it seemed to him a hopeful, exquisite act of using language to try to describe an experience that's in some ways beyond language. I was surprised by his invocation of hope. In his own life and writing and music, Michael L. lists toward the disturbing and the spare, and I wouldn't have thought he'd be attracted to the dynamic opulence of this piece. Then again, that was my own blind spot. Even in my admiration of his work, I often missed the tenderness that existed within the difficulty, and besides, he had to be somewhat in love with life to create at all. Lispector certainly was. We grabbed the sensual and spiritual richness of her writing in handfuls. Discussed her curious, almost cruel ambivalence toward the Christ-like hostess, her Spinozan fusing of essence and existence.

"Was that a real table? A metaphor? Both?"

"Milk and wine — intoxication and nourishment at the same time — an ideal state."

"Here we are complaining all the time, and here is all this bounty, right in front of us."

"Our expectations are diminishing us and how we experience the world. We miss too much when clouded by expectations."

"Being beyond desire is a kind of freedom, a transcendence."

The word "transcendence" drove me once more to *A Concise Dictionary of Existentialism,* where I found this from Simone de Beauvoir: "It is the existence of other men that tears each man out of his immanence and enables him to fulfill the truth of his being, to complete himself through transcendence, through escape towards some objective, through enterprise." (*See also:* Americanism; Being.) Though it was the lack of objective and lack of enterprise that brought about Lispector's transcendent experience of the meal, the quote did speak to the core of the ECRG project: the necessity of others in our search to find meaning in ourselves, of entering the unwalled city as individuals and receiving communal acceptance and succor. Lispector takes it further — her dissolution into a divine state is made possible not only through the presence of other people, but also through the presence of other beasts and flora and all of the gifts of nature. She ends this crônica:

We ate. Like a horde of locusts, we gradually covered the earth. As absorbed as those who cultivate existence, by planting and harvesting, by living and dying and eating. I ate with the honesty of someone who does not belie what he is eating. I ate that food and not its name. God was never possessed by what He is. Brusque, contented and austere, the food was saying: eat, eat and share among you. Everything there was mine. This was the father's table. I ate without affection. I ate without any feelings of compassion. And without giving way to hope. I ate without any trace of regret. And I was wholly deserving of that food. For I cannot always be my brother's keeper, nor can I be my own keeper. Alas, I no longer love myself. I have no desire to forge life because existence already exists. It exists like the ground we tread. Without a word of love. In total silence. But your satisfaction is akin to mine. We are strong and we eat. Bread is love between strangers.

I'd spent much of the morning of the December ECRG shopping, trying to echo the magnificence of the spread in "Sharing Bread." But it's nearly impossible in a typical American supermarket, where the fruit often has tiny stickers on it, printed with corporate logos, bar codes, and, most depressingly, websites. I searched for a pineapple of "malign ferocity" but the supermarket was like what Lispector wrote to a friend about Switzerland: "There are no demons here." The pineapples were all collared and tagged DOLE. The tomatoes were pale and bland or organic and overpriced, the grapes tidy and unsensual. But I did my best, which was also the opposite of the point of "Sharing Bread." I made the mistake of going to the supermarket with expectations, when it was the lack of expectation and desire that made such an extraordinary experience for Lispector at the dinner party. Even Lispector's hostess, when browsing the market stalls of Rio de Janeiro, probably did not have the expectation of creating a metaphysical experience for her dinner guests. I cobbled together a lame simulation, but passable among a group of friends who appreciated the effort, and the spread was bettered and enlivened by what everyone else brought — the wine, mini-cannoli from an Italian bakery, Christine's casserole, Ellen's rosemary cookies, Sara's elaborately frosted brownies. Our sons begged off bedtime so they could make multiple incursions on the special holiday bounty. As we talked, the food on the table diminished, but the real abundance lasted late into the night and we edged closer to the end of the year together.

———————

Six months later, though, I did finally find that ferocious pineapple, in a large covered market in central Mexico among hundreds of assiduously arranged pyramids of fruits and vegetables and incessant, melodic hawking. A fierce, spiky row of pineapples lined the top of one stall like a crude battlement. The recognition was immediate. I chose the most malign-looking one to bring back to Brad and the boys, its rangy crown taking up too much space in my market bag, threatening the overripe mangoes and thin-skinned tomatoes.

The day after I found the ferocious pineapple, we all took a long, steep walk high up on the *mirador* over the five-hundred-year-old town of San Miguel de Allende where old stone houses are built into an ancient stone hillside, took in the panorama of lakes and hills and blunt new developments on the outskirts, and then made our way back down through the untended beauty of the winding and plunging alleys and stairways with draping ivy and ankle-twisting cobbles. I was annoyed because Otto had chosen some kind of awful Cheetos *"extremos"* as a snack from a little store by the mirador, and his fingers and mouth blazed life-jacket orange. Was even more annoyed at myself because I'd let him, and had nothing to clean him up with. Then, turning a stairway where a large wedge of sky opened up between rooftops and walls, I saw some big snowy egrets swoop and dive. A little farther down, at the stairway's landing, was an enormous tree rising out of a small plaza below, filled with dozens of these egrets, branches clotted with their nests. Though egrets are common enough in south Louisiana, I'd never seen this before, in the middle of a town, so many high up in a tree. But I did recognize the sharp odor of their nesting. Two years earlier, during the *Deepwater Horizon* oil spill, on a boat in the Gulf of Mexico with some biologists and my photographer friend, skirting rings of soiled boom laid down to protect the flat barrier islands where birds nest, I had commented on what I thought was the hot, rank smell of the oil glimmering in sheets on the water around us. One of the biologists corrected me — it was from the birds. "I love that smell," she said. "That means they're nesting."

When we got closer to the plaza, we saw that the walkways with red curved balustrades and the street below were all splattered, layered, covered white with bird shit. The squawking commotion in the tree was constant, loud, and impressive, and as we continued down the stairs, the sound mingled with the familiar tonal drone of a Mass coming from a church, the Santa Cruz del Chorro, built onto the side of the hill in the seventeenth century. In the side courtyard stood a large wooden *santa cruz* (holy cross) painted with symbols of Christ's Passion, three dice that the Roman soldiers used to gamble for his garments, the fiery *corazón*, the spear. The church's façade was level with the assembly of egrets, its heavy wooden doors open toward it. On a small stone terrace in front of the church were a few benches where some older women watched kids too restless for the pews and a couple of young people sitting on the ground with their backs against the church, laptops open, absorbed in a different sort of congress. Did the church have Wi-Fi?

I stood on the terrace, my heart filling, my eyes stinging from emotion. All the world wordlessly, deeply connected through just — being. It was a Lispector moment, a felt accumulation of an intense year of loss, reading, thinking, talking, listening, a gift of the ECRG. At the Chorro, all these signs and all this activity were arranged into this one unexpected moment. Each one necessary, each one accepted into a wild harmony.

The people in the barrio could easily have gotten rid of the nesting colony, and I wondered what they thought of it, especially the person whose car was still parked (maybe broken down?) below the tree, guano-glazed from hood to trunk. But for now they tolerated the din and shit and the smell, and were rewarded with this spectacular vision, an auxiliary congregation of beautiful white egrets. During a quiet moment, maybe kneeling after receiving Communion, could the parishioners hear the birds behind them? When the priest raised his arms in benediction, could he see the birds framed in the threshold, messing with their nests in noisy pairs?

We hung around marveling for a bit, Otto and I in the side courtyard of the church with the santa cruz, strung with faded cut-paper decorations from a long-past feast day and lined with potted bougainvillea, as Brad and Silas wandered the shady terraces and porticos. When they signaled to us that it was time to move on, I knelt down, spit on my thumbs, and tried to wipe the awful orange from Otto's wincing face. We continued down, avoiding the shit-covered paths below the cathedral of egrets, which wasn't difficult, because there were lots of other paths to take.

NEW YEAR'S EVE

Tanks Versus Chickens

On the last day of 2012, I was a little hungover from a New Year's Eve's Eve party, having failed the Test of the Open Bar for about the hundredth time in my life. I was disappointed in myself, and it seemed that this year was going to end as it had begun, in a cloud of dull confusion. Was I ever going to learn my limit? Learn that just because there's so much being offered, I don't have to keep consuming? In a bid for productivity, I drove downriver through the lower Ninth Ward across the Industrial Canal, once breached and murderous, now repaired and functioning, to St. Bernard Parish to buy fireworks, because like a lot of things in Orleans Parish, fireworks are illegal but ubiquitous. When we were kids, Dad would drive across the parish line to buy fireworks twice a year, New Year's and Fourth of July, and return with big paper bags laden with lurid and exciting little packages, just waiting to be exploded. My excitement over fireworks has remained undiminished since childhood, and when those striped tents start appearing just outside of town, it makes me giddy to be an adult, with my own car and money and enthusiasms. Now I get to come home with the bags full of fun, rationing out the black snakes and smoke bombs over the afternoon until the sun goes down and anarchy takes over.

When I arrived home, I asked the boys for a little alone time, and shut the bedroom door, so I could at least dose myself with some reading, try to redeem a tiny rational part of my soul since I'd once again poisoned my body. *Fugitive Essays,* by Josiah Royce, had been mute on my bedside table for days now, and I thought I'd crack it open. I'd bought it the week before, after a holiday lunch gone bad.

Every year around Christmas, my sisters and I take Rachel's son, our nephew, to lunch at a nice white-tablecloth restaurant in the French Quarter. Our dad had been an imperfect father figure to him, by turns indulgent and overly strict. His steadiest, enduring father figure was the boyfriend whom Rachel broke up with before she killed herself, the generous and kind man who'd helped rear him since he was a toddler and has never left his life. Still, having been raised mostly by about a dozen auxiliary parents — aunts, uncles, grandparents — he must've felt like he was growing up in a swarm of opinions and judgment with no real authority.

I arrived at the Aunts' Lunch late and irritable because of traffic from some stupid bowl game being played in town and all the stupid tourists. We had a bad table, next to the service area, the nexus of tension in most restaurants, where harried back-of-the-house meets impatient front-of-the-house. And the scene was already strained when I sat down to the tepid Beefeater martini waiting for me. Apparently I'd missed some heavy exchange about *responsibility*. Since Dad had died months before our nephew's high school graduation, I imagine, we'd been overbearing in our concern. He was foundering, with school, with work, and we all hurried to right him. Soon, after the food arrived, a minor argument escalated effortlessly, and before you knew it, there was a dramatic exit from the restaurant by my nephew that caused head turning by the other dressed-up holiday diners.

Like my nephew, I was so over the holiday crush of family, the lifetime of associations activated each time we pull up a chair to the table. But my exit was more low-key. I threw down some money for the bill and left the others still seated, mid-entrée, mid-entreaty for me to stay. Alone in the French Quarter, early afternoon, I didn't want to go to a bar, didn't want to shop, already holiday-sick of consumption. Instead I went to an old used-book store nearby, with Parisian-high ceilings and shelves that require a sliding ladder on a rail to access. When I was younger, the store used to feel timeless and eternal, but that afternoon, older and feeling overwhelmed by how fast everything in the world was changing, I saw the cypress cabinets and shelves and the vellum, leather, cardboard hardbacks and pulpy paperbacks as achingly vulnerable, a match strike away from obliteration, fuel for an inferno.

Near the top of the narrow stairs, I was searching the philosophy section for potential ECRG material when I came across the essays by Josiah Royce, an American philosopher I'd never heard of but guessed I should have, given the amount of shelf space his books took up. The book was printed in 1920, its title embossed in thin faint gold on black. The table of contents held irresistible chapter titles like "The Decay of Earnestness," "Doubting and Working," "The Practical Significance of Pessimism." I randomly flipped to an essay, "George Eliot as a Religious Teacher," from 1881, and read:

> I have tried to show that George Eliot's effort to express the religious consciousness in terms of natural, not of supernatural, facts is, in part, a sequence from the philosophical movement of her age....She was an appreciative student of many systems, but she let none of them rule her. She heard what they had to say, and then went to actual human life to see whether the theory held good....Thus in her writings the best power of analytic vision is joined with depth of emotion.

I brought the book down to the register, one of the few reasonable post-martini purchases I've ever made.

In bed a week later, the afternoon of New Year's Eve, weighed down by lack of sleep and a little self-loathing, I chose one of the shorter essays, "Doubting and Working." The edges of the pages were deckled, blade-cut near the beginning of the previous century. The margins were nice and roomy, but the typeface a little tight. Royce begins with the basic problem of individual perception, from the physiological, like color blindness, to the psychological, like the "ghostly" projections of our public selves, and how that complicates even the simplest human interaction. For Royce, our inherent, myriad imperfections combined with our penchant for conviction is a real problem. "Exposed to the largest errors of observation, to the greatest defects of memory, to the incalculable interference of passion and prejudice, to the disadvantage of being surrounded by numberless obscure associations, we, thinking beings, live in this amusing chaos of our fleeting conscious states and spend our time in making assertions about the universe."

This skepticism wasn't new, it's something the species has been considering for millennia, but apparently we need to be reminded of it, often. Especially now that technology has exploded this "amusing chaos," turned it inside out and given it corporately owned plat-forms. It was already so difficult to see anything clearly, and now a fire hose of pronouncement and conviction, fact and analysis, mis-information and marketing, is aimed at our consciousness every time we turn on a device. So, do we give up having opinions? Give up on religious certitude and give in to nihilism? Give up social media? No, Royce admonishes from the nineteenth century, fountain pen in hand, we are active beings who just need to work at these things, find the right approach. Then he lays out what he feels is the most honest starting point for the *search*.

I admit that looking for truth implies a postulate that truth is worth the looking for, and a postulate that the world is such that it would be a good thing to know the nature of the world. Yet I still cling to my rule, and say, begin to search for truth by doubting all that you have without criticism come to hold as true. If you fail to doubt everything, doubt all you can. Doubt not because doubting is a good end, but because it is a good beginning. Doubt not for amusement, but as a matter of duty. Doubt not superficially, but with thoroughness. Doubt not flippantly, but with the deepest — it may be with the saddest — earnestness. Doubt as you would undergo a surgical operation, because it is necessary to thought-health. So only can you hope to attain convictions that are worth having. If you do not wish to think, then I have nothing to say. Then, indeed, you need not doubt at all, but take all you please for granted. But who then cares at all what you happen to fancy about the world?

Exhilarated by this, I read the passage a few times. But then I doubted whether I could commit myself to such strenuous doubting. Did I even have the time for the required investigation, for that first step, the one that threatened to derail every project? I lay in bed and thought of some things that were making the end of 2012 so awful: my inability to let go of childish sibling tensions; a gridlocked Congress about to drive us over some fiscal cliff; the slaughter of twenty first-graders in Newtown, Connecticut, days before Christmas; my own first-grader building LEGO zombie-fighting forts, militarizing his mini-figures; and even the overplayed Mayan apocalypse, people we knew fleeing to the countryside just to be on the safe side, in case that ancient prophecy of doom proved right.

I decided I was okay with ending my year headachy and foggy, with renewed commitment to doubt. Doubt was an invitation to the world, an openness to others, the same way that reading and conversation can be. The Royce quote seemed a signpost telling me we were on the right track with the ECRG. Through a full year of monthly gatherings and cases of wine, we'd built a perfect mechanism for creating doubt, for sustaining the search — a roomful of people willing to engage one another. Over the year, those who were searching for hard answers or group therapy had drifted away. At the December meeting, the twelve who'd remained decided the ECRG would continue on, excited about more opportunities to be inspired or challenged, ambivalent or confused. More opportunities to change our minds, to feel the pressure of the void on thousands of years of thinking. We'd continue on, to help one another out, to provide sustenance and comfort in the darker quarters of the unwalled city. That the ECRG had formed during a time of such grief and uncertainty for me was almost miraculous. All the words and ideas, written and spoken, nourished a deepening sense of what it means to be alive, to lose people we love, to think and feel through the loss.

By evening, I had vanquished my hangover with champagne and companionship, though not drinking so much as to poison the first day of 2013. We built a small bonfire in the field across the street from our house, and were joined by neighbors, friends, some ECRG-ers. The existential plumber arrived with his wife and kids, all of us good friends, and split time between fireside fellowship and standing on the edge of the field by himself, working through some arcane metaphysical problem and making sure the kids didn't run into the street. Case and Nina showed up together, reunited in what appeared to be an uneasy but affectionate truce, Nina bearing a goopy, delicious blueberry dessert and Case a subdued deference to Nina. No one pried, respectful of the special mystery of all relationships.

Tristan passed around a voluptuous bottle of brandy, and we took turns warming our insides.

The neighborhood had been exploding since dusk, and none of us gathered around the fire could recall so many fireworks being set off on one day. It was as though people wanted to obliterate 2012, drive it out with as much smoke and light and noise as possible. Brad said it reminded him of Cholula, Mexico, where we've visited friends a few times. In that town, fireworks go off year-round, night and day, accompanying processions and feast days celebrated by Cholula's many churches. According to legend, Cortés wanted to punish Aztec sympathizers by building a church to replace each of their 365 temples, one for every day of the year, but he only ever made it to about fifty, still a lot for a town that size. In the late sixteenth century, the Spanish built a basilica on top of the town's ancient pyramid, effectively merging native gods with Catholic saints. Sometimes it seemed like our apartment facing the main plaza was under siege, dawn often met with searing hisses and errant booms. When we finally asked a Cholulan, "Why fireworks? All the time?" he explained, "We're trying to get the attention of the saints."

For a moment I tried to connect this to Dad's pyrotechnic ebullience — what was he trying to get the attention of? The cosmos? The neighbors? After he would arrive home with the fireworks, it would take forever for the sun to go down so we could crowd the end of the driveway with glowing bamboo punks in hand, or clenched between teeth, Clint Eastwood–style, and start the raucous, sulfuric display, the only such one on our block of modest mansions. All eight of us would be out there, picking through the bags for our favorites. Roman candles, bottle rockets, garlands of firecrackers. Every year, we marveled at some novelty, like the spinning wheel nailed to the telephone pole that erupted with little Chinese lanterns, and every year some dud disappointed us, did not live up to its dramatic packaging. Mom would occupy the porch with Rebecca and Rachel — always littler, always apart — guarding them from the activity of the older kids, which was extra chaotic in the flashing dark and smoke. Dad alternately directed from a chair on the lawn or lit the Glorious Flower Fountain himself in the middle of the street while we looked out for cars.

Like me, he was probably just after some ephemeral, semi-dangerous fun, a semi-harmless spectacle. Whatever it was, for a few hours he kept us all attentive to the fuse, the spark, the payoff. Kept us looking up at the night sky in anticipation of blue green red glittering showers and down at the sidewalk for some small, bright transformation. Kept our ears open to the booming and crackling air. All of us together, a family in the moment, futureless and happy. In the morning, shreds of charred paper would litter the lawn and black starbursts would constellate the concrete. We'd be sent outside with a broom and a dustpan, fingers combing the grass for the night's debris.

As our neighborhood assaulted itself that New Year's Eve, Brad and some other dads, having inherited the tradition, experimented with the best lawn furniture to launch bottle rockets from. They dragged the gleaming chute of a broken playground slide from the back of the field, upending it to line up rows of rockets on its sloped edge and shoot them off together, like flaming arrows sent in unison from a castle parapet into the darkness, their smoky skeletons drifting afterward in the breeze off the Mississippi. Heavier ordnance like Black Cat's High Tower, Battle Star, and Fiery Fiesta fountained from the middle of the field. We armed the children with contraband sparklers, tiny cardboard tanks with wonky plastic wheels whose artillery sputtered weakly when lit, and tiny cardboard chickens shooting flaming "eggs" from their backsides. We pitted the chickens against the tanks; both sides had come all the way from China, where they'd been cheaply printed with the nostalgic hues of old hand-colored postcards — soft turquoise, yellow-orange, chartreuse, and dusty pink. In the battle of futile sparks and jerky, tentative movements, they were equals on the pavement, neither winners nor losers. In the smoke and the cold, we followed the directions on the boxes: did it all under adult supervision, found a hard level surface for our silly skirmishes, lit the fuses, and got out of the way.

ACKNOWLEDGMENTS

First, thank you to my fellow dark wood travelers past, present, and future, who made this book existentially possible — Brad, Chris, Susan, Ellen, Tristan, Kevin, Sara, Nate, Michael L., Christine, Michael D., Case, Nina, Tom, and Kyle. Susan, especially, for her relentless and indispensable note taking.

Much gratitude is owed my astute and generous readers over the years — Pia Ehrhardt, who made this book possible in many, many ways, Michael Jeffrey Lee, Chris Chambers, Mark Lane, Shawna Foose, Chris Lane, Sara Slaughter, John Gisleson, who was overly interested in my use of commas, and especially Lara Naughton and Andy Young, who kept me on track. Over the years, Ed Skoog, Eliza Borné, Roger Hodge, Jarret Lofstead, Joe Longo, David Rutledge, and Scott MacLeod all shared pieces of this work with their readers, giving me glimpses of light and hope along the way. Also thanks, Julia Leyda, for the life-changing invitation and lifelong friendship, and Michel Varisco, for taking me along and broadening my view.

The institutional support I received from the following was invaluable: the New Orleans Center for Creative Arts, the NOCCA Institute, Press Street Antenna, the Ragdale Foundation, the Rib Room (thank you, Soren), and Faubourg Wines (thank you, Cat).

I am crazy grateful to my wonderful agent, Emma Parry, for going out on a limb with this book and to my brilliant editor, Ben George, whose meticulous intelligence, energy, and faith strengthened the limb. I'm a little in awe of the assiduous Betsy Uhrig and Deborah Jacobs, for making everything as right as possible. Much, much thanks to everyone else at Little, Brown and Janklow & Nesbit for the thousands of decisions and actions that help put books into the world.

Finally, and always, Brad, Silas, and Otto — my boys, my heart.

APPENDIX: WORKS CITED

January: All Is Vanity

A Concise Dictionary of Existentialism. Edited by Ralph B. Winn. New York: Wisdom Library, 1960.

Epicurus. "Letter to Menoeceus."

James Joyce. *Dubliners.* New York: Random House (Modern Library Edition), 1993.

King James Bible, Ecclesiastes.

February: World of Stone

Simone de Beauvoir. "Selections from 'Towards a Morals of Ambiguity, According to Pyrrhus and Cinéas.'" Translated by Jay Miskowiec. *Social Text* 17 (Autumn 1987): 135–142.

Tadeusz Borowski. *This Way for the Gas, Ladies and Gentlemen.* New York: Penguin, 1976.

George Cotkin. *Existential America.* Baltimore: Johns Hopkins University Press, 2003.

William Shakespeare. *King Lear.*

March: The Belly of the Whale

1882 Annual Report of the Louisiana Board of Health.

Arthur Koestler. *The Act of Creation.* New York: Macmillan, 1964.

April: The Last Suffer

Georges Bataille. *Erotism: Death and Sensuality.* San Francisco: City Lights, 1986.

Louise Glück. *The Seven Ages.* New York: HarperCollins, 2001.

Vivian Gornick. *Fierce Attachments.* New York: Farrar, Straus & Giroux, 1987.

King James Bible, Gospel According to John.

Chuck Palahniuk. *Fight Club.* New York: W. W. Norton, 1996.

Shel Silverstein. *The Giving Tree.* New York: Harper & Row, 1964.

May: The Dark Wood

Dante Alighieri. *The Inferno.*

Hot Tub Time Machine (movie, 2010).

June: Voices over Water

John Cheever. *The Letters of John Cheever.* Edited by Benjamin Cheever. New York: Simon & Schuster, 1988.

———. *The Stories of John Cheever.* New York: Alfred A. Knopf, 1978.

July: The Least Dead Among All of Us

Alan Clayson. *Jacques Brel: La Vie Bohème.* New Malden, Surrey, England: Chrome Dreams, 2010.

August: The Metaphysical Hangover

Kingsley Amis. *Everyday Drinking: The Distilled Kingsley Amis.* New York: Bloomsbury USA, 1994.

Franz Kafka. *The Metamorphosis, In the Penal Colony, and Other Stories.* New York: Schocken Books, 1948.

September: The Walled City

Walker Percy. "New Orleans Mon Amour." Originally published in *Harper's,* September 1968. Reprinted in *Signposts in a Strange Land: Essays.* New York: Picador, 2000.

October: The Unwalled City

George Moore. *Memoirs of My Dead Life.* New York: D. Appleton, 1906.

Leo Tolstoy. *The Death of Ivan Ilyich.* Introduction by Ronald Blythe. New York: Bantam Classic, 1981.

November: Nineveh

Elizabeth Bishop. *The Complete Poems, 1927–1979.* New York: Farrar, Straus & Giroux, 1983.

Stephen Dobyns. *Velocities: New and Selected Poems, 1966–1992.* New York: Penguin, 1994.

Louise Glück. *The Wild Iris.* New York: Ecco, 1993.

Marie Howe. *What the Living Do: Poems.* New York: W. W. Norton, 1998.

King James Bible, Book of Jonah.

Everette Maddox. *I Hope It's Not Over, and Good-by: Selected Poems of Everette Maddox.* New Orleans: University of New Orleans Press, 2009.

Theodore Roethke. *The Collected Poems of Theodore Roethke.* Seattle: University of Washington Press, 1982.

December: Sharing Bread

Clarice Lispector. *Selected Crônicas: Essays.* New York: New Directions, 1996.

Benjamin Moser. *Why This World: A Biography of Clarice Lispector.* New York: Oxford University Press, 2012.

New Year's Eve: Tanks Versus Chickens

Josiah Royce. *Fugitive Essays.* Cambridge, MA: Harvard University Press, 1925.

ABOUT THE AUTHOR

Anne Gisleson's work has appeared in the *Atlantic*, the *Oxford American*, the *Believer*, and the *Los Angeles Times*, among other publications, and has been selected for inclusion in several anthologies, including *The Best American Nonrequired Reading*. She teaches in the creative writing program at the New Orleans Center for Creative Arts and lives in New Orleans with her husband and their two sons.